# CROWDFUNDING
## The Next Big Thing

## Money-Raising Secrets Of The Digital Age

GARY SPIRER

ISBN: 1492126225
ISBN 13: 9781492126225
Library of Congress Control Number: 2013914644
CreateSpace Independent Publishing Platform
North Charleston, South Carolina

# DEDICATION

Kaisa, Alexandra, Danielle and Gloria. Thanks for all of your love and support.

# ACKNOWLEDGEMENTS

Kaisa Kokkonen, Alexandra Spirer, Danielle Spirer, Gloria Spirer, Edward Wagner, Liam Spirer, Teddy Spirer, Robin Metz, Cathy Stewart, John Paine My Editor, Kirsi Kokkonen, Eeva Kokkonen, Irja Kokkonen, Martti Kokkonen, Lance Shuldberg, Elyse Shuldberg, Felix and Camelia, Don Burk, Tamora Burk, Douglas S. Ellenoff, Brian Kunzler, Matt Romney, Sandy Carter, Brent Wolfe, Deetz Shepherd, Gopal Gupta, Jonathan Libby, Heli Bergius, Teddy Garcia, Tyler Garns, Rodney S. Sampson, Brian Meece, Darlene Dion, Jonathan Stillman, Thomas Courtney, Hank Winchester, Robert Gonzalez, Kent Lovato, George Kontoravdis, Sampo Laine, David Weild IV, Chris Mitchell

# TABLE OF CONTENTS

# TABLE OF CONTENTS

# INTRODUCTION

We have all heard the stories. The Ouya video game console raised $8.5 million from 63,000 backers. Musician Amanda Palmer raised $1 million dollars from 25,000 backers to fund her new album. And we know about local efforts for good causes, such as the $10,000 Salaam Garage NYC raised for a book that featured homeless teenagers who have aged out of foster care. Crowdfunding is all the rage, not least because it shows how generous people really can be.

Crowdfunding rests upon the pitch and the search for the Next Big Thing—the blockbuster hit. Crowdfunding is the new *American Idol*, so to speak, for early-stage companies. Entrepreneurs, creative types, and small businesses go onto portals like Kickstarter and pitch their ideas for the chance to attract millions of dollars and a fan base that creates buzz about the project.

A significant change in crowdfunding occurred on April 5, 2012, when President Barack Obama signed into law the JOBS Act. JOBS is an acronym for Jump-start Our Business Start-ups. That's because early stage companies represent two-thirds of new job creation.

The JOBS Act has six parts, and one of them is titled "Crowdfunding." The idea is to spread the funding of new businesses beyond the old sphere of investment bankers, sophisticated rich angel investors, and venture capitalists who typically invest in early-stage companies looking for blockbuster hits. Now the crowd, or the average citizen, can invest in the same deals as the venture capitalists. Everybody has the opportunity to get in on the ground floor with the next Google, Twitter, LinkedIn, Facebook, or Instagram.

How is this different from the examples I listed at the start of the book? To eliminate any confusion, there are two types of crowdfunding deals:

1. Crowdfunding donations with rewards. You can "invest" in projects such as films, music, and games by donating money. In return, the amount of your donations entitles you to a certain level of rewards. For example, a cool watch to be manufactured, a coffee table book to be created, or a new music album to be produced. In this type of deal, you receive no ownership in the company to which you donate (no equity).
2. Crowdfunding equity. That gives you the opportunity to make money by investing in the next big thing. Unlike crowdfunding with donations or rewards, crowdfunding equity gives you actual ownership in the company itself.

On the positive side, crowdfunding becomes a global Internet-based laboratory for investors and entrepreneurs to learn and perfect more efficient ways to match investors and entrepreneurs with capital and ideas that can make the world a better place to live. On the negative side, though, crowdfunding becomes a grand experiment with enormous possibilities that will bring out the best and the worst—generosity and greed; donations and deceit; blockbuster hits and bombs.

You now can get in on the ground level of the next Google or other companies that will soar to be worth billions of dollars. It is true that these blockbuster hits are rare. Yet they are not as rare as you might think. The venture capital world has many more blockbuster hits than household names such as Microsoft and Intel. Have you ever heard of Internet voice-over protocol technology company Genband from Frisco, Texas, that raised $500 million of venture capital? What about the Internet-based service DocuSign, for signing and delivering documents, which raised $122.9 million? These are so common that the *Wall Street Journal* publishes each year its Top 50 venture-backed companies that have achieved multiple rounds of financing and valuations from hundreds of millions to billions.

There is, unfortunately, a dark side to this rosy picture. With all the trumpeting of crowdfunding's promise of new pools of capital, the brutal facts are that more than 75% of early-stage companies don't meet their initial projections. The majority of early-stage companies go out of business entirely—some within just a few years of their founding. Others continue to struggle and are acquired by another company for a much lower price than originally projected. Most investors lose all their money in the high-stakes, high-risk game of early-stage company investing.

That's why I have written this book. By comparing and contrasting the best venture capitalist approaches to early-stage company investment, *Crowdfunding: The Next Big Thing* reveals the best crowdfunding strategies and techniques for entrepreneurs and investors to beat the odds. No one strategy is the best. Each strategy has its pluses and minuses. Each can be successful, depending upon the risk versus the rewards you want and can emotionally handle.

For example, take two venture capital firms, Accel and Dag Ventures, which deploy different but successful investment strategies in early-stage company investment. Accel looks for entrepreneurs in the garage with a "next big thing" and usually seeks to be the first institutional investor in the deal. Dag Ventures looks to invest when an early-stage company is more mature and has already attracted other venture capital investors in previous investment rounds. Yet both have backed the most up-and-comers on the *Wall Street Journal*'s Top 50 Start-ups list.

Besides venture capitalists, you will also learn the best investment strategies of Warren Buffett, Peter Lynch, and Benjamin Graham to beat the market and how these insights can increase your odds of winning in early-stage company investing.

The book is designed to answer the questions of two different groups involved in early-stage companies. The first is the crowdfunding investor. How do you know which company will be a winner? How do you monitor the trends and not get caught up in fads and short-lived hype and gimmicks in areas such as games or technology? You will get answers to key questions about investing. For example, is the ability to find good companies based on your education, IQ, age, or having money to start? Here's another question: Which is more important—the idea or the entrepreneur? You see, once you step back from the glamour and excitement of crowdfunding, you are left with the cold, sober business of picking winners. You will want to weigh carefully how you can outperform the everyday crowd of investors and become successful like professional venture capitalists.

The other group the book addresses is composed of the entrepreneurs, small businesses, and creative types trying to get the money. In this book you will get answers for a wide variety of questions around crowdfunding. First, how do you get your idea funded? How do you draw instant traffic? How do you build a customer base (your list) or write and test your pitch for your product to get customers or investors to invest? A start-up company—and the savvy investor in that company—has to consider all sorts of baseline questions. For instance, how do you research new ideas for content and new products? How do you evaluate the potential competition? How can you increase your presence and influence on the web through social media marketing?

Make no mistake. The opportunities are potentially fabulous. Here's an example of how crowdfunding rescues companies and ideas that had no other way to get the initial financing. Choi Yong-Bae, the chief executive of Chungeorahm Film, has had several box office hits in South Korea, but finding film investors is never easy. Trying to fund his film *26 Years* became difficult because of its politically sensitive subject. Choi pitched the top entertainment companies in South Korea, then investment funds and venture capitalists, but got turned down. Finally, Choi set up a crowdfunding website and raised $404,000 of his $4.1 million budget from over 12,000 donors in exchange for movie tickets and small rewards. Through social media and word of mouth the crowdfunding project created enough fans to attract wealthy investors to fund up to 90% of the budget. The film was released in November 2012.

That's the allure of crowdfunding. The crowd is willing to invest in high-stakes early-stage companies that can soar in value and become blockbuster hits worth tens, even thousands of times your investment. In this new frontier of raising capital, crowdfunding investments by amateur investors bring a vast new pool of capital that can turbocharge entrepreneurs' dreams, creating the possibility of incredible wealth.

By now you may be asking, what qualifications does this author have to guide me through all these different areas of investment? To begin with, I have reviewed over 10,000 business plans. I have over

30 years of experience in finding deals, analyzing and investing and raising capital for them. You will learn the lessons and principles of successful investing and entrepreneurship that I have compiled from the best and the brightest. My track record for raising capital—over $125 million in current dollars—is 100%, in a wide variety of industries, such as coal mines, film, book publishing, online publishing, oil and gas, software, food, restaurants, the investment banking business, stock brokerage, and real estate.

I decided in 2008 to focus upon virtual real estate—the Internet. With the growth of the Internet and technology, the world of raising capital and building businesses has changed. Information, speed, and globalization have opened up new competition and new sources of capital, such as crowdfunding. Many of the books and articles on raising capital and building businesses are out of date in this new era of inbound marketing, social media, and mobile marketing and advertising.

Every company goes through different stages. In an earlier book I wrote about the seven steps involved in turning an idea into a million-dollar business. Every company goes through these distinct phases: Idea, Design, Discovery, Development, Pre-launch, Launch, and Post-launch. Within each of these stages are considerations about how best to make a company grow.

Those principles can help you understand early-stage companies, whether you are a crowdfunding investor or an entrepreneur. You will also learn valuable techniques for finding and analyzing deals in minutes using a formula that I call the Three Magical Ps. These are:

1. People. Who are the people involved in the transaction, including the customers?
2. Product. What's the product and how is it different?
3. Potential. What's its potential, including its profitability and its competitive advantage to sustain its growth and profitability?

An early-stage company presents many more mysteries to an investor, but once you know what to look for, you can see signs of the beginnings of a sound business and business model. I will show you how to assess and define more clearly your investment philosophy, strategies, and goals so you can increase your income. Then you'll learn how to invest in early-stage companies and increase the odds that you will pick a winner. For entrepreneurs, I will show you how you must pitch your business concept to get the money from investors, including those crowds out there willing to fund you.

Crowdfunding is an exciting new world for millions of people who live on Main Street. It holds great promise of riches, and at the same time it holds the hidden peril of losing your shirt. Let's start with the general principles of investing: What do you look for? You can learn how the game is played. You can arm yourself with knowledge. And when you get done with this book, you will be able to stand out from the crowd.

Please note that at the end of each chapter, I will summarize key chapter points or takeaways and add additional strategies, insights, tactics, and steps to make the material immediately actionable.

## CHAPTER 1

# HOW DO YOU FIND THE NEXT BIG THING?

Danger. Danger. Danger...Everywhere...By investing along with the crowd, the chances that you will lose all your money are greater than 50%. For most investors and entrepreneurs, that number can climb to over 90%. That's because most investors lose money.

Why? Because most of us have no real idea why we are investing or where to invest or how to invest.

What we do know is that we follow the crowd and we are terribly afraid to lose our money. Without an idea of how to make money, we chase after the next great thing, which usually turns out to be a dud.

The dream of being a crowd fund investor should have you running for the exits. If you can't make money investing in the stock market or bonds, what chances do you have making money in high-risk early-stage companies that are no more than an idea or just a start-up?

But wait. Surprise. You may have an opportunity to find the next big thing. Take a company called SendGrid. Founded in 2009, SendGrid was started to serve companies that send email messages that require either a confirmation or response. SendGrid helps prevent these emails from getting caught in spam filters and provides data about whether the email was read. It was originally funded by a company named TechStars, which calls itself "the #1 startup accelerator in the world." Today SendGrid is used by 40,000 publishers, has sent more than 2.6 billion monthly emails in 150 countries, and it has grown to 70 employees.

Imagine you were an original investor in this company. The chances you would have made a killing in SendGrid are very high. If you missed SendGrid or never heard of it, you can join the crowd.

In the newly proposed JOBS Act, the crowdfunding equity section allows you to invest in SendGrid just like a venture capitalist or angel investor. You can make the huge returns most only dream of. The returns which were virtually available to only the wealthy. That's because, beyond the crowd in crowdfunding, they are the insiders. This is the network of venture capitalists and wealthy investors who get to review the best deals, share their expertise, and invest together.

How does a SendGrid or Pinterest or any other deals like them come up? Do they have any common characteristics that give you a greater chance for picking the winners? How do the best early-stage investors pick more winners than losers and become the wealthiest individuals in the world?

Being presented with an idea for an investment can often mean nothing if you do not have an investment approach that makes sense.

Being able to invest is unlike other skill sets. You can see someone play a violin at Lincoln Center or throw a football for a touchdown to win the Super Bowl. You know you will never be good enough to do that. But in the world of investment, you don't need to have fine motor skills or eye-hand coordination. Instead, you can do the research, go to physical locations, ask questions, and observe.

Even more important, you need a why or a purpose. What do you want to achieve with your money?

The answer(s) to this question are what make crowdfunding such a game-changing approach for investors. and entrepreneurs, creative types (such as artists, writers, game developers, film makers), and small businesspeople.

Using the Internet, you as the investor can choose via crowdfunding to

- Strictly donate your money;
- Donate it for some reward;
- Donate it for an advance purchase of a product;
- Or, soon, buy part ownership in the company to which you give money (called equity-based crowdfunding, still being defined by the Securities and Exchange Commission, or SEC).

Each option can be for many reasons beyond money making. Your emotions may be stirred to back some good cause or get a cool game or give another fellow human being a shot a fulfilling their dream.

But if your choice involves money, you don't want to take risks. Who wants to give to a charity and find out they have been duped?

You are not alone if you have doubts regarding money and wealth building. Doubts and fears raise many questions, such as the following: Do you think you are too young to succeed? Larry Page and Sergey Brin were in their twenties when they started Google. Steve Chen and Chad Hurly were paid $1.65 billion by Google for YouTube — an 11-month-old company that allowed users to share videos. Mark Zuckerberg was 23 when he refused a billion-dollar offer from Yahoo for Facebook. Should you feel bad for the MySpace guys who sold out to Rupert Murdoch on the cheap for $580 million?

Maybe you think you need a great education to make money. Maybe you are thinking that you are not smart enough to be wealthy. Bill Gates dropped out of Harvard to focus on building Microsoft. Steve Jobs dropped out of Reed College after six months. A recent *New York Times* article reported on Eden Full, who dropped out of Princeton because a billionaire, Peter Thiel, provides $50,000 per year for two years for people under 20 who want to discover the next big thing.

Being a top investor or entrepreneur is not based upon age or education or talent or money or a number of other factors often cited by "experts."

What holds back many people is typically more personal. New studies show that people are predictably irrational. They will repeat the same mistakes that are counter to sound investing and business building over and over again. If they see others—the crowd—making money in social media, then they rush in. If they see oil prices exploding, they buy at the top of the market—before the price inevitably stabilizes at a lower value. Understanding your investing irrationality—your money-making blindness—will free you to see what the top investors and entrepreneurs see.

There is no strict formula or template that you plug in certain numbers and assumptions, and out come automatic profits.

You should realize that it is not only amateurs that get caught short. So do the pros—the venture capitalists. In 2000, venture capitalists in Silicon Valley could not plug enough money into the next dot.com company. Yet many of these new ideas proved to be a flash in the pan. Founded in 1997, online grocer Webvan was a huge dot-com flop. In 18 months, it raised $375 million in an initial public offering (IPO), expanded to eight U.S. cities, and built a gigantic infrastructure, including a group of high-tech warehouses. Yet they discovered that most customers didn't understand the idea of a web-based grocery store. In 2001, it filed for bankruptcy and laid off 2,000 workers.

That idea doesn't seem too hard to grasp, does it? People are used to shopping in grocery stores, so if you think they'll go to the web instead, guess what? That big idea lacked one essential ingredient: common sense.

Shikar Ghosh, a senior lecturer at Harvard Business School, told HBS's *Working Knowledge* why outside funding has the potential to turn a little failure into an enormous one. "The predominant cause of big failures versus small failures is too much funding. What funding does is cover up all the problems that a company has." He went on, "This lets management rationalize away the proverbial problem of the dogs not eating the dog food. When you don't have money, you reformulate the dog food so that the dogs will eat it. When you have a lot of money, you can afford to argue that the dogs should like the dog food because it is nutritious."

If you want to invest in start-ups or build them, then you can see that having enough money at the start is rarely the issue.

Crowdfunding can get many businesses off the ground.

The question becomes how to select the ones that have the best chance of success. These are the insights investors and entrepreneurs crave. They are the ones that will make you money.

So let's find out what only the top 1% know.

## TAKEAWAYS AND INSIGHTS

- You cannot avoid uncertainty and risk when you make investments. Think of currency risks and inflation.
- High risk does not mean you get high rewards. It means you can lose all your capital.
- Following the crowd can often lead to losses. You need to weigh when crowd opinions matter, such as a restaurant or product review. Ask how the crowd's opinion and feedback will impact your investment.
- A huge potential opportunity occurred on July 10, 2013, called Title II under the Jobs Act. The SEC voted to allow general solicitation of private placements to accredited investors. The total market is estimated to be over one trillion dollars and dwarfs the proposed Title III crowdfunding equity.
- Being an investor does not require the physical skills of peak performance.
- What is common to all peak performers—investors, entrepreneurs, athletes, artists—is their ability to harness their beliefs and emotions to excel.
- Being a top entrepreneur or investor is not based upon your age or education.

Click here for additional resources: http://bit.ly/19IzdMJ

# CHAPTER 2

# THE VALUE OF PATTERNS

Is wealth accumulation a matter of destiny? Will most of us just be wishful thinkers and also-rans in the game of money? More and more, a small group of experts believe that you can predict with a higher probability which companies will succeed. There is a science to wealth building. These experts describe the common traits that winning companies and their leaders and other stakeholders (employees, investors, suppliers, distributors, customers) have that the less successful or the outright losers don't.

Even so, many explanations of wealth building only describe symptoms, not the underlying causes. You can learn some of the important elements, but the roadmap to wealth is often still fuzzy and elusive. What you really want to know is the complete road map to wealth—from the original concept to the cash in hand. You want to know if there is a step-by-step approach, with checklists and ways to measure your progress.

Trying to follow most "how to" investment and business-building advice is like trying to land a plane in the dark without instruments. To land your plane, you need a context or framework or guideposts to know where you are. You want instrument gauges and lights on each side of the runway to guide the way down.

If you follow certain universal principles and patterns—the universals—your chances of success in investing or building businesses increase, sometimes greatly. Similar thoughts and actions can become the basis for your investment strategies if you are an investor. If you are an entrepreneur, these patterns can become the basis for future products and services and growth.

The history of human and economic evolution follows the same patterns:

- Differentiation—the difference or competitive advantage becomes magnified
- Selection—choice of the fittest
- Scale—the most selected and differentiated grow and become dominant

Think of the similar elements in the success of Sony's Walkman and Apple's iPod. The Walkman's mobile audio players with headphones set the stage for the future digital iPod. Each innovation evolved from prior innovations.

This same "standing on the shoulder of giants" is the basis for human innovation. The formulation of hypotheses, experimentation, and recording of similar findings is the foundation of the Scientific Revolution, the scientific method, and the idea of progress.

The same applies to the Internet. Many traditional businesses have succeeded online. Let's take Amazon, the giant for selling books, consumer electronics, and now any type of item you can name. There are different business models or different patterns or ways to invest or to build businesses. But in the end, they follow similar principles and patterns to get and keep customers.

*Wired* magazine interviewed the founder of Amazon, Jeff Bezos, and here is what he had to say about patterns. "There are two ways to build a successful company. One is to work very, very hard to convince customers to pay high margins. The other is to work very, very hard to be able to afford to offer customers low margins. They both work. We're firmly in the second camp. It's difficult—you have to eliminate defects and be very efficient. But it's also a point of view. We'd rather have a very large customer base and low margins than a smaller customer base and higher margins."

If you follow closely what Bezos is saying, each business has a culture and an idea of how to relate to each other internally and externally. Amazon believes in being customer-centric. Create great value for the customer, and the customer will come and stay. It's not building a field of dreams and they will come. You have to create a way for prospects to know you exist. You must be able to test your assumptions to discover what the customer values.

Of course, Bezos doesn't feel that is the only way to go. When asked why Amazon bought Zappos, the online shoe giant, he had this interesting comment: "Our version of a perfect customer experience is one in which our customer doesn't want to talk to us. Every time a customer contacts us, we see it as a defect. I've been saying for many, many years, people should talk to their friends, not their merchants." And yet he sees the value in Zappos' sales pattern, which is to bend over backward for the customer. "Zappos takes a completely different approach. You call them and ask them for a pizza, and they'll get out the Yellow Pages for you."

The investor and the entrepreneur have a common goal: a profitable, paying, happy customer who will reorder and recommend the company and its products to others.

You can find the patterns that indicate a successful start-up. Most early-stage companies have a tremendous need for customer feedback and sales to validate the business model. To be sure, certain Internet high flyers, such as Pinterest and Instagram, enjoyed a viral product that caught on with users—the crowd—and spread with little marketing effort.

Yet most early-stage companies do not have the good fortune of a viral product. They have to earn their success step by step. No matter which business model a start-up uses, it has to constantly search for better ways to:

- Increase or drive more traffic to their websites or offline businesses
- Turn leads or names into customers
- Serve their customers and follow up with superior solutions for clients
- Innovate with new ideas to develop better products and services
- Hire the right people

Finding these better ways is searching for principles and patterns that work and repeat. Once you recognize these, you can uncover the unique twist—sometimes small but powerful—that creates the distinction that makes one product favored over another. You can discover similar paths to success even in offbeat products that appear to have no relationship to each other.

Does the creation of Quicksilver surfer wear have anything in common with the creation of Red Bull? Actually, yes. The founders of both companies built their fortunes by initially marketing to non-mainstream markets. Quicksilver marketed surfer wear to those who wanted to feel part of the exclusive surfer world club—a non-traditional market. They sponsored top surfers, snowboarders, and surfing events. Red Bull targeted the non-mainstream world of extreme sports, hip bars, acrobatic teams and daredevil competitions. Red Bull likewise sponsored events in these non-traditional markets and became a huge winner for its investors and founders.

In the next few chapters we are going to break down these patterns so that you can start to see how they are predictable. Before going any further, though, I need to make one basic, but very important, distinction that you always must look for no matter what. This is the principle of the Golden Goose.

## THE GOLDEN GOOSE

If you decide to invest in crowdfunding, then you should understand the basic underlying principle behind all patterns. As an investor, I've examined many companies over the past 30 years. In terms of investing and in building businesses, one key area of confusion that I've found is the distinction between production capacity (PC) and the product (PI). This applies to investing via crowdfunding, the stock market, commodities, real estate, bonds, collectibles—in the world of investing, they're all the same.

What is production capacity? As an entrepreneur you want something to be producing income for you. Otherwise, you are the only means to making income for your company. You earn only what you can produce from your hourly work. You can't multiply past your own hours. And therefore a company can never expand if it does not have what I call a money machine.

That's the secret to investing and building businesses: you want to learn how to invest in and/or build a money machine. If you want to invest in early-stage companies, you're looking for what I call production capacity—the capacity to produce products and generate growing free cash flow. A business owner can keep doing the same thing over and over, thinking he's building something efficiently when he's just turning the hamster wheel.

Another name for the money machine is the Golden Goose. The Golden Goose has two parts. The products are the golden eggs (PI), but what you need is the production capacity (PC)—the ability to keep producing those eggs.

You want to make the Golden Goose work for you instead of you always working for it. If you're the machine, you never build wealth, because you can't sell yourself. You are the business. The minute you stop, your business stops. People wake up one day and say, "When I retire, what do I have?" Well, if they don't have any production capacity beyond themselves, they better not stop working.

An entrepreneur needs to build a portfolio that is going to deliver real income and residual wealth over a period of time. Everything that you set up within the portfolio, you should examine it and say, "Is this going to work for me, or am I going to work for it?"

Another way of seeing the problem is that most people don't make a distinction between an investment, a business, and a job. They are the job; they're the vehicle, and there's no leverage in it. You can't leverage yourself. You can't leverage your hours. When you own a Golden Goose you purchased or are building, you attract investors. You can start leveraging their money and others' skills, talents, and know-how. Investors will give you more and more money and the company will grow, as we saw with SendGrid. The cash flow you're generating from the money machine (or the potential money machine from a user base growing virally, as with Pinterest) produces multiples of income, leverage through others' contributions, and residual wealth.

Can you run a one-person business and succeed?

Yes. But you should have a goal as to what defines success. Ask yourself questions such as the following: Is your business goal always to remain solo? How much growth is enough in terms of revenue or number of clients or total hours worked in a week? What's your real net income on an hourly basis? For example, if your monthly income is $6,000 but you work 60 hours a week (240 hours per month), then your hourly rate is $25 ($6,000/240 hours). That's not what I would call a successful business model.

"Just because you're a great technician at what you do doesn't mean you'll automatically be a great entrepreneur, too," says Marla Tabaka, a business coach who writes the *Successful Soloist* blog for Inc.com. "They're two totally different hats to wear."

## SEVEN STEPS TO SUCCESS

Finding patterns can be broken down into smaller pieces because of the very nature of business growth. Whether you decide to start up or invest in a business, you should be aware that every company has common problems, challenges, and solutions at each stage of development or growth. Every business must go through a seven-step process to turn its concept and vision, however small or large, into reality.

As an investor, you want to be aware of where the business stands in its development and how well it has executed the seven-step process.

Why?

Think of development as a fetus or newborn. This is a time of great risk. Will the child be born healthy? When born, it is very fragile and needs a lot of nurturing and care. It's a time of joy and much care. Who's going to raise the child? Can you afford to raise the child? Do you have the experience, the temperament, the time?

It's a stage when risk is very high. The entrepreneur similarly starts up her baby and hopes for the best—a healthy, growing business.

You as the investor must realize the risks and uncertainties of early-stage companies and value them accordingly. The seven-step process gives you a road map so you can quickly evaluate where a company stands—its strengths and weaknesses.

Of these seven steps, we will discuss in the next few chapters the three initial steps to evaluating an investment and building a business. These steps are the setup or the base upon which everything is built:

1. Idea
2. Design
3. Discovery

Before a business even starts, it must have these three components. How solid they are will go a long way toward determining if the company succeeds or fails. Think of the opportunities you have seen on crowdfunding sites. Did you recognize a good idea right off the bat? Did the way the product was designed, or packaged, strike a chord with you? Did you read the comments of other investors who had already discovered the product?

Let's see how to apply the first three steps as they related to investing, crowdfunding, and business building. As you get more adept with these initial three steps, you will begin to recognize the good and eliminate the bad. You will have more time to focus on fewer deals and not feel overwhelmed by too many options. This ability to cut through the basics of investments and businesses will save you tons of time and money.

This is not rocket science; it's common sense. Or maybe it's uncommonly good sense. Because once you grasp these three steps, you are going to look at a new business in a whole new way. You, not the crowd, are going to see the right patterns.

## TAKEAWAYS AND INSIGHTS

- The Golden Goose represents the business machine—what produces the Golden Eggs or products that are sold, donated, or exchanged to get the money.
- Most people confuse a product for a business and often they are the product/service.
- With only so many hours to sell, the potential to expand is limited.
- True entrepreneurs build Money Machines that can be leveraged by attracting other people and have the upside to attract venture capital or angel investors whose goal is to make 5x, 10x or more on their moves in 3-5 years and exit. Some will go on further in time.
- Customer-centric business cultures like Amazon and Zappos are very good business models to follow, whether at low margins or high margins respectively.
- Start-ups need to develop customers by finding out what they want by getting out and interviewing them.
- The Idea is important, but it's only a guess or hunch until it is Designed and matched against the competition through Discovery—marketing and customer research. The Idea, Design and Discovery are the first steps to a sound business foundation.
- Patterns and principles often repeat and give you guidelines or a roadmap to follow.
- Today, determining seeks to find insights and patterns from analyzing who people are, what they do and why. Investors analyze markets, companies, customers, and other stakeholders to get a competitive edge.

- Getting the competitive edge mirrors evolution and the survival of the fittest (which can mean collaboration and teamwork):
    - o Differentiation
    - o Selection
    - o Scale
- Innovation typically comes from improving on what others have done—sometimes dramatically or disruptively.

Click here for additional resources: http://bit.ly/19ICPP0

CHAPTER 3

# GREAT IDEA, GREAT DESIGN

The first thing you are looking for is a good idea. Everything starts with an idea. Human beings possess the most powerful wealth-building mechanism of all: the ability to envision an idea and turn it into a reality. Ideas can come by accident, such as Alexander Fleming's discovery of penicillin. Or they can come through determined effort and thousands of versions, such as Edison's idea of an incandescent light bulb. Or by copying and improving upon an idea, such as Howard Schultz of Starbucks, who on a trip to Italy came up with the idea to imitate Italian coffee bars. Ruth Handler was traveling to Lucerne, Switzerland, when she came up with the idea for the Barbie doll from Reinhard Beuthien's racy comic strip character Lilli.

Here's a solo entrepreneur who came up with an idea for a business and left his full-time gig as chief technology officer of the Internet site Tumblr to work at home. FastCompany.com reported: "Marco Arment started Instapaper, because he wanted to be able to read the Web pages he'd saved during the day on his train ride home." He used his coding skills to develop a way to bookmark those pages. Once his "Read Later" button is dragged to a customer's Bookmark toolbar, it creates a reading list. "It was pretty basic," he insisted. "Just a place to put everything you find when you can't or don't want to read right then."

What if he went to a crowdfunding site and asked you to donate or soon invest in his business? Would you do it? Well, you still don't know anything past the fact that he has a great idea. But you could tell—right away—hey, as a customer, that's something I'd like to have.

The idea is where it all starts. Finding the next big thing—the killer application—is the aim globally of top investors, entrepreneurs, and myriad support companies that emerge and prosper from hitting pay dirt. Find the right idea and you can quickly have a gold rush on your hands.

You first need to come up with what I call a Huge Tipping Point Idea. I took the principle from a book by Malcolm Gladwell called *Tipping Point.* What does it mean? "The tipping point is that magic moment when an idea, trend, or social behavior crosses a threshold, tips, and spreads like wildfire. Just as a single sick person can start an epidemic of the flu, so too can a small but precisely targeted push cause a fashion trend, the popularity of a new product, or a drop in the crime rate." You can see how crowdfunding fits into this idea. It has a unique advantage in that its success depends upon the crowd liking the idea and voting with their dollars and spreading the word to others.

In business, a Huge Tipping Point Idea is needed for a product or service to make that happen. Clearly, few ideas tip, but it's a goal to which you want to aspire. You want to ask yourself as an investor or entrepreneur the question: Will this idea take off?

As an entrepreneur, your idea differentiates your product from others like it in the marketplace. The idea is what gets you as the investor interested. The idea is what attracts the prospects and the customers. You might use a simple test: Does the idea excite you? Would you go home and tell someone about it? Would you start to think about it and its possibilities? Some of the stuff about ideas is not rocket science. The real issue becomes who else has the same idea or may be working on it. You can find out some of this information by getting on the Internet or asking your network of friends and business associates (see the Discovery step). But you'll never know whether a big competitor is working on the same idea and yet to release it. Nor will you know if some start-up is building some version of the Idea in a garage or basement. Few good ideas exist without others recognizing them at the same time.

Based upon the Idea, the entrepreneur has to develop a compelling offer, or value proposition, that grabs the customer's (and investor's) interest right away. You need to tell your customer:

- What your product does
- How much it costs

- What benefits are in it for the customer or how he can use it to solve his needs and wants
- Why she should believe you and buy from you
- What makes your customers—the crowd—demand more and more

Let's look at each of these points, because they are important considerations for both the entrepreneur and the crowd-funding investor.

**What your product does:** Think of the actual functionality, mechanics, or features of your product or service. For instance, a car transports you from one place to another. A cell phone enables you to call someone rather than use a land line. A cookie is a type of dessert. A survey asks questions to get your opinion and/or feedback.

For example, I have a software company called Questionmine. Its product is an interactive video survey and interactive mobile video survey which clients can use to ask questions and get feedback in real time while their prospect or customer watches a video.

**How much it costs:** A prospect or customer will want to know the price of that car, cell phone, cookie, or video survey that you or others are offering. In part, price normally is matched to features and benefits (translated into perceived value), such as horsepower, design, radio with a CD or not, miles per gallon, size of the fuel tank, or seat fabric, to name a few. Your cell phone provider gives you different plans tied to usage or number of minutes, plus texting or not. Different quality cookies have different prices. Credit cards have different levels of credit: American Express has green, gold, silver, and black levels. Questionmine has prices based upon usage (video views) and the number of videos.

Determining prices takes a lot of work when you first start up a company. The first question is whether the prospect will pay anything for your product or service. Next, will he pay a price that gives you a profit? At the price you propose, do you have to get a few customers or lots of customers to generate the revenue you are projecting? For example, if you are selling products to large customers which take months to close, then you must be able to charge enough to cover the months of overhead you are paying while you get the sale and then the cost of delivering and serving the customer.

Another way to approach this is to determine the cost of acquiring a customer (CAC) versus the lifetime value of the customer (LTV). There are many variables in calculating your CAC, but generally it's all the costs related to getting the sale,, such as the marketing and sales, salaries, promotions, traffic sources, affiliates, or JVs. Your LTV is what revenues the customer will bring to you over the lifetime of your relationship. The CAC question is one of the most asked on *Shark Tank*. Here's how it normally goes:

Shark: What are your sales?

Entrepreneur: None or some figure, say $100000

Shark: Is that this year? Over how many years?

Entrepreneur: Last year we did $25000.This year we already have done $75000 and we have 6 months to go?

Sharks: Nice. So what are you costs to produce the product?

Entrepreneur: $1

Shark: And you sell it for?

Entrepreneur: $4 wholesale Retails for $8

Shark: And your cost to acquire a customer?

Entrepreneur: Fifty cents

Shark: And do they reorder?

Entrepreneur: Yes. At least twice a year.

The point: the Sharks and any smart investor want to know if you understand your numbers. If you do understand them, then they are asking if you have tested the market enough to know what it costs to acquire a customer. Next, they are asking if you have the appropriate margins to cover your other costs, such as producing the product itself, distributing it, the operating costs, and any financing costs, such as paying money for equipment or a line of credit. Are customers reordering the product? If it's a big-ticket item, then what is the length of the sales cycle (from initial time contact is made with a prospect to an actual purchase) and on what terms?

When we started up Questionmine, we had to lay out all the features and the different ways we could charge based upon the benefits (solutions) these features produced. We had to look at the competition and how much different market segments were accustomed to paying for services in our category. We were much more than a survey company, since, in addition to video surveys, we offered interactive video polls, quizzes, assessments, scheduled recorded webinars, and video slide presentations such as Power Point or Apple Keynote, all of which you could make interactive by overlaying any of these videos with questions and answer choices. These questions and answers could be timed to appear to the second over the video (usually across the bottom 25% of the video), or the questions and answers could be timed to appear below or to the side of the video.

In other words, how we presented Questionmine's features and benefits—the overall value proposition—affected greatly how customers perceived whether they paid a price that gave them a very high return on investment.

**What benefits are in it for the customer, or how can he use it to solve his needs and wants?** An easy way to distinguish a feature from a benefit is to add a "so that" after the function or mechanics of your feature statement. I purchase or lease a car "so that" I can travel from place to place rather than waste the time it would take to walk there. I get a silver American Express card "so that" I receive the extra services and the prestige associated with the color when I go to pay with the card.

Benefits equate to the most important question of your prospects or customers: *What's in it for me?* Here's a very important statement: People don't want to be sold. They want to buy. Buying is mainly an emotional decision that is then rationalized by the thinking part of your brain after the product is purchased. One day I was on a call with a top salesman of customer-relationship management system (CRM) company Eloqua, (required by Oracle) with whom my company Questionmine partners. He stated to me, "The bottom line is, we have to find out for our customers who their customers are and what they do." That was his benefit statement to why he'd partner with us. Questionmine would deliver the video metrics and analytics Eloqua's clients needed "so that" they could know their customers better—who they were, what they did, and why.

**Why should they believe you and buy from you?** In the end, your customer has to trust you. Trust and competence go hand in hand. You want a surgeon that you can trust (integrity) and that can perform the open-heart surgery (competent). You don't want an honest incompetent surgeon, carpenter, dentist, or mechanic. Nor do you want a dishonest doctor who knowingly charges you for procedures you don't need.

When you pitch a product, the person you are pitching is asking: Can I trust this person and/ or company, and are they competent? In other words, can they deliver on their promise or on their side of the exchange if you deliver on your side?

As a software company, Questionmine has to establish trust by delivering its service, being reliable, and generating the features and benefits the customer wants.

Reputation and word of mouth spread very fast. As a company you have to be extremely vigilant in how you are perceived when you pitch prospects and customers.

Investors examine carefully your pitch—what you say and what is for real. If you misrepresent who your company is and/or what it does, then you will be labeled untrustworthy and/or incompetent, resulting in investors rejecting your deal.

**What makes your customers—the crowd—demand more and more?** In the case of crowdfunding, your investors or donators can also be your customers. To reiterate, investors and customers want to be excited. Typically, life is stressful and often boring. Investors and customers want to invest and buy things that are different, cool, and add something different to their life. In effect, they are seeking what's new. When we had a food company, we'd have a booth at the Fancy Food Shows in San Francisco, Chicago, and New York City. The most popular area was entitled "What's New?" Food buyers, food distributors, food brokers, the media, and competitors flocked to observe and admire the new packaging and the new flavors.

In many different ways, you are pitching what you have to sell, whether it's a product, a service, a cause, a project, or some type of relationship with others (romantic, business, or otherwise).

Your pitch encompasses your presentation, positioning, and performance. On the *X Factor*, you present by singing on a stage or platform. The judges initially in the auditions and elimination rounds and then the live audience and the viewing-at-home audience (the crowd) want to be wowed. They want to discover the Next Big Thing, the What's New, the Susan Boyle-type of surprise performance that defies expectations and is "remark" - able: something you will *remark about* or tell others—your friends—about, and they will *remark about* it and tell their friends.

As I will show you, the new world of online social media and offline mobile capability has opened up an enormous opportunity to get the money, increase your customers dramatically, and build a sizeable monthly income and net worth. You need to understand and be able to implement it: to translate what your product or service does; what's its price; what's the benefit, or what's in it for others (the value proposition/the irresistible offer); and why they should trust you and feel you are competent.

But all this has to be accomplished by knowing where, when, and how to present and pitch so that you can create awareness, get traffic, arouse interest and desire, and convert prospects to paying customers.

## CREATING STAKEHOLDER VALUE

The place to start that process is not you, but your customer. What is the importance of creating value for your customer? At the heart of investing and business building is an exchange of value. As an entrepreneur, you are exchanging value with numerous people—your stakeholders, such as your suppliers, customers, and investors, who want to assist and support you if you in turn give them value by paying them money or giving them something in kind which represents value to them.

As a crowd fund donator, you are often purchasing the company's product and thus you are a customer as well. As a crowd funder under equity-based crowdfunding, you are investing in a company. You are purchasing shares in the company and expecting to receive more value than for which you paid.

As an entrepreneur or small businessperson, your customer for your products is paying you for a perceived/expected value. If the customer receives the expected value or more, you have a happy customer. You have fulfilled the promise of your value proposition and your exchange.

In order to evaluate how good your value proposition is for your customer and other stakeholders, you need to look carefully at what's going on in the marketplace, or the Arena. (see the Discovery step to follow shortly) Why do you feel your idea represents an improved solution over what is in the market? Do you believe your idea can change the world? Do you have a solution to a pain/problem which the market immediately recognizes and for which it will pay you a high-margined profit? Or will millions will pay you a lower-margined profit so that you still make lots of money (think Costco, BJs, or Wal-Mart). Or, do you have to educate your market to make them aware of the value of your product, which can take a lot of time, money, and resources?

Take Nuance, which seized upon an answer to an age-old office problem: transcribing dictation notes into written copy. How did they solve the problem of the two-step, time-consuming process of dictating into a dictation machine and then having to retype the dictation notes into a word-processing document? They developed a software program called Dragon Naturally Speaking, "so that" businesspeople can talk into a microphone that translates their spoken words into written words on their computers. Today they're recognized as the premier dictation program in the marketplace.

## HOW TO COME UP WITH THE NEXT BIG THING

In a *Wall Street Journal* article, "How to Come Up With a Great Idea," the description says, "There is no magic formula. But that doesn't mean there is no formula at all...Where do the eurekas come from? At the heart of any successful business is a great idea...But those great ideas don't come on command. And that leaves lots of would-be entrepreneurs asking the same question: How did everybody *else* get the inspiration to strike—and how can we work the same magic?"

Here are some of the ways great ideas are discovered:

- Observe things in your own life that are frustrating you and ask the question: is there a better way to... (fill in the blank).
- Think big, not incrementally. To raise money, investors want ideas that impact people's lives by simplifying or improving things.
- Look at how things are done routinely in other industries and bring those practices to a different industry.
- Test things incrementally, where you are not risking large sums of money. This saves you money and gives you the flexibility to move forward or make a large change or pivot if something is not working out.
    - Note this important point: The more money and time you commit to an idea, the more you can get locked into that idea or solution—and this often leads to failure. Your ego and emotions become involved as an entrepreneur, creative type, small businessperson, or investor. You must prove you are right and stop listening—tune any wise advice out from consideration.
- Give your subconscious mind time to work: keep thinking about coming up with an idea related to something on which you are working. or just be very observant when you are seeking an opportunity and keep asking your mind to notice something different—a big improvement. Then do other things—go off and relax. Sometimes, even when you are doing boring stuff, the idea comes to you.
- Plan A often morphs into a totally different idea as you test the market and get feedback. Many of the most successful companies, including PayPal and Hewlett Packard, started out with a completely different vision.

What many older people may find inspirational in the article is a quote from Vivek Wadhwa of Singularity University: "Typical entrepreneurs are middle-aged professionals who see a market need and start up companies with their own savings...The average age of successful entrepreneurs in high-growth industries such as computers, health care, and aerospace is 40. Twice as many successful entrepreneurs are aged over 50 as under 25 and twice as many over 60 as under 20."

Here's one of the best tips for building a great company, whether you are a solo entrepreneur or you want to build a team and a hyper-growth company:

Imagine more than your business idea. From the day you start thinking of an idea for a business, imagine you are an investor and a customer in your own business.

What idea or solution to a problem would make them feel they are getting a ten-to-one return so they are compelled to invest in your company and buy your products? Remember: everyone wants to feel she got a bargain and tremendous value in an exchange with you. Share the wealth and you have a much better chance of attracting investors, customers, and other supportive stakeholders.

## DESIGN

So that's the first step: a Huge Tipping Point Idea. But a great idea will go nowhere without a Design. The Design step moves you toward making your idea a reality. Without the right design, your Idea will fail. Design means much more than what you see on the exterior of a product. As Steve Jobs, renowned founder of Apple, showed, there is a lot that goes into Design beyond the product itself.

His design philosophy permeated how he built his companies—Apple, Next, Pixar—and his remarkable products. Business design and product design merged and were inseparable. Often, you might feel that the Idea determines the ultimate success of a business. But in fact, the Idea triggers a question: What if this Idea became a reality? And what would this idea look like?

Most people start fiddling with the Idea and do a few sketches, sometimes on a napkin. They may tell someone they trust or sit down with a designer or design the Idea themselves at first. Most of the time, the Idea originator focuses almost exclusively on the product itself. Yet most fail to face the equally important part of Design.

As biographer Walter Isaacson wrote in his book *Steve Jobs*, the Apple chief built his products and his companies "endowed with his DNA, that is, filled with creative designers and daredevil engineers who could carry forward his vision.... He built a company where leaps of imagination were combined with feats of engineering." From the very beginning, Jobs would think how to make the product "user friendly, put it together in a package, market it, and make a few bucks." Jobs was a perfectionist, a trait he learned from his father, a cabinetmaker. That passion for a good-looking as well as well-functioning device would carry through all of his unique products: the Macintosh, the iMac, the iPhone, and the iPad.

As reported by Cliff Kuang for Fastcodesign.com, "Mike Markkula, one of the first investors in Apple, wrote a one-page memo—'The Apple Marketing Philosophy'—that stressed three points. The first was *empathy*: the focus on customer feelings and needs. The second was *focus*: eliminate all of the unimportant opportunities. The third was *impute*. People do judge a book by its cover."

You can see a consistent theme. In a way perception is everything. It's not enough to have the best product; it's also how you package it. Markkula and Jobs were way ahead of their times. They realized customer focus and customer experience were the keys to the design of a company's product and the business itself, inside and outside. That's one reason why Jobs had the knack of understanding what consumers needed before they did. He wanted to let people experience his devices intuitively, a hallmark of all Apple products.

I myself quickly learned in the food business that your package on the supermarket shelf is your salesperson. You only have a second to catch buyers' attention, interest them, evoke desire, and get them to take action and buy. That is the classic marketing formula of AIDA: Attention, Interest, Desire, Action.

From the very beginning, an entrepreneur wants to start designing the company's look, feel, positioning, and messaging by constantly asking over and over and seeking answers to the following fundamental questions:

- What is my product?
- What does it do?
- Why would people buy it? (What's in it for them?)

- Why would they buy it now? (Why would it be a priority in the buyer's mind? This is very important.)
- What price point would get them to immediately want to buy if my product was a priority in their minds?
- Why should they believe or trust me and my company, project, or cause?
- What will I name the product? My company?

All these questions need to be asked up front because it is often, at this point, that you make a crucial decision based upon the Idea alone. You tune out everything else because you see big dollar signs as an investor or entrepreneur; imagine the press calling you a genius or big crowds applauding you. At the Idea stage, you can fall prey to the ridiculous, as seen on CNN's *Anderson Cooper 360°*: What was he/she thinking? You don't want to be part of the conversation in which others might comment: How often do smart people do dumb things? My point is: there are enough unknowns and risks at the Idea step to at least start asking some fundamental questions at the Design step. This won't ensure success, but it will open your eyes to the challenges and problems you will face. Constantly trying to ask the right questions will give you a good head start in the right direction.

By asking questions, you keep yourself at the Big Picture or Forest (from the trees or details) level. This often enables you to avoid having a knee-jerk reaction (the entrepreneurial urge) and jumping blindly into a bad investment or business idea.

## SIMPLE VERSUS COMPLEX AND SIMPLIFYING THE COMPLEX

What is common to all aspects of business and capital raising is that it is a complex process. What appears simple on the surface becomes quickly complex once reality confronts us and questions are asked of us. Suddenly, you realize there are many unknowns and a lot of risks.

Getting the money and pitching for millions is a process of:

- Taking what seemingly is simple at first: the business itself, the product, and how to describe its features and benefits
- Realizing that it's complex to articulate all this when a business start-up asks the right questions
- Working day and night to return to the simplicity of the original Idea through the right business, product, and messaging design

Design can be laying out a plan and strategies for a company as well. Design can include the overriding vision and structure of the company: Who will be the potential partners? Who can help the company get the Idea off the ground? What does that start-up have to explain verbally or graphically to communicate, present, and pitch their Idea? Does the company have to get someone's or a group's permission to proceed with the Idea? What if they say no? All these issues should be addressed at the Design step.

Now let's turn back to products and services: Design can be a sketch for a house you want to sell or for a retail shop or for the container or box of the product. Design can be the name, the trademark, or the formula. Design is limited only by your imagination. You might talk your Idea out with someone you trust: someone who won't try to immediately talk you out of the Idea but will listen and ask questions. The key is to take action. Talk it out. Make your idea concrete and physical, e.g., sketch it on a napkin or write up how you would describe and picture the product on a sales sheet.

One design that affects millions of people today is based upon the Gausebeck-Levchin test. When you purchase an item on a website, you see a box with crisscrossed lines and weird letters and numbers. You have to look at the box and decipher the squiggly letters and numbers. You then type the letters and numbers into another window to prove you are purchasing the item.

The design was created to solve PayPal's biggest problem, which was the fraud being committed by PayPal's user base. Russian mobsters were using PayPal to steal credit card numbers and launder money. PayPal was hardly alone, since similar fraud issues had toppled other online payment companies. Levchin and 75 engineers entered into a 24/7 dogfight to counter the Russian mobsters, maintain consumer confidence, and save PayPal.

Here are some additional critical insights about Design:

1. Technology is essentially made up of ideas and design.
2. A business itself is an idea and design that works with physical technology (tools) and social technologies (ways of organizing).
3. There is always a conflict between design and functionality. For instance, too many websites are designed to look very creative, but the way they function gets in the way of the user engaging and doing business.
4. Simple trumps complex.
5. Design creates and builds wealth. Design can differentiate a company and make it the one selected. Think once more of Apple iPods, iPhones, iPads, and the Apple Store and website. How a company designs its name and its logo is very important.
6. Design sets the tone and the experience and evokes the emotions of the company's customers. This attracts new customers and keeps existing customers coming back. Think of Starbucks and Amazon.

The key principles of Idea and Design are the first two assets that any promising company, or investment, must have. Without a striking idea, or advance on an old idea, you have no core at the center. Without a striking design, you have no presentation and/or packaging for the idea. Yet another crucial step is needed: testing out the idea.

To craft your pitch (your presentation of your Idea and Design):

- Convince yourself first. You should sell yourself. You should not, as I have pointed out, just jump at an idea without stepping back and looking at the Big Picture and asking the right questions over and over.

- Examine and test the Idea and Design of your business and its product(s) by reviewing the Three Magical Ps: people, product, and potential. Ask yourself: Who can help you get the business and product off the ground? How will you test your idea/solution with potential customers? What will you have to show them? What questions will you ask them?
- Who will you sit with first and ask for advice?
- Can you design the product or can you show what products or services exist and how you would better them?
- Before you or others can be convinced of your Idea and Design, you need to know if and/or how the marketplace responded to a similar idea and design. Who already is out there with a product or service that competes with yours?
- Again, most start-ups believe they know the competition well. They do some investigation and conclude there's a simple road to big money with their product idea and design. Ironically, the more you delve into your product and what it requires, the more you start becoming aware of how many competitors already exist. In other words, how complex the world in which you want to start up your company truly is.

That leads us to the Discovery phase.

## TAKEAWAYS AND INSIGHTS

- Design your business as a product itself as much as the products or service you are marketing.
- From the very beginning view your Idea and Design as if you were an investor.
- The biggest challenge to success may be your fear of it—even more than your fear of failure.
- The 7 Steps are not linear. You keep coming back to them in different iterations at different levels of your business individually or in different combinations and sequences to fit your specific challenges and problem.
- Marketing is about communication and conversation.
- The key to finding great ideas is to be an observer—typically an outsider and/or a peak performer who becomes so immersed in a subject that he/she sees the nuances that make the difference.
- The one-page memo by Mike Markkula, one of Apple's first investors, is brilliant in stressing three points; empathy, focus, and inputs (look or design)
- From building Questionmine, I learned you can have the greatest product but look, feel, and usability are integral to success.
- The Lean Start-up has become very popular among entrepreneurs and investors alike. In part, Lean Start-up views your Idea as a hypothesis, guess, or hunch as to what may be a valuable solution for customers. Then, like a scientific experiment you go into the marketplace (see Discovery step) and test incrementally your hypothesis and its supporting assumption.

- To give you another structure or framework to evaluate your company or investment, use the Lean Canvas, which has many designs itself.
- Ideas are just ideas until they are implemented. But great ideas help a lot. Often, your original idea keeps changing as you get input.
- Sometimes, you have to change your idea dramatically, or pivot.
- Likeability and warmth are keys to generating trust in leaders, customers, investors, and other stakeholders.

Click here for additional resources: http://bit.ly/19Iz5gv

## CHAPTER 4

# DISCOVERY

In Discovery, a start-up company has to uncover who its competitors are and then calculate how well its product—it's Idea and Design—will be accepted by the marketplace. That's why Discovery is so important. It's the point where a company tests out its idea and basic design concepts to get feedback. Two good examples of the Discovery process are, ironically, two of the largest crowdfunding sites, Kickstarter and Indiegogo. Both companies and their founders understood that the Internet provided a new way to raise capital by reaching smaller, non-wealthy investors who wanted to pledge or donate money to causes or projects without owning a piece of company. This was an Idea and Design radically different from traditional private equity funding, which is limited to only wealthy investors under strict SEC regulations.

Kickstarter and Indiegogo both saw that they could get a piece of the fund-raising pie by owning the best crowdfunding portals. The way Kickstarter makes money is to charge 5% on money raised from donors, mainly to creative types such as authors, film makers, and musicians. Indiegogo charges 4% for successful campaigns, although that figure goes up to 9% if the funding goal is not reached. Kickstarter operates on an all-or-nothing principle, which means you must raise the full amount of money you are seeking or you receive no money, whereas Indiegogo allows you to receive any money pledged to your project but at the higher rate if you don't raise all the money. In their cases, their Discovery process discovered a new niche in their marketplace. Yet they will not be alone for long. An estimated 500-plus crowdfunding portals will be created in the upcoming years.

That surge of competition is one of the most important aspects of the Discovery process. Radical Ideas and Designs can be very appealing at first. But then the brutal reality of global competition will rear its head. No one is immune from current and future competitive threats. There are two theories on this: first mover advantage and fast copiers which we will cover later.

For now, you want to be aware that often what happens is that companies do a quick competitive analysis. They congratulate themselves on the lack of competition. But after investing a lot of time and money, they discover from an analyst or prospective investor that they have a number of very formidable competitors. Without an ability to respond to the newly discovered competition, the company may struggle, find investors reluctant to invest, and fail.

So a new start-up now has to go into the marketplace/arena with a watchful eye. The arena is where an outfit finds out in the real world what and who else is out there. The question you repeatedly have to ask as an investor and entrepreneur is: Does someone else or do many others have similar Ideas and Designs? Most likely, the fledgling company will have competition or substitutes for their products or services, i.e., other solutions. In fact, the entrepreneur wants some competition to validate that others believe there is a market for its product.

Therefore, in Discovery, the maverick has to evaluate how it is going to differentiate itself. Ironically, as noted previously, Harvard lecturer Ghosh notes that many companies fail because of *overfunding* based upon often arrogant entrepreneurs (jockeys) who think they are right about their product idea and design and do not leave themselves room to test assumptions and pivot (make radical changes rather than incremental ones) when the market is not buying what is being offered.

A key element involves positioning, such as being a premium brand or a service, i.e., unique enough to charge a price and get high margins, such as Microsoft Windows, versus a low-margin commodity such as ordinary salt or rice. This is a very important point that few anticipate. One of the key things that hurt businesses is a product that can be easily duplicated. Or, the distinction or the unique difference is not articulated well. As a result, competitors can manipulate their own positioning and make product claims which appear to have the newcomer's unique solution. They are not above promising people solutions they can't deliver.

The newcomer can't just say that because an established company doesn't have a good product, it's not going to be a competitor. These competitors may have very good copywriters and marketers who are skilled at manipulating people into buying their products with false claims. When customers buy something from them and find that the product doesn't deliver as promised, the customers are going to be more gun-shy of buying a new company's product if it makes similar claims. Therefore, a young company must clearly and emphatically distinguish itself in the marketplace in its presentations, pitches, and messaging so that it gets above the noise in the market and doesn't look like a "me-too" product in comparison to its competitors.

## COMPETITIVE ADVANTAGE

As an entrepreneur or an investor, you need to consider four key questions when reviewing a company's product and its promised solution to see if it has a sustainable unfair or competitive advantage:

1. What makes the product special?
2. Can it charge high margins (get monopoly profits)?
3. Can this special advantage be sustained over time? Does it have what Warren Buffett calls a wide economic moat (competitive advantage) around the castle (product or service)?
4. Is the special product advantage proprietary or protected with a patent or trademark, or is there some other special license or agreement that gives the product an unfair advantage?

In the Discovery process, one of the most important things for most investors who are looking to invest in a company, or for an entrepreneur who's looking to build a company, is the competitive advantage.

As mentioned, when people start off, they often fail to really evaluate the competition carefully enough to see what they're doing well. A neophyte needs to check that if it comes out with a new product, can the competition copy or substitute quickly for it and take over that idea and make it their own? Understanding the competition is important, but a company also needs to create strategies that set it apart.

## LISTENING

Listening well is crucial to being effective in life. Listening to other people's feedback—their perceptions, evaluations, interpretations—can provide valuable guidance. Benjamin Franklin said, "Love your enemies, for they tell you your faults...Who is wise? He that learns from everyone."

Many times, people distort reality—a little or a lot. An entrepreneur's task is not to take the feedback and/or criticism so personally that he likewise distorts the truth.

Above all else, what a new company is looking for is a competitive advantage, or the "castle and the moat." The castle is the product or service, and the moat is the differentiating factor—the competitive advantage. Great investors like Warren Buffett look mainly for a company's competitive advantage—the edge. In other words, what advantage does it have in the marketplace that's going to be the moat which protects it as competitors try to duplicate what it has?

In many businesses, the moat allows for high profit margins to be maintained. Consistent high profit margins are indicative of a strong competitive advantage. Make no mistake: the market wants to push a new product to be a commodity, a product whose price can be undercut.

An idea that has great margins is premium and is perceived as having value. Typically, most businesses either want to be the premium player or the cheap player, but a business rarely wants to be in the middle. As a commodity, the edge is small and the profit margin is normally very small, because the ability to substitute for that product is easy. Many times, access to the market is easy, so there's little barrier to competition.

For example, many new technologies start out with premium or even monopoly-like pricing, but then as competition enters the market, the price drops and the high profit margins get eroded. You can see the competition heating up in the tablet wars. Apple's iPad mini was announced and now competes with Google's Nexus 7. Apple believes its superior quality will offset its higher price. Yet Brian Tong of C/net.com begged to differ. He compared the two competing tablets using *six criteria: design, controls and user interface, features, web browsing and multimedia, performance, and value.* He concluded that Nexus 7 edged out the Apple iPad mini by being more competitively priced.

When you watch the two tablets being analyzed, you are struck by the innovation—the Idea and the Design—but also the fierce competition between Google and Apple.

Their competition attracted new players and *new criteria* for who is winning and why. Here is a headline from a *Forbes* magazine article by Todd Hixon: "Why Android Is Winning the Tablet Wars." Hixon asks: What is happening and where is this going? He sees four driving forces:

1. Tablets are more than a media consumption device now.
2. Android has matured.
3. Samsung is on the rise.
4. Tablets have been democratized.

Then there is a survey, which asked the question: What do you use your tablet for most?
Usage categories:

- **Work** = spreadsheets, word processing, and presentations;
- **Communications** = email, web browsing, and social media;
- **Media/games** = movies, e-books, music, and games;
- **Specialized** = administering surveys, reading college applications, etc. (Source: Data was collected May 8 to May 10, 2013, from 1,444 responses from US individuals using the CivicScience web-based opinion research platform).

Here are huge players Apple, Google, Samsung, and Amazon going toe to toe. What chance does a smaller competitor have against these highly competitive giants?

Rule: as an investor or entrepreneur, avoid markets where you compete or potentially can compete against giant companies that have tremendous resources.

It is much easier to sell distinctive products and services to *niches* which avoid competing with the giants. Many times that uniqueness is the deciding variable that makes an investor willing to invest in a company. For example, if I controlled most of the rough-cut diamonds in the world, as De Beers has, I would have a unique competitive advantage—in fact, a monopoly. If diamond users could not substitute for my diamonds or find an alternative supplier, I could keep raising my prices and increasing my profits. I would do this until I found the optimum number of users and profit margin.

Till the 1980s, De Beers accounted for 90% of all rough diamonds sold by value, and controlled an empire that extended from the mines of South Africa, Australia, Canada, and Siberia to the sorting rooms of London, Antwerp, and Tel Aviv. Today that share has whittled down to some 35%, courtesy of a series of rapid changes in the world of luxury and mining...These tectonic changes are taking place at a time when there's pressure on sales in a shrinking market; De Beers's total sales in 2012 decreased 16% to $6.1 billion. Meantime, competitors like Alrosa of Russia, BHP Billiton of Australia, and Anglo-Australian mining group Rio Tinto continue to chisel away at De Beers's monopoly. Rio Tinto increased sales by 12% in 2012.

> While rivals have evolved a distribution system that mimics that of De Beers, the hitherto virtual monopoly is no longer able to "punish" its customers for buying diamonds from other companies. "We embrace the fact that we operate in a competitive marketplace as we believe we have an exceptionally strong offering for our customers," says Varda Shine, CEO of Diamond Trading Corporation (DTC), De Beers's marketing arm. "We understand that our sightholders [or dealers] will purchase diamonds from other producers and we see this as a perfectly healthy situation for the industry to be in." (Source: economictimes.indiatimes.com)

On the other hand, if I produced a very common product, such as ordinary nails available from innumerable suppliers, I would have little competitive advantage. My margins would be low and I would have to sell in volume or survive as a very small, low-overhead operation. I could try to differentiate myself through service and quality, but as an investor, there would still be little competitive advantage for me to rely upon.

Of course, there are many successful commodity-type businesses, but they usually are in a defined niche or segment of business, and that niche is their competitive advantage. Often, they have built up relationships over the years that keep competitors out. Since these relationships are often personal, they can erode quickly if a key member of the business dies or gets in a disagreement with a long-standing customer.

Ideally, you want to invest in a company that has a unique niche product for which there is strong and growing demand.

## UNIQUE SELLING PROPOSITION

Think of your pitch as beginning with words that immediately tell others—your stakeholders, such as investors, employees, suppliers, distributors, and customers—why you are different or possess a competitive advantage.

Coming up with your simple statement of why you are different is very challenging. In fact, getting your positioning correct is vital to your company's survival and growth.

In any area of life, especially in raising money such as through crowdfunding, you must be able to articulate quickly and precisely why you are different.

During the Discovery Phase, you want to ask yourself as the investor or entrepreneur: What is the new company's unique selling proposition? If we take the words by themselves, they'll give a clue as to what these terms mean. One, *unique* means that a product is different from anything else out there. Second, *selling* means that this *uniqueness* has to be sold to somebody.

Here's a test. Ask what "job" your product or service does or solves. If somebody buys it, he is hiring your product or service to do a job or solve a problem.

Third, the *proposition* is effectively the offer. The offer must be irresistible to such a point that somebody *must* have your product or solution, rather than it's just *nice* to have.

One of the key criteria I use is to ask the question: Is this a "must-have" product or a "nice-to-have" product? "Must have" versus "nice to have" makes all the difference between a winning company and investment and a losing one.

Think of it this way. A must-have product is a compelling product that makes itself a priority in the customer's mind.

Let's go further. Whether you are an investor or a business owner, you need to ask questions constantly as you compare your product to the competition in the Discovery step. These questions help shape the company's strategies and tactics. You become aware of how others have attracted or are attempting to attract customers.

## DOES YOUR PRODUCT HAVE AN EMOTIONAL COMPETITIVE ADVANTAGE?

Products and companies have to attract others and excite them emotionally. Ask what appeal a product or solution has. Does it have an overall story? Does it have positioning? Does it have ways to get attention and stimulate interest and desire? Does it have an attribute that's going to create an emotional bond with the customer so that there's an authentic relationship? Will it have an online relationship or offline or both? Will it maintain a dialogue or conversation that is ongoing, rather than a self-serving monologue that keeps telling the customer, just as other companies do, that it's the world's best or the fastest or the cheapest?

A company must keep its customers engaged. Effectively, the attribute you're looking for is emotional engagement. More and more, a brand depends on relationships; it's reflected in the logo and the design, like the iPad. But these brand elements are part of an entire essence or gestalt or feeling which connects the customer to the brand.

These elements—story, a remarkable product/solution, an appealing look or design, and an ongoing, two-way, authentic conversation—collectively give a product and company a competitive advantage—its uniqueness in the marketplace

It is the uniqueness turned into the unique selling proposition which makes the product one about which others want to tell their network of friends and associates.

## DO YOU POSSESS AN EXCITED FAN BASE OR NETWORK?

A company's network may become more and more the deciding factor that tips the scales in its favor. Today even having a great product or solution is not enough. It's a necessary key to success. But without a supportive network, a company will find it hard to compete.

Up to now, venture capitalists' and wealthy investors' main appeal besides money has been their network of connections. They can open doors to accounts that entrepreneurs may never be able to reach on their own.

With crowdfunding, entrepreneurs, creative types, and small businesspeople have an opportunity to become visible, make others—the crowd—aware of their unique selling proposition, and create their own networks and following.

For an entrepreneur in the world of crowdfunding, it's about appealing to and building your network—your relationships. Relationships are the new currency. The crowd becomes your network or relationships. The crowd takes on many roles. They become your customer base, your investors, and your evangelists who are going to tell new customers about you.

Crowd sourcing and crowdfunding are the outgrowth of social media. Social media employ web- and mobile-based technologies to support interactive dialogues or conversations between and among organizations, communities, and individuals. Your unique selling proposition is integral to your story. Your story and your unique selling proposition are vital components of your presentations, pitches, and positioning and building your relationships of supporters, customers, and investors.

As I will repeat over and over, early-stage companies must go through defined stages of growth and must perform many different tasks at the same time to reach meaningful milestones. The 7 Step System and the Magical P's and other models I will show you are guidelines or a map to show you how these roles and milestones fit together. Companies, which follow these stages and steps are deemed to be consistent and normally succeed much more than inconsistent companies that try to bypass the patterns models and steps I am revealing to you. It's like a baseball player trying to win by running to second base without touching first base. To get the edge and succeed, you must touch all bases, beginning with your Idea and Design. Then get out and interview customers to find out if your product solves a real problem for them and who else has a similar solution (part of your Discovery step).

During the first steps—Idea, Design, and Discovery—you are gathering information and talking to and building you network. You are finding out if your product provides a satisfying solution for the customers. *Good to Great* author Jim Collins says, don't go into a business unless it can be the best in the world. Business writer Guy Kawasaki similarly asks about a product's uniqueness: Is it going to be the best in the world?

## BEING ABLE TO BOIL THE OCEAN IS NOT A COMPETITIVE ADVANTAGE

Here's one of the biggest challenges I have found in my own start-ups and in advising others. I call it the "boil the ocean" error. When you or I are asked who is our customer, we struggle with an answer. Deep down, we believe everyone should want our product. If only we had enough money and resources, the entire world would buy our great product.

Well, the entire world doesn't buy Apple, Google, Samsung, or Amazon products or advertise on Google's search engine or join Facebook or use Twitter. In fact, the more you dig into your research in the Discovery step, the more you realize that there are other very strong competitors with solutions similar to yours. You have to find your sweet spot or niche where you can be clearly the best. This is where you want to define your unique selling proposition and appeal and activate your network—the crowd—to get behind you.

To be the best in the world, a start-up also has to look at the niche it occupies. It can't try to conquer too big a market, i.e., it can't boil the ocean. A niche product is one that appeals to a subset of an already established market where larger companies already dominate. As mentioned and should be repeated, a newcomer typically wants to avoid going head to head with the larger company that has the resources and connections to quash the competitive threat to their market dominance.

For example, LuluLemon Athletica is a typical niche retail company which specializes in exercise equipment, athletic wear, and exercise accessories mostly for women. LuluLemon states that it makes technical athletic clothes for yoga, running, working out, and most other sweaty pursuits."

Here's their history: "After twenty years in the surf, skate, and snowboard business, founder Chip Wilson took the first commercial yoga class offered in Vancouver and found the result exhilarating. He felt yoga had a feeling close to surfing and snowboarding."

Chip possessed a passion for technical athletic fabrics which he used to substitute for the cotton yoga outfits which were being used at the time.

He offered the new yoga outfits which started an underground yoga clothing movement. He discovered what yoga clothing appealed to the yoga market by asking for feedback from yoga instructors who were asked to wear the products.

Using discovery, the LuluLemon name itself was chosen in a survey of 100 people from a list of 20 brand names and 20 logos. The logo is actually a stylized "A" that was made for the first letter in the name "athletically hip", a name which failed to make the grade.

Next LuluLemon opened its first real store November 2000 in Kitsilano, the beach area of Vancouver, British Columbia. LuluLemon developed with their trainers a lifestyle community approach that focused upon healthy living which included yoga, diet, running/cycling and mental outlook.

Notice how LuluLemon has a founding story, a niche, a unique selling proposition which combines to creates its competitive advantage.

This is not to say that larger companies can't seek to dominate niches within their market as well. Examples are companies such as Canon and Hewlett Packard, which target the home office market with all-in-one copiers-scanners and faxes as well as the small nonhome businesses and the large corporate market.

## DO YOU HAVE A SUSTAINABLE COMPETITIVE ADVANTAGE?

If a product doesn't have an emotionally exciting story, a uniqueness, an unfair or competitive advantage, and the ability to be the best in the world in a niche, smart investors aren't going to put their money up. Why put money into something if there isn't an advantage that it can sustain?

A lot of times just being faster or better is not enough of a differentiator. Many people make the mistake of just thinking that being cheaper than their competitors is enough. Would Lululemon be around if it just sold based upon being the cheapest or even first in its category? Faster, cheaper, or even better alone doesn't necessarily mean a company will have a *sustainable* competitive advantage; what if the competition engages in cutthroat pricing until the new competitor is driven out of business?

The big challenge I see today is whether the advantage can be sustained. Even looking back five years, products which seemed unbeatable suddenly fell from the grace of the crowd. Think of Nokia. What about BlackBerry smart phones? Are they on their way to becoming cultural artifacts, relics of a prior age? Or how about Atari computers? They didn't remain state of the art for very long.

Other examples in the fast-moving world of technology are legion. Take AltaVista, a very popular web search engine owned by Yahoo, but whose popularity dropped off with the rise of Google. Yahoo shut Alta Vista down July 8, 2013. Yahoo itself would be out of business if it had not shifted its strategy to become a content provider. As a home page, many would argue, it still maintains an advantage over Google.

Having a sustainable competitive advantage is a key investment criteria for Warren Buffet. Except for his investment in IBM, Buffett has avoided investing in technology companies. The reason is that sustaining a competitive advantage in a fast-shifting marketplace is extremely difficult.

The problem with many businesses is they are product- and profit-centric. They tout the features of their products in one-way monologues. Both start-up and large businesses will struggle if they do not recognize the dramatic shift to a world of social media. Here the crowd—the customers—rules. The customers carry on conversations with their peers and gather information about products. They don't trust most companies to tell them the truth.

Your objective is to stand out more clearly and favorably in your customers' eyes. They have to see an advantage in your unique selling proposition over your competition because you offered them more benefits, features, and a larger bottom-line payoff. But, this still is not enough to get the edge and win. The way to win and get the edge is to show that you are listening to what the customers need and want and that you genuinely care about them. That you want to engage, entertain, and educate them. That with your product and company, their lives and experiences will be better.

When you take this customer-centric ongoing engagement and conversation approach, then you can enact your Unique Selling Strategy successfully.

## UNIQUE SELLING STRATEGY

How is a Unique Selling Strategy different from a unique selling proposition? The unique selling strategy centers on the question: does the company make money when its product or service is sold at a certain price point? In other words, does it have a true profit margin? Even if a business is just beginning, it can project selling at a certain price and achieving a certain gross margin (sales minus cost of goods or product cost) at various levels of volume. Then, after subtracting expenses, such as marketing, sales, and operations, from the gross margin, would the company really make a decent profit?

As I have tried to point out, the company will be able to obtain attractive margins if it can find a niche or crowd and deliver it a unique solution which solves a pain point, problem, or need it has—even if the need is purely to be entertained.

Just because the crowd buys the unique selling proposition, it does not mean that the company has a true competitive advantage. For example, on *Shark Tank*, an entrepreneur presented a teddy bear product on which you could record your voice or music for your child if you were away, or grandparents could do the same. When asked about sales, the entrepreneur first stated he had significant growth. When asked about his marketing and selling strategy, he admitted his sales came from Groupon. He could not prove that customers would pay the full price where he could make and maintain a sufficient, attractive profit margin.

Pricing is as much an art as a science. Often, it takes a lot of experimentation when you have a new product. Often, you price your product or service very low or give it away to get trial and feedback.

Here are some of the challenges I discovered with a family food company we started from our kitchen. Traditionally, biscotti is an Italian hard, twice-baked cookie that is often dunked in coffee, tea, or wine to soften and enjoy it. We had developed a unique easy-to-eat biscotti cookie to which we added American flavors with names such as Cranberry Orange Zest, Double Double Chocolate, and Very Vanilla Almond.

I went into business with a master salesman. Marty worked for a large food distributor in New Jersey and had his own small food brokerage and food distribution company on the side.

I kept asking Marty for the sales from his big food distributing company. One day, Marty walked into my office. He seemed very enthusiastic. Here's the order. For a moment, I was ecstatic until I looked more carefully at the price.

"Marty, you got to be kidding me. We can't sell at this price. We won't make any money."

"What are you talking about?" he questioned.

"Those are cheap cookie prices. We have to double-bake the biscotti and we don't own the bakery," I pointed out.

Right then I realized I had made a huge blunder in the Discovery process. I had projected sales based upon Marty telling me he could sell two million dollars worth of cookies. But, I just assumed the sales would be at the premium price. But, to Marty and his distribution company, a cookie was a cookie. We could charge a little more but not the premium prices I projected. And the distributor wanted a large cut to cover their costs and make a profit. Then, there was the food broker. Even worse, I discovered that to make biscotti you'd have to tie up double the number of ovens since they were double-baked cookies. Few bakeries in the country would bake biscotti, and they wanted volume commitments to even consider baking for us. We didn't have the volume. We needed lower prices to get the volume. We had a classic chicken-and-egg problem.

The lesson I learned firsthand: many entrepreneurs and investors make the error of not realizing that they're losing money on each unit sold until they're too far into the company.

Instead, they start up and bring in investors into their deal. Everything appears promising. Suddenly, they discover either customers won't pay for their solution or they won't pay enough or buy in enough volume. As a result, they struggle, and most go out of business.

This is why you have to develop your customers from the beginning. But, the challenge is that you may get customers initially at low-volume premium prices. However, when you try to scale your business, you can't get the premium prices or your realize your distributors or partners want too big a cut.

Growth itself can be good or bad. As I demonstrated, growth is bad if you are failing fast by selling each unit at a loss or too low a margin to sustain and grow the business. Growth can also get ahead of your resources. Often, growth means you have to anticipate the production capacity, the staffing, including customer service, to support the growth.

## COST OF A NEW CUSTOMER AND RAPID GROWTH

An entrepreneur needs to identify the number of new customers per month. If you allow terms and have to pay for items up front before you get paid, then you have a cash shortfall. For example, prospects visit the company website or call to get more information that has to be sent out, such as a physical catalog or samples such as cookies. The company needs to factor in the cost of maintaining and sending out marketing literature and materials, physical product samples, and the average monthly cost of promotions. This includes online and offline promotions that are one time or continuous.

As a company grows rapidly, it may find that it underestimated all these costs in its pricing and sees its profit margins under pressure and its cash flow becoming more and more drained.

You have to either adjust your pricing, which may get a lot of resistance, or come up with new product add-ons to increase your revenues.

The lesson learned: developing a Unique Pricing Strategy is dynamic process. Your pricing strategies must constantly be reviewed against your competitors moves and your own growth needs and their associated costs.

## HOW TO INCREASE YOUR SALES

Your Unique Pricing Strategy affects the three ways to increase your sales:

- Increase the number of customers
- Increase the average size of the sale per customer
- Increase the frequency of purchase

If you increased each of these three ways to increase your sales by just 10%, you would get an overall sales increase of approximately 33%. If you increased each of these three ways by 25%, you would double your sales.

These three ways to increase sales are why companies are constantly giving promotions in the form of coupons, discounts, and loyalty programs. A reduced price increases the number of customers if there is a true demand for the product. Or, with add-ons you can increase the average size of the sale per customer, such as: Do you want fries with your burger? What about a soda or a shake? Frequent flyer miles and other loyalty programs are designed to increase the frequency of your purchases. Each of these strategies should be tested; some variation can be incorporated into your optimum pricing strategy.

An important note: beware of too big a coupon discount or the "groupon effect" where you get a lot of customers but few repeat customers at your full price.

Another important note: Your competitive advantage can be its superior selling system. For instance, Amazon sells its e-books through a unique selling strategy. CEO Jeff Bezos said: "We want to make money when people *use* our devices, not when they *buy* our devices."

Underlying Amazon's low-margin pricing strategy is a customer-centric approach to marketing and selling that focuses on ease of doing business. Amazon increases the average size of the sales per customer by related product suggestions and by offering shipping breaks for larger purchases.

Note: Amazon has added services such as CreateSpace to help you publish and market your books and set them up on Kindle and with other distributors. This complements Amazon's book-selling business, its sale of e-books, and Kindle itself.

## COST AS A COMPETITIVE ADVANTAGE

As you saw in my bakery company example, I need a lower cookie cost which I developed over time by automating our entire double-baked biscotti-making process.

While the focus may be on increasing sales, you should never overlook your costs. Cost is a big factor in businesses. Certain manufacturers have a competitive advantage because of their production capacity, delivery, and supply chain systems, such as Walmart. Walmart excels in their information systems tracking supply, products on the shelf, and the ability to manage cost. Once we automated our biscotti baking process, we put together a co-brand with Walmart. Quickly, we learned that Walmart would not tolerate being out of stock, since that equated with lost sales and lost money. Imagine 4,500 stores and how much Walmart would lose if an item is out of stock storewide even for a few minutes. We had to plan way in advance for Yellow Trucking to pick up our baked goods to arrive precisely at the time Walmart said to have the goods ready to go into their distribution centers.

Like Walmart, Costco, BJs, and others have low-margin, high-volume operations that rely upon many efficient suppliers. If a company has this type of business model, cost is the driving attraction and the competitive advantage.

Companies that have a competitive advantage over time develop a cost advantage because of the way they perfect their internal systems. Greater cost advantages enable efficient companies to deliver products over distances and still undercut the local players. Greater reach because of their supply and cost systems has enabled companies like Walmart to expand nationally and internationally. Way back when,

Andrew Carnegie developed methods to produce steel cheaper than his competitors. He shipped steel to local markets at prices the local steel makers could not match.

## PRODUCTION CAPACITY

The next component in terms of looking at a company is what I call the production capacity. If a business depends upon outside vendors, especially contractors, it's relying upon somebody's production capacity. If the company doesn't have the capacity to produce more, then as a business scales up, it won't be able to meet its customers' demand or refill orders from new customers. If it can't find other suppliers, then it has to get its current suppliers to expand their production capacity. If this expansion involves additional space, additional equipment, additional suppliers, there will be a time lag that could be significant.

The next question you want to ask is: What is the supply chain? One of the main errors in business is relying upon a single supplier. As mentioned, we had a complicated product to make—a double-baked biscotti cookie—and only a handful of bakeries had the equipment to automate the production. We essentially relied upon a single supplier at a time because it took months to set up and perfect the baking process. When you need systems that require a huge infrastructure and multiple skill sets, you're basically at the supplier's mercy. And we were. We had little negotiation power.

Lesson learned: make sure the company has different sources of supply. This is often a challenge when you begin companies, such as software, that have a small set of programmers who know the code. Unless the code is well documented and the source code protected, it can be a difficult situation, similar to having a single supplier.

Another lesson learned: always get three bids when you seek to hire an outside vendor. The lowest bid is not always the best bid. More often than not you get what you pay for. On the other hand, vendors will take advantage of you if they feel you are ignorant. Another reason is that they are too busy and lack the production capacity. They decide if you will pay a very high price, then they will take the job. When you get three bids, a lot of these issues come out if you ask the right questions and compare apples to apples.

## DELIVERY CAPABILITY

One of the big issues in crowdfunding will be the ability to have suppliers who have the production capacity and the ability to deliver the product on time and at a cost that doesn't eat up the projected profits and cash flow. The delivery/fulfillment issue must be considered in the Discovery step: How is the new company delivering the product? If it's sourcing a product in Australia or China, then the product is most likely to come by boat. Then it has to have a certain lead time to get its products. The more time delay, the more inventory the company will require to cover increasing demand. The company may need to have two or more months of inventory on hand. Since inventory can tie up a lot of capital, cash will be needed.

Depending upon when the product sells and when the money is collected, a company can have a negative capital position. This means the faster it grows, the more capital it needs to lay out in advance of sales and collections. One of the main things it wants to know is what the delivery mechanism is.

As an investor or entrepreneur, you must assess and lay out the supply chain step by step in detail. Find out how long it takes to move supply from the manufacturer to the point of being able to be sold. Look at whether a company has a competitive advantage in its distribution. When it has physical products, every time a company moves a product, that move entails a cost. In today's world, if it has to move products using trucks or rail, it is subject to a number of variable costs, such as fuel. If it has a distribution pattern that has a lot of middlemen, then its ability to maintain a high margin is eroded. That's because a middleman is getting a cut of the proceeds.

What makes the Internet so attractive is that a company can eliminate a lot of the middlemen and can sell direct. And if it can do that, then its distribution becomes a competitive advantage as more people buy the product.

What makes crowdfunding so attractive is that it too is using the Internet as its delivery mechanism, and it will cut out lots of middlemen.

Under the traditional capital-raising scenario, an entrepreneur seeking to raise capital outside his own resources will go to friends and families first. After friends and family, the options to get capital drop significantly. Banks are difficult since the company has little or no track record. Sometimes the entrepreneur can get terms from suppliers or even get suppliers to become their partners. But, the entrepreneur is at a disadvantage since the supplier knows everything about the entrepreneur and how desperate he may be to get supplies or funding.

The entrepreneur starts down one or two main paths: try directly to interest venture capitalists or angel investors or both, or the entrepreneur can attempt to interest a broker/dealer or investment banker to raise capital for a fee.

In crowdfunding, the portal or site takes on the role of the investment banker (middle man) and brokers the deals listed on the site or portal. With crowdfunding donations with perks or rewards, the money raised is typically very small, less than $10,000 on average. But with the proposed crowdfunding equity-based money raises, up to a million dollars can be raised from non-wealthy investors potentially much faster with fewer middlemen.

Equity-based crowdfunding can be a more efficient way for early-stage companies to raise capital. It may be more efficient, but it will still be very challenging as you will see. If you continue to follow each of the 7 Steps and the other models I lay out, you will learn how to face and overcome these challenges.

Under the JOBS Act Title II, private placements will become much more efficient since they can now be advertised across all media offline and online including social, mobile, and the web.

## CUSTOMER FOCUSED

The next clear competitive advantage is a company's customer base.

In an online business, the main focus is upon building a list. A list consists of prospects who opted in (typically gave their email or name and email) to get some free information from the company or actual customers who purchased products from the company. If a company or a single-person operation has a responsive list, it can mail to its prospects or customers at a low cost on the Internet. This can lead to prospects buying products and customers reordering products. Because of the low Internet delivery costs and the high margins that can be made from cutting out middlemen and selling directly, large sums of money can be made.

What is key to recognize is that many offline businesses, such as coffee shops, have few prospects and low-priced items. It is more difficult to generate the sales and bottom line that information marketers can generate with high-priced training and coaching programs. But even small business can build a list by offering free and paid information product and bundling them with their lower-priced items. In exchange for coupons or free information, small businesses can collect emails and cell phone numbers. Then mail or text to prospects or customers and create new sources of income.

Building a customer list is not enough. Customers today are very fickle. They are being bombarded with images and ads every minute online and offline. An early-stage company needs to design its business to be customer focused like Amazon or Starbucks.

Why?

The company that knows and engages its prospects and customers best wins. Imagine if you were a prospect and customer mind reader, the advantage you would have as a marketer and seller of products. It's a huge competitive advantage once the customers recognize that they're being listened to cared about and serviced well.

Amazon and Starbucks have developed unique value propositions and delivery systems that are based upon precision personalized marketing. Their marketing addresses the individual, not just the general niches of book buyers or coffee drinkers. Instead, Amazon drills down to what specific books you like and offers related ones, or, with Starbucks, what specific coffee drink you want instead of general one-size-fits-all coffee drinks served elsewhere. In certain Starbucks, if you are a regular, they will attempt to remember you and the drink you like the next time you order at the same Starbucks.

A company needs to keep in mind what challenges and obstacles its customers face. If you want to attract customers, then you must find ways to relate and empathize (remember Apple's investor Mike Markkula's one-page memo of the points—the first being empathy) with the customers' core identity—their true desires and dreams as well as their doubts and fears they have about achieving what they want. The more you know about your prospects and customers, the more you can shape your products and services to give them the insights and solutions they want.

Listening and getting to know your customer better is what is driving data-driven automated marketing today. Companies are seeking to learn as much as they can about who their customers are and what they are doing. They are probing to even find out their customer's deepest "why."

Again, the companies which will succeed will combine the science and art of listening to and getting to know their customers well.

## THE REPUTATION ADVANTAGE

One of the biggest challenges for an early-stage company is few people typically know anything about it. Unless the company is started by founders with successful track records, the entrepreneur is the new kid on the block. New companies and new ideas are treated with skepticism. Rightfully so, since most ideas, designs, and companies fail. People and companies are naturally self-protective. They don't want to take unnecessary risks with their time, money, and resources.

I've always taken the approach that you cannot build a company by yourself, especially in today's competitive world. Even if you are a single person, you should collaborate and create a team around you. You need to assess your own strengths and weaknesses and find those with complementary skill sets.

The big question of others about a company's products and its people becomes: What's in it for me? Who is this person or company?

Or, put a different way, what is this person's or company's reputation? Even harder to decipher, what is this person's or company's character?

The pivotal questions come back to: Are the person and company trustworthy and competent?

I know many people and companies that have built positive reputations and command influence but have little character and often are incompetent. What most business transactions come down to is trust and competence. When trust is established, things often move much faster.

In *Speed of Trust*, by Stephen M. R. Covey, his father, Stephen Covey, states, "The greatest trust-building key is 'results.' Results build brand loyalty. Results inspire and fire up a winning culture. The consistent production of results not only causes customers to increase their reorders, it also compels them to consistently recommend you to others."

A good reputation normally, but not always, signifies the attributes of integrity and competence, and this also leads to name recognition. Here is what Kristal Lutz wrote in "What Makes Patagonia the 'Coolest Company on the Planet': Insights from Founder, Yvon Chouinard":

"If you want to succeed, you have to have integrity. Integrity can't be taught. Integrity is a value—something you hold inside yourself to be very important. Your goal is to invest in a company or build one as an entrepreneur that has as its goal a values-based culture. When successful companies are analyzed over time, researchers have discovered that what is constant and survives, no matter what a company's ups and downs are, is its values. Companies like Patagonia are driven by a certain philosophy, purpose, and value system. Patagonia's founder, Yvon Chouinard's guiding design principle came from Antoine de Saint-Exupéry, the French aviator:

> Have you ever thought not only about the airplane, but whatever man builds, that all of man's industrial efforts, all his computations and calculations, all the nights spent working over draughts and blueprints, invariably culminate in the production of a thing whose sole and guiding principle is the ultimate principle of simplicity?
>
> It is as if there were a natural law which ordained that to achieve this end, to refine the curve of a piece of furniture, or a

> ship's keel, or the fuselage of an airplane, until gradually it partakes of the elementary purity of the curve of the human breast or shoulder, there must be experimentation of several generations of craftsmen. In anything at all, perfection is finally attained not when there is no longer anything to add, but when there is no longer anything to take away, when a body has been stripped down to its nakedness."

Early-stage businesses create a history by their actions, but, like Patagonia, you need to consciously develop a guiding purpose, philosophy, and value system which can make the difference. When things get rough and challenging, as they always do in business and life, it is often your purpose, philosophy, and value system that give you the motivation to persist through the dips to reach and sustain success.

Like a ball team, a business can have stars with great track records and integrity and still fail. Often, the failure can be traced back to a lack of chemistry among the team members. They don't have a true camaraderie, purpose, or philosophy. It's more about their individual achievements. Most great individual athletes who succeed today have supportive teams around them. A solid team provides competitive advantages, such as leadership, culture, know-how, innovation, and entrepreneurialism.

Of course, it helps to invest in a team that has worked together in the past and has demonstrated success and integrity. But, don't rely on their claims or even their press. Check carefully into their backgrounds to find out how they worked together with others and if they truly created the results which they claim on their resumes.

## THE SWITCHING COST

Another competitive advantage is switching cost. People won't switch from one product to another because there is a cost to do so—monetarily psychically and/or physically. Microsoft once had a switching cost advantage since its operating system, Windows, became the standard. Even if somebody comes along with the greatest operating system, look how long it took people to scrap their investments in Microsoft to get some advantage with a new player like Google. In mobile phones, the iPhone has the advantage of developers creating more and more applications for its products. Switching cost becomes a major factor in trying to compete with larger players. Will people make that investment to switch?

That's why an entrepreneur or investor needs to do her due diligence. That involves the investigation of a business or a person prior to doing business with her. I always begin putting together a business thinking of what investors or other stakeholders would require to do business with my company or me. Probe deep enough to determine whether your competition's competitive advantages are a reality; often, businesses appear at first to be leaders, but in time someone else comes along and does it better. They had the idea, but somebody came in and took away the market because the original company did not get it right. When AOL came in, they banked on dial-up, but they did not really anticipate the broadband revolution to come. They tried a strategy of being an island. Google types came in and had an open system of information, and AOL never recovered. They thought they would create a competitive advantage with Time Warner, but in reality it was illusionary. Today, I will point out, the pendulum is swinging back to less open applications and portals like Facebook.

* * *

Possessing a competitive advantage has been found to be one of the most important components of a business. It makes little business sense to claim, "I've got a great idea and a terrific product and business design," if you can't articulate a sustainable competitive advantage. As an investor or entrepreneur, you should not invest in a prototype without being convinced that you have a unique selling proposition that clearly states why you are different and that the odds are in your favor that customers will see value and purchase your product.

As Jack Nicklaus says about a golf swing, 85% is in the setup and the preparation. When you begin the golf swing, you have a much greater chance of success if you set up right. When you don't have the setup and preparation, it is almost impossible to have a repeating swing that produces consistently good to excellent results. Same for any part of a business, or the products and services it looks to sell.

Successful businesses follow the same pattern that evolution follows from Darwin's survival of the fittest. As with evolution, businesses that survive have *differentiation* (a competitive advantage). They are *selected* by customers and investors. They survive and thrive, or *scale.*

The prior three steps—Idea, Design, and Discovery—are all vital components that any entrepreneur or investor needs to consider before committing to move to the enough to give you a profit Development/ Execution step.

Your question as an investor does the business' unique selling proposition and Unique Selling Strategy amount to a sustainable profitable business model that can scale.

When you undertake the Idea, Design, and Discovery steps, think of them as being the basics similar to what peak performers would practice to perfect their fundamentals and create a foundation that will hold up under the pressure of the actual game or competition.

The mantra is *prepare, practice, and test everything over and over. Building a company or finding investment opportunities is an iterative, circular, not linear, back-and-forth process.* Constantly review, question, test, measure, and refine your ideas, designs, and discovery process (research, due diligence, competitive analysis). Then, begin the development (see the next chapter) of your product while continuing to evaluate and choose carefully the people to support your efforts. Continually step back and look at your overall business and the assumptions behind it—in preparation for the pre-launch and actual launch of the product in the marketplace.

## TAKEAWAYS AND INSIGHTS

- Intellectual property such as licenses, patents, or other rights may or may not be competitive advantages as significant resources may be needed.
- There are many competitive advantages. The question is whether a company has a true sustainable advantage when competitors realize the opportunity and can devote significant resources to copying the advantage.
- Evaluate if the advantage is sustainable broadly or better focused upon dominating certain vertical markets, such as financial services or health care, and niches within those verticals.
- Discovery is about due diligence: finding who is already in the market and what customers are using without your Idea/Solution and Business and Product Designs. Like a scientist and detective you are seeking clues and evidence as to whether your hypothesis and its underlying assumptions make sense; have real value and others will pay you.
- What makes businesses work are attractive value propositions which can be articulated in a clear, concise, likeable way. Perception is a key to success.
- Being customer-centric—listening, caring, being appreciative, and responsive like Amazon and Zappos are critical components of business today and can become a strong competitive advantage.

Click here for additional resources: http://bit.ly/1caLz1e

## CHAPTER 5

# DEVELOPMENT

"Messy" is the word that comes to mind when I think of the Development step. Raising capital and building a business are not neat undertakings that follow some prescribed plug-and-play formula. Coming up with a cool Idea or a Design of a product and business and learning during Discovery how unique an Idea and Design are versus the marketplace are challenging enough. Add to that forming a team that can Develop a product, and you have the makings of an uncertain, risky, early-stage company.

Development is the *transitional step* where a company goes from its initial setup into fully manifesting its unique selling proposition, even if the USP is still vague. Think of Development as where the tire meets the road.

The Development stage, the fourth step in the 7 Steps model, brings up a fundamental issue related to crowdfunding. Is the company an asset builder—one that builds a Golden Goose or Money Machine that attracts capital? Or is the company one that pursues development of merely a Golden Egg or product that is focused more on income than long-term assets and building a sustainable business?

Let's take a concrete example. Mechanical-watch restoration expert Leo Pardon decided to run a two-month Kickstarter campaign to raise $20,000 for his new Vuelta, a "reboot of the gentleman's mechanical-wind timepiece," with a waterproof leather strap and a transparent bottom for watching the internal mechanism in motion. Pardon reached his funding goal in two days and went on to raise $98,022 from 264 backers, who gave him feedback as to how to improve the watch's design.

The question is: What did Pardon envision? Did he plan to develop a watch (a Golden Egg product) for a limited sale or a company (a

Golden Goose or Money Machine) that builds gentlemen's mechanical-wind timepieces?

Here's why this distinction is so important when it comes to money raising, especially crowdfunding. Crowdfunding donations with rewards or perks offered on sites like Kickstarter and RocketHub are mainly aimed at funding Golden Egg projects of creative types—not Golden Goose companies where you get ownership.

In fact, entrepreneurs that are looking to build companies don't do well at crowdfunding donations with rewards. The cofounder of RocketHub, Brian Meese, told an audience interested in crowdfunding that entrepreneurs often don't do as well with the rewards type of crowdfunding because they are not as experienced in building the needed networks or followers as, say, a creative-type rock group. Rock groups know that to survive they need fans to buy their records and tickets to their concerts. Nor, Meese said, do entrepreneurs' companies typically have the emotional appeal of the specific creative-type projects, such as a new rock group's debut album, that succeed on RocketHub.

Remember, in crowdfunding donations with rewards, you back projects by giving them money and get some reward in return, such as the product for which you backed or donated money—for example, the rock group's debut album or a T-shirt or a cool watch at a presale discount. Again, you don't get any ownership of the project or company.

## WHAT IS YOUR DEVELOPMENT AND MONEY-RAISING STRATEGY?

Crowdfunding is one strategy, as I will explain, to get some initial seed capital. When you begin to formulate your Idea/product/solution and Design steps and evaluate your solution against the competition and test it with potential customers via interviews in the Discovery step, you must decide on how you are going to fund the Development of your project, campaign, or company from the very beginning.

This brings up your purpose. Why do you exist? What is your vision? How do you want to impact the world? What is your strategy for accomplishing your goals? Who is going to help you get from here to there?

There is no right or wrong as to what purpose, cause, project, or company you decide to create or build. The real question becomes how you are going to amass the time, energy, money, and resources to develop your vision into reality. Once you decide on a strategy, you will impact your life, those close to you, and those you ask to help you get where you want to go.

The issue of money and wealth building is very emotionally charged. Some people just want to do well or create and don't want to deal with money issues. Unfortunately, money is needed to support causes and medical, scientific, or artistic endeavors. That's what makes crowdfunding donations or crowdfunding donations with rewards such an exciting mechanism to get creative-type projects funded.

## INVESTORS WANT TO OWN COMPANIES, NOT IN YOU, INC.

Here's an important point. *You* may decide to start and develop a company as an entrepreneur for many reasons, such as *you* hate working for someone else or *you* were fired and have no other alternative or *you* have a passion to solve some problem which frustrates *you* or *you* love the thrill of creating and growing companies.

As you will see, investors want to know your story: Why are you starting up this company, and what makes you tick?

But, for the most part, no matter how much investors may like you and your project on an emotional level, they want to make money. Often, lots of money!

Here's the bottom line: investors want ownership in companies so they can make tons of money for taking a risk and betting on you and your start-up company.

The key to wealth building is ownership. But the bigger key is the ownership of a business, not an individual.

Let's dig down even further. The real riches are made by owning a certain type of company that I call a Golden Goose or Money Machine.

Investors want to invest in and *own* Money Machine-type companies run by a *team* that can generate Golden Eggs over the long run. In other words, investors want to back the right people, the right product, and the right potential. That's how they can end up making 10 times or more on their money.

Investors normally do not want to invest in individuals, or what I call You, Inc. *You* can get hit by a bus, *you* can walk out the door and decide not to come back, and *you* only have so many hours in a day. Instead, investors want to invest in an ongoing team and business. Many top investors feel there are numerous ideas but the team has to develop and execute them. Even having a great idea and team does not ensure success. For example, the early stage carries more risk because the company usually rests on one or a few founders or key executives. Accidents or arguments have derailed many a promising start-up.

What about superstars? Aren't they You, Inc.? Yes, in the beginning, they may be. But star power only goes so far. Many movie stars and celebrities are not single practitioners or You, Inc. The more savvy performers, such as Oprah Winfrey, Jennifer Lopez, Steven Spielberg, James Patterson, and Clint Eastwood, took their earning power and invested it in Golden Goose-type companies with teams that create and develop assets such as records, films, fashion lines, TV shows, and books. In addition, these stars also get paid royalties for many years from products they created with other companies.

Another key point: in the Development step, you as an entrepreneur want to create and own businesses or assets that work for you and that you can sell for a lot more than you invested in money, time, and resources. Even if you are a very talented individual with high earnings, you should look to turn those earnings into solid assets and businesses.

Experienced investors want to invest in assets that they can own and have some level of control and protection. They want to leverage their money by investing in a company that becomes an asset. I define an asset as something that puts money—cash—in your pocket whether you work for it or not. They want companies that generate positive cash flow and earnings that grow so they can get higher and higher multiples on the earnings and higher and higher stock prices.

## DEVELOP HIGH MULTIPLES AND SUPER MONEY EXITS

Ultimately, you must realize you are developing your product and company to sell part of it or all of if you seek venture capital or angel money. The investors' goal is to sell out their investment in your company as soon as possible when the investors feel they can achieve the maximum return on their investment. You are rarely going to be able to buy your investors out. As I will cover later, the investors' exit may occur through a merger or acquisition, an IPO, a secondary, or a recapitalization. Don't worry about the meaning of these terms, as I will define them later. The important point is you will have to sell part or all of your company in the future, depending upon the exit strategy, how successful your company is, and how much control you maintained after one or more rounds of funding.

Investors want legal protection of their investments and a degree of control so they can get out or exit to realize these high *multiples* if they materialize.

What sort of multiples are we talking about? The best-known stock market metric is called the price/earnings multiple. If a company's earnings are $100,000 and its multiple is 10x, then the company's stock is worth $1,000,000. If the company's earnings grow to $500,000, then the company's value is $5,000,000 with the same 10x multiple. But if the company's multiple rises to 15x, then the values become $1.5 million and $7.5 million, respectively.

This is the secret of Super Money. Invest privately at a low multiple of earnings and go for a public offering at a much higher multiple. Invest in a company whose earnings are $100,000 at a 5x multiple ($500,000 value) and go public with $1,000,000 earnings at a 20x to 100x multiple ($500,000 becomes $20 million to $100 million).

As an entrepreneur, if you want to raise money and build significant wealth, then you must understand that from the moment you conceive of the Idea and Design and go through the Discovery step and begin Development, your goal is to build an early-stage Golden Goose-type company that can generate growing cash flow and high multiples on that cash flow and become potentially worth a fortune.

Note: Companies such as Instagram and Twitter have multi-billion dollar valuations based upon their number of users and not based upon on their revenues and earnings. In the case of Facebook's acquisition, Facebook acquired Instagram for its growing user base and as a defensive move so Instagram would not pull users to it from Facebook. Facebook's business model is to generate revenues by selling ads to advertisers who will pay more for a growing user base. Instagram also gave Facebook an engagement tool to keep Facebook users on their site.

## DEVELOPING UNEXPECTED GROWTH

Most of the time what you plan does not happen. The projected sales or growth or popularity of the campaign or project does not materialize.

But sometimes the opposite occurs. You get fast growth. Fast growth can be a good sign if you set up the company to handle it. However, most start-ups don't have the systems or experience to service the growth. They may not be aware of their real costs of getting and keeping customers. As a result, they may be losing money and not know it. They may end up failing fast and going out of business or being acquired. They may become arrogant thinking growth in revenues equates to being a successful business and turn off people. Fast-growing companies may attract numerous and some very large competitors, as Groupon did.

The point: don't just develop a product in theory and put down a bunch of people in a financial projection. Instead, think through carefully how many people you will need to support your growth. Next, calculate how much time and money will it take to hire and train the kind of people you want representing your company. From my experience, there is a strong tendency to underestimate the time and cost of support. Remember, this includes systems to process orders including credit cards that fail and the time to get updated so they can be charged.

Keep in mind that it will take a lot of time and money to develop your products to meet the demand, the needed suppliers and contractors the features, and fixing and servicing things which are broken.

Here's a fast-growth example where things turned out positively. Sometimes things became much bigger than you ever anticipated and you keep expanding. The television show *Undercover Boss*, for instance, profiled a family-owned sports bar franchise called the Tilted Kilt—using the tartan to outfit sexy waitresses—that just kept growing and growing.

The first Tilted Kilt Pub & Eatery was opened in the Las Vegas Rio Hotel and Casino in 2003 by restaurateur Mark DiMartino and business partners and co-founders Shannon Reilly and John Reynaud. The concept was a "contemporary, Celtic theme sports bar, staffed with beautiful servers." It took one hour after the concept meeting for Harrah's to contact DiMartino and inquire about immediate development. As of November 2012, Tilted Kilt has 70 locations and 20 in development."

## PITCH DEVELOPMENT VERSUS BUSINESS DEVELOPMENT

I want to move into a critical area of business and personal success.

I can point out what investors and want. But once you have your basic Idea, Design and Discovery mapped out, you have to keep in mind a very important distinction input versus output.

Input people can study and develop and develop, but nothing ever seems to become an output or something you can use, test, and evaluate.

As discussed, you have to develop your product based upon potential customer feedback from meeting and speaking with them.

The output you are seeking is a minimal viable product (MVP).

Here's the critical point: view the Development step as the creation of multiple minimal viable products such as your pitch, positioning, and presentations in different formats such as text, voice, video, photos, and images.

As we move through the development step: note that there are numerous inputs being shaped into outputs or MVPs on a mental, emotional, social, spiritual, and physical level.

The challenge is to know what to develop, when, and with whom. Many of the developments occur at the same time.

Keep in mind that you as a person and your team will be faced with an overwhelming amount of variables without an exact formula as to what to do.

Here, I believe, the difference comes from the artist within us.

Your intuition, instinct, and imagination must fill in the gaps which experimentation and testing can't.

This brings up another very important corollary point: each component of your business affects the other just as one area of your life affects the other. In life, you take on many roles, but in the end it's still you. How many times has some negative personality trait like being overly competitive, too sensitive, too critical, too fearful, or too hostile reared its head and sabotaged a promising relationship or potentially lucrative deal?

In a business, there are many people and many roles, but in the end each business takes on its own distinct business personality, look, or brand. In a large business or bureaucracy, some people can "hide." But over time, the business or organization develops a culture, value, belief system, and attitude, just like a person. If people who interact with the business find its dealings too dishonest or incompetent, then over time these personality traits become associated with the business.

In my course, "Invest in Your Destiny," I call this business personality, the group mind, or the We. I compare the group mind to the individual mind, or the I. The I and the We both have positive and negative traits.

In a start-up business, you are developing the business's personality as well as the business' products and services. The founders are like the parents and the children at the same time. Their behavior greatly affects the success of the company. Investors look to back the CEO and carefully evaluate his/her personality. Most rank integrity as the key trait since it's hard to teach once a person reaches a certain investors age or stage of development. The same can be said of the business itself and the rest of the team which the CEO and founder selected.

The key point: during the Development step the business personality is developing as well as its founding story, its customers, products, positioning, messaging, and business model. All of these elements, along with the stakeholders, are developing at different speeds, some better and some worse than others.

The collective whole becomes the basis for the business's or project's or campaign's pitch. Whether you think of it this way or not, the pitch begins as soon as the Idea for the business project or campaign pops into your head.

From the very beginning of coming up with an Idea for a business, project, or campaign, you start pitching or talking to yourself and then with others. In the largest sense, you must pitch or sell yourself and then others. As I just pointed out, there is a lot of developmental and personality psychology involved here: belief, doubt, fear, faith, attitude, and social and emotional intelligence. Without being facetious, you might come to the conclusion that the best investment in a business might be a business psychologist or psychiatrist, similar to a sports psychologist. Many so-called business coaches I don't feel are qualified. Experienced mentors can definitely help if they are willing to put in the time and effort.

Think of it this way. While you are seeking to develop a business, you are in parallel developing your pitch to potential customers, investors, partners, employees, suppliers, and other stakeholders.

When you develop the right business psychology and build the right business foundation step by step, you are also setting up the elements necessary for successful presentations and pitches which will raise you the capital you need.

Your pitches:

- Communicate and articulate your Idea and Design.
- Incorporate what you found out during the Discovery step, such as whether you have the unique solution and competitive advantage that potential customers want.
- Translate to your development team the product attributes they must create to deliver your unique solution.
- Become the basis for your marketing, sales, and customer service.

Think about how critical the pitch is to your success in raising capital. Venture capitalists invest in less than 1% of the deals that are presented and pitched to them. Venture capitalist David Rose estimates VCs invest in one out of 400 deals pitched to them. That means 99+% of businesses that created, presented, and pitched Ideas and Designs and developed minimal viable products and business models are rejected. Imagine this business is your baby, and the VC is saying your baby and 99+% of the other babies he examines are ugly and he rejects them.

Much of business and life is perception. How you market and sell or present and pitch your business, project, or campaign often has as much to do with your success as the actual product. Think of how many times Simon Cowell on *American Idol* or *The X Factor* or Usher on *The Voice* talked about the performer's stage presence, her confidence and command of the stage, her delivery, and her song choice. The same elements are evaluated on *Shark Tank*, except the business presentation and the business pitch is the equivalent of the song choice. Body language, voice tone, and the words all come into play, similar to any speaker on stage. Yes, the business terms are part of the presentation and pitch as well as many other elements I will cover later.

Granted, market trends, market timing, randomness, and luck all affect the success of business pitches. But markets do not go down to zero. Deals can always be made even if the terms are less favorable because of market conditions. So, at some point, when you need to survive or get to the next level, you will have to keep your wits about you, present, and pitch. Over time, no pitch will overcome a product that doesn't work or is not competitive at all. However, I'm sure you are aware many inferior or average products succeed over much better products because of politics, the ability to influence and persuade, and advantages such as switching costs.

The bottom line: master the art and science of presenting and pitching to raise money and succeed in all areas of your life.

## DEVELOP AND MASTER THE FOUR BASIC PITCHES

What are these four basic pitches? They are: the elevator speech, slide show, executive summary, and business plan. Each type of pitch is a different way to explain how an early-stage company is designed to be a Golden Goose that can produce Golden Eggs and potentially be a blockbuster hit.

What should be contained in each type of pitch will be covered in the next few chapters, but I wanted to make sure that you were aware of the importance of developing your pitches while you are developing your customers and your product(s).

To develop the *"right"* business psychology and personality, business model, products, and pitches, you need to develop the *"right"* mind-set or psychology, which I call the Entrepreneurial Mind.

Note: There is no right mind-set, but it's an approach to business and life that has certain positive characteristics that appear more often than not in highly successful people. The Entrepreneurial Mind represents a composite of these success traits, which may be in various proportions in different people.

## THE ENTREPRENEURIAL MIND

If you begin to feel overwhelmed as I bring up different concepts, then you are experiencing the challenge of investing, creating, and building early-stage companies (or projects and campaigns).

It takes a certain mind-set to deal with myriad unknowns, risks, and variables when there is no cookie-cutter formula or recipe to follow. I call this mind-set the Entrepreneurial Mind. The Entrepreneurial Mind must take all these disparate parts and organize them into a clear vision which can be spelled out clearly in the four pitch types.

The best Entrepreneurial Minds, both as entrepreneurs and as investors, are able to separate the wheat from the chaff—the true value and focus points of a new venture from the wannabe entrepreneurs and investors.

It takes a certain mind-set to understand how to create a Golden Goose-type company. When you are using the Entrepreneurial Mind, you will realize the one constant that must run through all your thinking. A company must create in its product or service *value* for the investor and customer.

To win and get the edge, the Entrepreneurial Mind focuses on delivering value. The Entrepreneurial Mind sees value ahead of others and then amasses the resources through leverage (other people's skills, money, know-how) to achieve the envisioned value. Value is developed in a series of steps by reducing risk the inverse of value. In effect, the Entrepreneurial Mind sees a number of value points into the future and sets out to manifest them. Investors call these value points milestones on which they peg their investments.

Let's define value. Value is the driving force underlying most transactions or exchanges. What does value mean exactly? It is a fair return in an exchange, whether it be goods or money. The reason the Entrepreneurial Mind separates wealth builders—the top 1%—from the crowd of also-rans is because it not only conceives of the extraordinary idea (the Huge Tipping Point Idea) but sees the *value proposition* for a Golden Goose-type asset or company ahead of the marketplace.

What exactly is a value proposition, and why is it so important to wealth building? Investopedia.com provides a dictionary of financial terms, and here is their definition: "A business or marketing statement (pitch) that summarizes why a consumer should buy a product or use a service. This statement should *convince* a potential consumer that one particular product or service will add more value or better solve a problem than other similar offerings."

An entrepreneur needs to state, in simple, direct terms, why a buyer needs/values his product. Not only that, but he needs to back up that statement by citing proof. That includes the people working for the company, why the product is different and better, and how the product is going to be sold.

## TO DEVELOP RELATIONSHIPS, SHARE YOUR VALUE

The best way to sell anything these days is to realize that relationships are the new currency. Social media is the new marketing. The right relationships brought to a company by its advisers can gain it the visibility, influence, following, customers, and ultimately the money as a result. The process is all about people.

For an entrepreneur, *the way to pay for new relationships and maintain existing ones is to share the value you are creating with your stakeholders* so they will support and multiply your efforts. You have to repeatedly assure your partners and followers. You must constantly articulate what value has been created and your vision for the potential value that will be created.

As I will show you, at every step of developing a product and building a business (all 7 Steps from Idea to Post Launch, as I will show you) of developing a product and building a business, you repeatedly have to craft offers or value propositions that give those involved with your company—your relationships—a payoff or a piece of the value. This payoff can be in the form of simple praise, bonuses, stock options, and other incentives.

This pitching of the value created and to be created is vital to success. It is one of my main capital-raising secrets. I call it the *buy-in process*, and I will cover the subject extensively when discussing the four types of pitch because it is so important.

## DEVELOP EXTRAORDINARY VALUE IN THREE WAYS

For now, let's drill down into the specifics of the value proposition or solution the Entrepreneurial Mind needs to envision in a product to develop it and test it with potential customers. To make a bet with his time and money, the true Entrepreneurial Mind seeks to get beyond the ordinary value. He envisions extraordinary value that can be sold one of three ways:

- High prices, high margins in low volume, such as a handcrafted boat
- High prices, high margins in high volume, such as the iPhone or iPad
- Low prices, low margins in high volume, such as Amazon or Costco delivers

There are different variations of these three value models. But what is common to all of them is they are the basis for creating an *irresistible offer*, or a compelling value proposition articulated in a well-scripted pitch. In the irresistible offer, the extraordinary value exceeds the definition of ordinary value. A Bill Gates or Jeff Bezos or Mark Cuban or other members of the top 1% club envision and find the means to develop high-value products with irresistible offers.

## DEVELOPMENT MISTAKES TO AVOID

Most entrepreneurs, small businesspeople, and creative types—as well as most investors—make the following mistakes:

- They jump into projects, campaigns, and companies without understanding the different business models or ways money can be made.
- Instead they choose business models that are short lived, i.e., the products or campaigns will run for a short time before another product is created, leading to spikes and severe drops in revenue.
- Result: such irregular, inconsistent revenue cannot create the sustained, growing earnings and wealth that investors seek and often pay high multiples to own (unless they get the asset at a bargain price, and then either they or their management team turns it into a Golden Goose money machine).

There are always exceptions where someone falls into an exceptional deal or trade out of luck. But this is very rare.

## DEVELOPMENT OF CROWDFUNDING PROJECTS: WHO WINS?

Take the example of two films the same producer, Jeremy Walker, financed on Kickstarter. As Chris Hewitt reported in the *Pioneer Press*, part of TwinCities.com, Walker figured he could finance more than one of his films if he was successful with getting the first one financed on Kickstarter. "Walker financed his first film, called *Triumph67*, in October 2009, raising $12,000, exceeding his goal of $10,000. But no one got paid on *Triumph67* and it was important on the next film, *Death to Prom*. With more awareness and a track record, Walker raised, in a last-minute squeaker, his $45,000 funding goal from 400 donors to start shooting his film. The $45,000 did not cover his entire budget, a risk to his 400 donors."

Let's look at Jeremy Walker. He's a creative-type film maker. He used an entrepreneurial approach to get his first film financed and exceeded his funding goal, but no one got paid. Then, he went back to Kickstarter and raised $4,5000 from 400 donors, but not enough to cover his budget.

Who wins here? Definitely Jeremy Walker. Do the donors win? It depends upon their mind-set and what they wanted from Walker's film projects. It may have been as simple as "we want to help Jeremy Walker" or "we like his films." But the donors received no ownership in Walker's films if they succeeded.

What becomes evident is that crowd-funding projects such as Walker's can be hit or miss. Crowdfunding donations with rewards deals are not designed to give ownership in sustainable, ongoing businesses. Rarely will crowdfunding donations with rewards deals help finance the early-stage blockbuster-potential companies that venture capitalists and angels are seeking. But crowdfunding donations with rewards does serve a purpose—funding causes, scientific and educational projects, and creative types in general. It's not all about the money.

The key point: to succeed, whether you are seeking to develop products for crowdfunding donations with rewards or equity-based or loan-based crowdfunding or private placements, you will need to create the Entrepreneurial Mind extraordinary value approach and to follow the 7 Steps, the Magical P's and the other models and guidelines I have laid out for you.

Keep remembering: if you want to make tons of money, one way is to own pieces of early-stage companies that become blockbuster hits.

## THE OUTSIDER VERSUS THE PREDATOR ENTREPRENEURIAL MIND

When you trace the history of blockbuster companies, their leaders had Entrepreneurial Minds that did not follow the crowd or herd. They were not the darlings of the crowdfunding world of today, written up in the press as models of success. They were outsiders or predators or both.

Take the following story of Yelp's co-founder Jeremy Stoppelman, the Outsider Entrepreneurial Mind, versus Google, the Group Predator Entrepreneurial Mind. Note: these are more archetypes to illustrate personality types than saying Stoppelman is an angel and Google is all evil.

Look at the tactics used by Google, narrated in a *Fast Company* article, "Power," by Max Chapin, written about Stoppelman. Google offered Yelp $550 million when Yelp was being battered by the new rage, Groupon. Just before Stoppelman signed the deal, he was offered $750 million by Yahoo. Then Steve Jobs called while Stoppelman was talking to Elevation Partners, founded by U2's Bono, about raising another round of capital. Jobs said to Stoppelman, who went out of the room to take the call, "Don't sell...Google is evil."

*Business Insider* reported, "Jobs urged Stoppelman, who revered the Apple chief as a visionary, to 'stay independent and not sell out to Google.' Jobs was not a fan of Google and had accused the search giant of stealing Apple's smartphone and tablet technology."

The *Fast Company* reports picks up again: "Spurned by Stoppelman, Google [the predator] tried to crush him. It started up Google Places—renamed Google+ Local—a Yelp knockoff that includes links to pretty much every online review site but Yelp...Stoppelman testified before the Senate Judiciary Committee investigating antitrust accusations against Google in September 2011 that his company received threats that Google would remove Yelp from its search index."

## DEVELOPMENT: OUTSIDER LESSONS IN BUSINESS AND LIFE

In developing a business and your products, you have to decide whether you are going to be an "evil" predator or an outsider looking in who still can find the Sure Thing Opportunity.

The Outsider: "If a man does not keep pace with his companions, perhaps it is because he hears a different drummer. Let him step to the music which he hears, however measured or far away"—Henry David Thoreau.

Being a successful entrepreneur constantly challenges your inner being and moral compass. If you want to win in a very competitive world and still try to do it in an honest, Outsider way, then here are some things you should heed:

- Know how to pitch your ideas clearly and concretely.
- Play the championship points: under extreme pressure, find a way to win.
- Strive to maintain your character and integrity in your dealings, and honor your word.
- Have the conviction to make courageous decisions and bets that align with your company's culture and values and your own, even if such decisions and bets may threaten the existence of your business.
- Develop win-win strategic relationships that reduce each other's risk and increases dramatically each other's upside.

Note on strategic investors and alliances: The appeal of a venture capitalist or superangel investor or a strategic partner is their experience, guidance, and powerful relationships. The real problem is many investors and strategic partners promise these value-added benefits beyond their monetary investment but then don't deliver once the deal is made. To counter this, research carefully and interview others who have done business with them where similar promises were made.

**More Outsider Lessons**: Many times in my life I walked away from powerful people and companies. In the near term, it cost me a lot. It would have been so much easier to make the deal. But I felt that, as Jobs said, some people and companies are evil. I didn't want to sell my soul. Over time, I rarely regretted the decisions to go a different direction. They have given me a certain sense of freedom. Monetarily, I may be poorer, but as a person I am much richer.

## DEVELOP CUSTOMERS FIRST, THEN PRODUCTS

The true Outsider actually thinks *"out of the box"* about getting customers first before developing her product. The outsider literally *gets out* of the office and interviews potential customers on the solution to some problem the outsider believes the customers want solved

This pre-product development process begins in the Discovery step and carries over into the Development step with Designs of the Idea created in the Design step and refined. Now the sketches and the white board drawings begin to be transformed into a minimal viable product to be tested with the potential customers.

To raise the money and build a successful company, an entrepreneur needs to develop:

- Potential customers that want the solution
- A minimal viable product that can be tested with customers
- Customers who will pay for the product
- Customers who will pay a profit for use of the product

**The Challenge:** The product types must be matched to different market types that require different strategies and time lines to become viable. I will review these product and market types later.

**The Lesson:** The key here is to recognize that early-stage products have different hurdles and obstacles than products created by existing larger companies that know their market. Early-stage companies are in search of markets to fit to their problem-solving product, whereas large companies know their markets and try to find the right product to gain market share.

## DEVELOPMENT STEP GOALS

- An extraordinary product (create/own or control it).
- An extraordinary team and Golden Goose-like company if the goal is to attract venture capitalists and angels.

- An extraordinary value proposition/an irresistible offer articulated in extraordinary pitches.
- An ability to find and pitch powerful allies and strategic partners that reduce your risk and make your deal more of a sure thing.
- The mind-set to walk away from a deal when it is not right culturally, morally, and spiritually, even if you feel there are no other alternatives.

## START-UP DEVELOPMENT STAGES: A HISTORICAL PERSPECTIVE

The history of coffee provides an excellent example of the stages a start-up company goes through. As narrated at coffeego.com, in 850 an Ethiopian herdsman named Kaldi observed that his goat went wild after chewing on some red berries. Kaldi tasted the berries himself and experienced the same exuberance as his goat. Kaldi showed it to his chief monk, who threw them in the fire, calling the berries the work of the devil. But the aroma attracted a rebellious monk, who grabbed the beans out of the fire and mixed them with water. He pitched his Idea to others, and the rest is coffee history.

Over time, the Idea tipped, went viral, and multiplied around the world into the global coffee market we know today. The story of coffee reads more like a thriller as kings and powerful groups tried to corner the coffee market and create a monopoly. But through sexual intrigues, murder, trickery, and thievery, coffee spread.

Several centuries after the rebellious monk's discovery of coffee, an enterprising Arab trader took the coffee to what is now Yemen and planted it in large plantations. By 1453, the Ottoman Turks introduced coffee to Constantinople, and by 1475 coffee shops opened where lively discussions and debates took place (the ancient Starbucks).

By 1570, coffee came to Venice. At the time Muslims enjoyed a monopoly on coffee production. Their laws forbade the export of fertile beans. But in the early eighteenth century, the mayor of Amsterdam gave a young coffee plant to King Louis IV of France.

In 1723, a French naval officer took a clipping from the coffee tree and took it to Martinique. Within three years coffee plantations spread all over the island. This little tree became the spark of 19 million trees in Martinique over the next 50 years and was the stock from which coffee throughout the Caribbean and South and Central America originated.

The history of coffee demonstrates that over time human beings follow similar patterns to find and control blockbuster money-making deals.

1. They are always observant or aware of what maybe different or an opportunity as the goat keeper was of his goats' unusual behavior.
2. They test the Idea to their own satisfaction as the goat keeper did.
3. Expect resistance to new ideas as the chief monk wanted to maintain the status quo.
4. They are a rebel or outsider (the hero's journey/story) persists with an Idea and pitches it to others—*People*—who see the opportunity (and become emotionally hooked).
5. They perfect the *Product*—the coffee itself:
6. They develop *Proprietary* information (the competitive advantage) such as the *Process* of making the beans into coffee (the technology, the know-how).
7. They take control over the *Production* (monopoly).
8. They seek High *Potential opportunities.*
9. They look for high *Profitability* (High margins).
10. *Proliferation*—the ability to scale (grow and distribute to many) is a necessary criteria.
11. Can achieve from a cutting (small input), a disproportionately large (leverage). In effect, the costs per unit drop with a greater and greater volume.
12. You get compound growth as trees produce more trees. In 50 years, 19 million trees in Martinique (compound growth)

## CROWDFUNDING EQUITY: SEEDS THAT GROW INTO PUMPKINS

In a similar fashion to coffee, companies start with seeds or Ideas. Crowdfunding equity enables the ideas to be funded by seed capital, which is rarely available at this stage of the development cycle of a project or business other than from friends and family. Crowdfunding opens an entirely new source of capital for Ideas that might never get funded.

Just think of what this means. Some Ideas and seed capital can grow into Microsoft, Google, Starbucks, or new medical advances and spread across the world.

It comes down to which seed to bet on. In *The Pumpkin Plan*, Mike Michalowicz shows that the farmer with the most extraordinary pumpkin in the field wins the prize at the county fair every time. The winning pumpkin farmers "hold 'the secret formula' for big-time entrepreneurial success: plant hearty seeds, identify the most promising pumpkins, kill off the rest of the vine, and nurture only the pumpkins with the biggest potential." You can't grow a huge pumpkin from an ordinary seed. All of the car-sized blue-ribbon pumpkins you see on TV came from a lineage of seeds called the Atlantic Giant variety, developed by Howard Dill of Nova Scotia, Canada. There is no substitute. The blockbuster seed was the Atlantic Giant.

Venture capital, angel capital, and crowdfunding equity are ways to buy into farms at different points in the planting cycle before the harvest (the projected exit where the investor cashes out and make money).

From seed to harvest, there are many risks and uncertainties that may kill your company (farm) and its crop (coffee or pumpkins) or product. Michalowicz says the aim of the entrepreneur is to find the giant pumpkins—those Ideas with the most potential—and focus on those. The winning Ideas are built upon your core strength or sweet spot, made up of your uniqueness, area of innovation, best customers, and a systematic approach. To create winning businesses means killing off the weaker, diseased pumpkins (bad ideas /bad clients), which drain your resources and spread you too thin. You have to avoid or get out of the entrepreneurial trap of being You, Inc., where you try to be a jack-of-all-trades but end up being a master of none.

The bottom line to achieve success: you have to prune the pumpkin vine by immediately making a list of all your clients, their revenue, and the time and hassle to service them. Get rid of the terrible clients that pester you, don't want to pay you, and eat up your time and resources. Focus on servicing only your top clients or customers. Allow more time to service their needs, which they've expressed by your interviewing them personally about their industry, their business challenges, and where they need solutions. The result is that you will make a lot of money servicing fewer accounts. Once you identify and learn to service your best customers, you can systematize this process and grow your business with the help of your team.

Interestingly, one significant advance in farming itself was reported recently in the *New York Times.* Jesse Vollmar and Brad Koch, just out of college, started up a farm management software called FarmLogs that received funding from Y Combinator, a seed fund. The software can track what is planted on each field. A click leads to a log of what was done on each field, filling in the date, fertilizing on that date, spraying on another, with the data stored in one place. FarmLogs does not charge a setup fee, but charges farmers by the month. That marketing tactic sets it apart from its competition.

In a similar way, if you want to get the money, you must from the very beginning start crafting in the Design step your own system to help you create (seed), build, and manage your own farm/business.

Design, Discovery, and Development, however, don't occur in a vacuum. Just as you can't plant pumpkin seeds and just let them grow without weeding out the weak and diseased pumpkins, you have to constantly be testing ways to better your crop (product, project, business, and pitch). Weed out what does not work.

You can't avoid testing. What I am showing you in the 7 Steps accelerates the process by pointing out the right steps and what to look for.

## ONLY AN EXTRAORDINARY PRODUCT SUCCEEDS AND ATTRACTS INVESTORS?

So, you might be wondering, what makes for success in business? Does it all come down to creating an extraordinary product?

Contrary to popular notions, Michel Vilette and Catherine Vuillermot, in *From Predators to Icons: Exposing the Myth of Business Heroes*, contend that businesspeople who succeed do not provide superior products to their customers from the very start. "In many cases, the goods and services provided early on by companies with the most spectacular growth and profitability were mediocre. The mail order furniture sold by IKEA in the early 1950s was of very poor quality...the first Wal-Mart stores were badly organized, squalid warehouses selling at low prices clothing that had gone out of fashion in big cities."

What they are saying is that concepts evolve. You plant, test, prune, and weed out what does not work in an ongoing process. You start with a minimum viable product—the poor-quality IKEA furniture, for example. You start with Plan A and test the product and evolve to Plan B. In *Getting to Plan B*, John Mullins and Randy Komisar assert that most business plans are ill-conceived and are based upon flawed, untested assumptions. To avoid wasting years of time and investors' money, they put forth a field-tested process to rigorously test your initial business idea so you can make quick corrections and turn the odds in your favor. They state that if your "initial hypothesis does not pan out, such as Google's first licensing deals, chalk it up to learning and move on to Plan B. Google's revenue model was copied from Overture...Shanda's first games were licensed from South Korean gamers. You don't have to reinvent the wheel to create a successful new venture."

The development process becomes one of testing ideas and concepts and changing them in response to the market. The key is to respond and change in a way so that you elicit feedback with a group or crowd that finds what you are doing attractive enough that they feel they can be part of your product development process.

Development should not be a haphazard affair. Besides having a unique product, a USP, a value proposition, and an irresistible offer, you need a systemized approach to creating and testing your products and project or business itself.

As an entrepreneur takes his initial Idea and goes through each of the 7 Steps, he has to understand that the process of creating a viable business model or project model is not simply linear. The entrepreneur has to develop his project or business by thinking ahead strategically and laying out goals, milestones, and tasks. He must constantly adjust each step of building his business and his business model by rigorously testing of all his assumptions. Wherever possible, each assumption should be tested with numbers that can be improved upon.

It is very important to ask the right questions and set the right criteria and numbers to test. Often, entrepreneurs focus on vanity numbers, such as more customers, without looking at the quality of the customers. Are they profitable, easy to work with, or do they eat up your time and resources so that you are stuck working 80 to 100 hours a week with no life and lots of unhealthy stress?

The entrepreneur has to be more than a visionary. She has to lead, set up, and deploy a systematic development process, even if it is very rudimentary in the beginning. To repeat, she has to have a way to measure success and understand failure. This deliberate, repeated testing approach enables the entrepreneur as leader and her team to keep going deeply into every aspect of the business to discover the nuances and the structural holes that create the sustainable competitive advantage and a successful business model.

## DEVELOPING YOUR OWN PRODUCTS OR NOT: THE PROS AND CONS

One of the biggest questions for starting up a business or a project is whether to develop your own products or represent someone else's.

Briefly, there are different product development strategies that involve different risks:

1. Create your own
2. Buy, license or sell others' products
3. Copy others

Creating your own gives you more control and higher margins, but you have to spend a lot of time and money with no assurance anyone will buy your product.

Clearly, taking others' products and services is easier, but you have less control and lower margins.

Copying others makes you a me-too product. Some do very well with the copycat strategy and predators rip off others' hard work. Most successful products are unique twists off other products that already exist or have been conceptualized.

You have to develop a disciplined and creative approach that assumes hard work and a lot of experimentation if you are creating any projects, campaigns, or businesses.

Most entrepreneurs, creative types, and small businesses fail to get the money at the beginning of the development stage because there are so many unknowns. The investor views this as highly risky. Investors are aware that product developers completely underestimate the time, resources, and hard work it takes to create an ordinary working prototype—not even an extraordinary one.

## THE DEVELOPMENT OF AN IRRESISTIBLE OFFER

To attract investors other than friends, family or yourself and customers early in the Development step, you must create a pitch that contains an irresistible offer. Note that in crowdfunding donations with rewards you are essentially pre-selling a product which is just a concept or Idea with a Design or a prototype or MVP. So, you win or lose more on your Idea and Design, i.e., your pitch, than on your product being fully developed.

Since crowdfunding is Internet-based—and soon will be more and more mobile based as well—let's look briefly at what are the components of an irresistible offer and how to develop one for the Internet and crowdfunding specifically.

An irresistible offer has four main components and must incorporate a compelling value proposition:

- What does the product do (feature)?
- How much is it (price)?
- What's in it for me (must be an emotional and compelling proposition: benefit or value versus the price)?
- Why should I believe what you are telling me (credibility: competence/integrity/reputation)?

As discussed under the Discovery step, every product has a value proposition poor, good, great or extraordinary. Your questions become your value proposition and make it compelling, and has it been crafted into an irresistible offer that can be pitched successfully on a crowdfunding site such as Kickstarter, Indiegogo, or RocketHub?

How do you know? The first test should start with yourself. If you can be unbiased, then ask, would I jump at the offer? Is it a wow? Then test it with many people. Ask them what would make your offer or proposition compelling and irresistible.

In the end, you have to test it with the crowd. If your close group won't back it (donate), then your chances for a successful campaign are very slim.

Without creating an irresistible offer for a crowdfunding project or campaign that can be presented and pitched in the right way to friends, family, and then strangers, the odds of getting the money are very low.

## DEVELOPING YOUR MONEY-RAISING STRATEGIES

As I have demonstrated in the Development step, there are numerous developments going on at the same time from you're your own mindset (the Entrepreneurial Mind) to developing a team and a business personality.

In addition, I want to point out that there we have focused upon crowdfunding donations and crowdfunding equity. But there are other money-raising strategies.

In fact, there are five main money-raising strategies and many variations within each depending on a number of criteria such as the risk involved collateral and business experience.

The five main money-raising strategies are:

1. Crowdfunding donations or perks
2. Launching products on the Internet. Product launches are very similar.
3. Crowdfunding Equity–based
4. Private equity
5. Crowdfunding lending or borrowing from others

The first three are online strategies. You craft a very well-written pitch/sales copy articulating your irresistible offers and display them on landing pages (pages for generating leads, or where a prospective customer takes action, such as signing up for an offer to get a free e-book).

Normally, strategies number one and number two will not create the type of businesses that venture capitalists pursue.

However, some crowdfunding donations with rewards projects or campaigns can raise millions of dollars (strategy number one), and some Internet marketing product launches (strategy number two) can also raise millions of dollars. But few of the projects that raise money using these two strategies possess the potential blockbuster companies or assets with earnings potential that the venture capitalists will pursue.

Yet strategies number one and number two can be used to test ideas that may evolve into Ideas that can attract venture capital, like the Pebble watch campaign on Kickstarter.

For an entrepreneur, having Developed a prototype (or having some control over it by contract or other arrangement), the crucial step is to bring it before others for possible seed funding. Think of *Shark Tank*. You see everything from prototypes that have no sales to full-blown companies seeking the Sharks' connections, advice, and money.

You must know the various pitches and what the essential parts of each type are to get the money, build your company, and make the money.

So, the pitch. What makes for a good pitch? Or should I say, what type of pitch would you prefer?

## TAKEAWAYS AND INSIGHTS

- When you look at the big picture, the Development step confronts you with reality on multiple levels: personal, career, and business.
- In the Development Step, you are faced with who you are: your talents, skills, possessions, resources, passions, strengths, and weaknesses.
- Like a business model, you have a personal model where you give to receive things back in monetary and non-monetary forms.
- As psychologist Victor Frankl wrote in *Man's Search for Meaning* so well, what motivates us is our search for meaning.
- To have meaning. You need a purpose as an individual and an organization.
- The challenge for many people is they struggle to find a true purpose or meaning, or they find themselves in careers mismatched to what they really want to do.
- In the book *Escape from Freedom* Erich Fromm states that most people are afraid of freedom and desperately want to be led. The concept is to be emancipated from an overbearing authority/set of values, which leaves us empty and anxious until we use our "freedom to," which involves creative and true authenticity. In other words, to become the artist and connect with others as our true selves.
- In *The Outsider* by Colin Wilson, the struggle is how to deal with our boredom (or our failure to see a purpose and feel trapped or not free), alienation, and how to belong when we feel we don't. "The Man who is interested to know how he should live instead of merely taking life as it comes is automatically an Outsider."

- In the Development step, uncertainty and risk many times increase as the reality of taking ideas and designs and turning them into concrete things strikes. But even if that can be done, the questions becomes: does the developed product make enough meaning and create enough value where enough customers will make you a profit?
- When you see the Development step from multiple perspectives and dimensions, you can understand more clearly what's in the mind of other stakeholders—their fears, their motivations—desires and needs.
- These multiple development levels frame the challenges of early-stage companies since success in the beginning rests on a few key people. This is why professional investors focus so much on the team, their track record, and what milestones they have achieved toward the company's vision and purpose.
- Like the story of coffee, it starts with a seedling and the uncertainty and risk of whether the seedling will ever grow into a coffee tree that will produce coffee beans to be harvested.
- In the Development step, you want to lay out even daily what are the different elements which **must** be developed versus what would be nice to develop. Put the development steps on a time line and assign who—one or more people—are responsible for their accomplishment and when.
- From my experience, it takes 2x to 3x the estimated time and cost, and you similarly get 33% to 50% less revenue projected.
- The five major money-raising strategies are: crowdfunding donations or perks; launching products on the internet; crowdfunding equity; private placements and crowdfunding lending or borrowing.

- With the Development step challenges in mind, then you will see why pitches and presentations must address these issues.

Click here for additional resources: http://bit.ly/18WBHq3

# CHAPTER 6

# PREPARING FOR THE PITCH

Imagine you are an investor and you receive a call from an entrepreneur. Let's take this a step further. Say you are famed venture capitalist Peter Thiel, one of the founders of PayPal, and you are pitched synthetic meat. What would you expect Thiel to do? How polite do you think Thiel would be with this entrepreneur visionary? Would he slam down the phone? Would he ask how the entrepreneur got his private number?

Pitches as seemingly crazy and offbeat happen every minute somewhere on planet earth.

In real life, Modern Meadow co-founder Andras Forgacs had these facts to work with in his short pitch, or elevator speech. One quarter-pound burger consumes 6.7 pounds of grain, 52.8 gallons water, 74.5 square feet of land, and 1,036 British Thermal Units of fossil fuel. What he wanted to do was make meat in the lab. That would result in a 96% reduction in greenhouse gas emissions and use 45% of the energy, 1% of the land, and 4% of the water compared to rearing animals.

As reported by Nate C. Hindman in the *Huffington Post*, "Thiel's fund is pitching the company as a small step forward in saving the planet. Printed meat is 'an economic and compassionate solution to a global problem,' Lindy Fishburne, executive director of Breakout Labs, a project of the Thiel Foundation, said in a statement."

Now think about starting up a crowdfunding campaign on Kickstarter. This Internet portal symbolizes what crowdfunding equity is trying to accomplish: provide entrepreneurs with early-stage funding that venture capitalists and angel investors may reject. Many solid business ideas go unfunded because entrepreneurs do not have the network to reach the most likely investors for their company.

In a very difficult economic climate, businesses need cash. Even more pressing is the need for seed and start-up capital. A wide range of start-up projects and businesses of all sizes must turn to others for cash. Make no mistake: without cash, you're out of business.

One of the crucial elements of crowdfunding equity is its enormous potential for creating seed money for worthy companies that are starved for capital to grow.

Yet think of what that means for you. Even with crowdfunding equity, few entrepreneurs will get the money because they don't know how to pitch their deals. The reason is that they don't understand that investors are also their customers.

So I'm going to spend a few chapters looking at what insiders—venture capitalists and angel investors—look for in a young company. You can then craft your pitch—or, as an investor, examine the merits of a pitch—in a way that you can get the maximum numbers of dollars.

I'll start by making what should be an obvious point: most people don't like asking others for money. Add standing in front of people and pitching them for money like a public speaker, and you have ratcheted up the fear and discomfort many times. But what if you can become comfortable with your discomfort? What if I could show you that the solution to your discomfort lies in a simple strategy? You deliberately practice your pitch on the many people you meet in the normal course of a day. That's not counting your pitches when you attend conferences, trade shows, and other networking events. You can become an expert in pitching over time before you present to your key targeted investors, which dramatically increases your chances of getting the money.

Other people will give you valuable feedback unknowingly. I call one key method my glazed-eye technique. At first I tell people about my proposed deal, and I see if their eyes glaze over with confusion or disinterest. Normally, I'm long-winded. But I note carefully which words resonate with a person or audience.

Refining your unique selling proposition or short elevator speech is easier with some products, and others can take a much longer time. For example, our software company Questionmine, a customer listening and video metrics software platform, has many applications. The benefits: precision personalized marketing that identifies and responds in real time to your best customers and increases your sales-ready leads and sales. Questionmine's unique selling proposition is evolving, and your eyes may have glazed over. But my team keeps working on perfecting what our unique selling proposition is.

My friend Doug also has a software company for which he wanted to raise capital. Recently, he called me and asked, "Gary, how do you get the money?"

"Doug, here's my secret. I kind of stumbled on it years ago," I said. I realized that I had never said this just this way.

"Raising money is similar to casting a movie," I continued. "Some years ago, I raised money for a film fund that tied up movie scripts. What I quickly learned was that decisions in Hollywood rested upon a number of elements:

1. The script
2. Who wrote the script
3. The producer
4. The director
5. The actor(s)
6. What hit movie was similar
7. The budget

"The more of these main movie elements you had tied up, the more attractive the package was for the studio."

It dawned upon me that raising money in Hollywood is very similar to venture capital and, now, crowdfunding.

"In early-stage business financing, a transaction, project, or deal rests upon the same critical elements as a film deal. The cast of characters—*who (people)* is involved in running the company? What's the story—the deal or *product* concept or the product itself? Why is it different (the sustainable competitive advantage)? What's the *potential*—the upside—and who makes what for investing time, money, resources, or some combination of these?"

Notice, we're back to the magical Ps: *people, product, and potential.*

After I explained this to Doug, he said he had never thought of raising capital this way, but it made a lot of sense. I made a mental note to relate Doug's story to you since it confirmed my premise of testing your pitch while laying out one of my key "how to get the money" secrets.

In Hollywood, as in venture capital, everyone wants the blockbuster. A few blockbuster hits make tons of money and pay for the majority of losers, break-even deals, or barely making your money back—an inadequate return to warrant the risk inherent in providing funding for early-stage companies.

So that's your first assignment: view your company or the company you've chosen as an investment as a movie and lay out the elements it contains:

- Who are the lead people on the team?
- Do you have any bankable stars (a team) that investors would immediately back? What about an active board of advisers with top proven players in your industry?
- What's your story? Your purpose? Your Why? Your Passion?
- Why should anyone care about seeing your company become a reality?
- What's the script or plan to implement your company?
- What's the budget—where does the money come from and go?
- Who owns what percentage of the company? Who gets their money out first?
- How would you present your company idea to a group of executives and investors?

I am going to take this Hollywood blockbuster concept a step further to show you a model that will dramatically help both entrepreneurs and investors thrive in today's new world.

Success has three essential ingredients. It takes (1) talented, determined people who (2) follow a system and/or plan (mental and written, even on scraps of paper or stored online) and have (3) the ability to evaluate in real time what is going on—get feedback and refine assumptions, even pivot from one plan to another until they get the pitch right.

The most savvy business operators know the current climate, understand the rules, have a plan, and are flexible to shift or respond to find the right path to deal with uncertainty and minimize risk as much as possible. Andy Grove of Intel said success relies not as much on being pro-active as being able to respond in the right way to a constantly shifting environment.

We are now in an interesting business climate. I call it the "Performance Economy." These days speed is the new drug. Everyone wants everything immediately—people insist on instant gratification and hate to wait. People live at breakneck speed; everything is done in a blur. The line between business and our personal lives has virtually disappeared.

The Hollywood blockbuster model is representative of the Performance Economy. Hollywood is about stardom and blockbuster movies. Similarly, TV networks are about blockbuster TV shows, including a number of reality shows that discover the next stars.

Today, people are obsessed with celebrities and everyone wants to be a star. Star power creates financial power—big stars bring in big bucks. In the movie business, Hollywood executives often feel stars' box office appeal can reduce a film's risk of failure (but not eliminate it, since a bad script or director can't save it), like insurance policies, and increase the odds for blockbuster hits.

The Performance Economy is about the search for the Next Big Thing. In this light, let's look at *American Idol*, *Dancing with the Stars*, *America's Got Talent*, all the cooking and reality television shows, and the endless designer labels. Star-based goods and services dominate the markets and make gazillions of dollars.

The Performance Economy is based on a simple formula that has filtered down from the top. Business operators on every level—huge to tiny, local to global—want to be stars. They want to become celebrities and build name recognition, and the secret is that they essentially follow the same plan. When you understand that formula, it will help you reach the top.

Let's examine *American Idol* and its format in more depth. I'm sure you know how the show goes, but let me describe it in business terms.

*American Idol* is a contest to find the next singing superstar. Contestants enter to land a recording contract and launch singing careers. Hopefuls line up by the tens of thousands to audition in select major cities and appear on the show. Those who make the cut go to Hollywood, where the roster is further whittled down. After a few weeks the show finally gets rolling, and the public votes on which singers will be eliminated. Each ensuing week, one candidate is eliminated, and the last one left standing wins. He or she is the American Idol.

Great formula. Remarkably popular and successful show!

So how can you use its success to help you in your business dealings?

*American Idol* uses a formula that I call *core magnets*. This is the product or service that attracts you—customer, investor—to a business. Core magnets are the stars of the show, the reason you come to watch or to buy or to sign up from someone else. Without core magnets like an iPod or iPhone, where would Apple be? Where would Google be without its search algorithm and its AdWords system?

Core magnets are the key to all successful businesses—the vital links that all businesses need to succeed. Core magnets have targets—objects that they attract.

*American Idol*'s "target" is the audience, the people out in TV land. Like all TV shows, *American Idol* wants to attract the largest possible audience. The "target" for businesses is customers (its audience). Without customers, businesses fail. To reach their targets, businesses need core magnets.

Just as *American Idol* contestants must stand out, so must a company. On *American Idol*, not only must contestants shine, but they must continually convince their targets, the voting audience—the crowd—that they deserve their support. Week after week, they must demonstrate that they have the star power make it to the top.

To win in most businesses, you need to use your talents, knowledge, and skills in a similar way. Do you have a unique personality and style? What about your products and services? Then are you willing to take a risk and get onstage and build a following—an audience or crowd that adores you?

Let's continue to use the *American Idol* analogy to see how a business can attract people. To become the next American Idol, a contestant must display a combination of talent, style, looks, personality, and likeability. The *Idol* winner must:

**Be able to sing.** Singing is each contestant's product—his or her stock in trade. The reason the singers sing is to entertain. To win, a singer must entertain and be as good as or better than the competition. The *American Idol* audience wants to be entertained, and those who can't sing a lick won't win.

Now let's look at business products. The products being sold must provide what customers want—Tupperware must withstand being used over and over again, and food must be nutritious and taste good. Quality counts. If the products being sold are not top notch, you picked the wrong business or investment.

**Have a unique style.** A contestant must be distinctive to emerge from the pack. If everyone operates similarly, no one will stand out. Likewise, if customers can get the same result from everyone, they won't have any reason to buy from your company over others, and you won't be able to build loyalty and long-term relationships.

Customers remember and gravitate to distinctive items—those that have special qualities and stand out. They want to buy unique items to distinguish themselves and show that they have good taste. For example, many people like to get into new trends early and buy "designer" goods, as they believe that it gives them a certain status.

Distinctive items reflect people's personal styles and how they wish to project themselves. Distinctive styles top the charts in the Performance Economy. They get people press coverage and make them household names; it's how singers on *American Idol* land record contracts and parts in Broadway shows.

**Choose the right songs.** They say "Timing is everything," and it frequently is. Most people don't want to buy winter coats in the summer; they don't even want to try them on. Entertainers must offer what audiences want, like the type of music they want to hear. The most brilliant young classical cellist would be voted off *American Idol*. Similarly, a business must provide what its customers want and need. If you're trying to sell a water filter that is so complex to install that your customers need to call a plumber, how many water filters do you think people will buy?

**Connect with the audience.** In a world of choices, we tend to gravitate to a select few. Often, we can't articulate why we're drawn to them, but we just seem to connect. Certain people stand out and are more *memorable* (how many times has Simon Cowell used this word?); they make a stronger impression on you. That same principle can be carried over to a business in a practical fashion. Market research is essential. Identify your audience and learn what they want. Find out your competitive advantages and build your sales around them.

**Have star quality.** People want the best and will often pay a premium for the best. Look at the luxury market and the unbelievable prices people will pay. Become the star of your level, the best in class or group. Make your products or services better; provide more value for the price; have great customer service, few returns, and the most pleasant employees; find ways to stand out.

In business, customers vote with their time, money, and resources. Simply put, for businesses to succeed they must attract (magnetize) their targets (their customers), and once they hook them, they must retain them.

## WHY EARLY-STAGE INVESTORS INVEST IN A COMPANY

What's going to get investors excited about your deal?

**Chance. Fear. Return on Investment**. The chance to hit the Next Big Thing (the Hollywood or TV-like blockbuster)—and the fear that they could reject or miss out on the Next Big Thing. The other key motivation for venture capitalists is to maximize their return on the money they invest.

**Emotional Appeal.** I should point out that angel investors have many emotional reasons to invest beyond just making money. They may be attracted to causes such as disseminating the best information on a type of cancer.

**The Sketchy World of Prediction**. How in the world do they pick the winners? Prediction is at best an inexact science. Nate Silver, in *The Signal and the Noise*, points out the dangers of extrapolation—a basic method of prediction. This basic assumption simply states that a current trend will continue. Yet the fallacy in this mode of prediction is obvious. Trends change. For instance, in 1894 a writer predicted that as cities grew, so would the use of horse-drawn carriages. By the 1940s, the amount of projected city horse manure in the city of London would be nine feet tall city-wide. But then along came Henry Ford and the Model T. The predicted crisis became a non-event. You can easily see how this idea applies to today's rapidly evolving world of technology.

**The Bootstrapper's Benefit**. When you pitch as an entrepreneur, you want to show that you know how to handle money. Better yet, you have to demonstrate that you are willing to put up your own money or that you bootstrapped the company with little money or sleep.

The benefit to this bootstrapping approach is that the longer you can carry a company to the point that you have proved the concept works and can raise revenue, the more potential value you can create. Why? Because as you reduce risk through proof of concept and revenue generation from customer use, you are increasing the value of your company. In turn, you give up less control over your company and maintain a greater percentage of ownership. Plus, you more likely can say no to an unfavorable offer to fund your company.

**Staying Power**. Another way to view bootstrapping is that it is a way to create staying power. One of the keys to moving the odds in your favor as an investor or entrepreneur in early-stage companies is staying power. The fuel of any company, especially a start-up, is cash flow. Cash from sales reduces the need from other cash sources, such as investors.

Yet there is the Cash Paradox. Too little cash and a company runs out of fuel. Too much cash and a company can lose its agility to pivot. The company becomes committed to a certain product line or business model it cannot change. If the company bets wrong, it burns up its cash by scaling up to meet a market demand that does not exist.

A *Harvard Business Review* article titled "Beating the Odds When You Launch a New Venture," written by Clark G. Gilbert and Matthew J. Eyring, provides one example of pursuing the wrong path that would involve wasting large sums of money or time or both. In the early days of E Ink, a supplier of electronic paper display technologies in Cambridge, Massachusetts, they had to decide "whether its electronic 'ink' would best be used for large-area display signage, flat-panel screens for e-books, or the more ambitious radio-paper products, which could be programmed and updated remotely." If the company made the wrong choice, it could lose millions of dollars. "Rather than choosing one path and hoping for the best," the articles goes on, "E Ink reduced the cost of pursuing all three by outsourcing its marketing and production capabilities." When display signage proved less successful, the company was not locked into a single market. It ended up licensing its technology for none other than Amazon's Kindle.

New ventures constantly come to strategic forks. Many of them raise lots of capital and commit to a certain path without adequately testing their assumptions. The entrepreneur's, and often the investors', egos are on the line, and they forge ahead, ignoring the market demand for their product. The result is throwing too much money at the wrong product, and the company runs out of money. Paradoxically, too much money caused the company to fail.

Nor is this problem limited to small start-ups. Corporations who launch new products can also be guilty of arrogance. Here is how that *Harvard Business Review* article put it: "Corporations typically allocate money for a new venture all at once, hoping for a large payoff fairly soon. The more money that is sunk into a project at the outset, the less patience the company tends to have and the more people believe in the validity of their original approach, even in the face of evidence to the contrary."

Given all these variables, no one really knows in the early stage of a company whether it will succeed. If we did, we would have a lot more millionaires. That doesn't stop people from trying, though. Frans Johansson, in *The Click Moment*, points out another paradox. We admit to the uncertainty of everyday life, but we still believe we can pick the winners. This overconfidence becomes the investor's and entrepreneur's Achilles' heel. Johansson feels the world is too random and complicated to distill winners from losers through "strategy, planning, and careful analysis." Instead, he points to a common pattern in which a focused individual trying to find the best solutions for growing his or her company comes upon an unlikely outcome that turns into success.

The stories of inventions and discoveries are often not the result of an idea coming to mind and an immediate workable solution. Think of Thomas Edison's hundreds of tests to find the right material for the light bulb, often the symbol of invention. In this pattern an entrepreneur tries laborious tests until a general idea or hypothesis becomes a valuable solution. That concept/idea/solution in turn attracts consumer demand and delivers substantial profits over many years.

Jim Collins and Morten T. Hansen speak of the same turning-point success pattern in *Great by Choice*. Despite uncertainty, chaos, and luck, some people and companies thrive much more consistently than others. The researchers discovered that successful companies and leaders were "more disciplined, more empirical, and more paranoid." They were not were more visionary or risk taking or more creative. The difference did not lie in innovation alone but in the "right blend of creativity with discipline and the ability to scale the innovation."

The key point is that you want to prepare and practice deliberately over and over to develop the "right blend of creativity with discipline and the ability to scale the innovation." By deep or deliberate practice, which all top performers undergo, you as the entrepreneur will recognize more and more patterns and relationships among information and data unique to your business. This constant practice and diligent awareness prepares you to handle surprises, see the turning-point opportunity, and have the stamina and resources to withstand bad luck and struggles so you can stay in the game and win in the Performance Economy.

All early-stage companies must innovate while maintaining a focused approach:

1. They must be more agile because they must keep testing their assumptions and pivoting until they find the right solution and business model that work and can scale.

2. By deliberating running through numerous scenarios, early-stage companies become more and more sensitive to nuances in their marketplace. From this constant practice of trial-and-error testing of assumptions, they can discover a competitive market advantage that others don't see.
3. The winners not only see the turning-point advantage, they are prepared to act on it. While others are funding too many competing projects, the winners stockpile their resources so that they can back the winners that they end up choosing.
4. Ultimately, the winner is not who comes to market first but who gets it right first. To maintain a competitive advantage involves identifying and handling risk from the earliest stage of a company's development.

Most investors and entrepreneurs seek magic formulas to find the blockbuster deals. Instead, they have to develop an approach that recognizes the uncertainties inherent in companies, especially start-ups, and how to offset these risks as best as possible.

## PITCHING FOR MILLIONS

If you want to make millions of dollars, you must understand the mind-sets of both the investor and the entrepreneur. Many investors are successful entrepreneurs who have faced and may still be facing the same issues that you are encountering.

If you want to beat the odds, you need to develop your own *margin of safety* in your pitch or presentation itself. Everything you do will be scrutinized, so you should prepare for this brutal examination ahead of time by deliberately practicing.

Once you go on "stage" or start building your platform—start up a company or look to invest or both—you are being sized up as to who you are and how you can benefit others.

When you present your company to venture capitalists or an angel network in person, you have to anticipate what can go wrong with your pitch:

1. What if they tell you your idea is unclear?
2. What if the time you have to present is reduced or lengthened?
3. What if you are interrupted by an impatient investor?
4. What if a prior presentation was extraordinary?

**Tell a Great Story.** First and foremost, an entrepreneur needs to tell a story that speaks to the heart, not the head. Film producer Peter Guber, in his book *Tell to Win*, relates how he once tried to pitch the mayor of Las Vegas, Oscar Goodman, on building a new stadium for a Las Vegas minor league team that was part of the Los Angeles farm team system. The problem was, Goodman wanted a major league team, not a minor league affiliate. At first Gruber tried to overwhelm Goodman with facts and figures. "No dice," the mayor said. Gruber tried again and again, in vain.

Gruber reflected afterward on losing out: "My efforts proved that you never get a second chance to make a first impression…The number one lesson is to distinguish a data dump from a well-told story."

Another valuable tip concerning a pitch is that it takes time and practice to tell your story clearly. To win at the game of pitching, you need to plan, practice, and prepare. You can't make presentations off the cuff and win very often. Virtually every successful investment or company has started with or evolved through numerous versions of their pitch until it was able to articulate a definite purpose and USP within the context of an emotionally appealing story.

Take the story of Crowdtilt. As reported on Entrepreneur.com, in the article "Crowdtilt Makes Group-Funding Available to Everyone," by Gwen Moran, co-founder James Beshara started off working for a nonprofit development in South Africa. Based on that experience, he initially wanted to create a site that could fund charities and community projects. But by carefully observing the nuances of his new site, he noticed a pattern. The site was being used more to raise money for vacations and parties. So he and co-founder Khaled Hussein decided to expand the site's pitch to "group fund anything." Crowdtilt took off because it came up with a unique selling proposition that appealed to its social media users—its crowd—who quickly spread the word.

One of the aspects of the pitch that needs to be refined is its length and clarity. With attention at a premium in today's speeded-up environment, no one has much patience for a complicated or long-winded pitch. Anything that appears difficult to comprehend normally creates confusion and the sense that it's a hassle and that it's not worth the time. The result: complicated, long-winded pitches immediately drive investors and customers away.

Your core story and core idea must be simple. For example, Southwest Airlines positioned itself as "the low-fare airline." Herb Kelleher, the CEO of Southwest Airlines, said he could teach the secret of running the airline in 30 seconds, as recorded in the book *Made to Stick*, by Chip and Dan Heath. All decisions were weighed against the core idea "the low-cost airline." If someone in the organization said, "Why don't we add chicken salad to the menu?" the answer was no, because the chicken salad didn't add to Southwest becoming the unchallenged low-cost airline.

## KNOW WHAT WORKS FOR YOU

Your pitch has to have a definite aim or goal, such as getting an investor interested. But your pitch also has to express your own purpose for starting up the business. Your purpose and passion have to connect with the investor. Think of the TV show *Shark Tank*. In many cases the Sharks walk from deals because the person pitching irritates them. On the other hand, tears and passionate pleas have turned noes into yeses.

To have a successful outcome and increase your odds of getting the money, your pitch must have an emotional hook tied to your purpose to engage prospects, customers, and investors alike. As an entrepreneur, you should ask the following questions:

- What will the achievement of your definite purpose mean to you?
- Why are you passionate about your purpose and the business you envision?

- What will this mean for you, your team, and the world? Why can you be the best in the world at what you do?

Business has been compared to war. Pitching means waging battle after battle—presentation after presentation—in the competitive war of business, where entrepreneurs compete against the best and the brightest to get the money.

The book *The Launch Pad*, by Randall Stross, tells the story of Silicon Valley's most exclusive school for start-ups. In the summer of 2011, 2,089 teams applied to investment firm Y Combinator for seed capital and a grueling three-month session of guidance and evaluation of their software start-ups by Y Combinator's founder, venture capitalist Paul Graham. From the 2,089 applicants, 170 teams were interviewed, and only 64 accepted and funded. They were given three months to build a viable start-up.

What can an entrepreneur take away from this example?

- Notice how many times they had to compete by pitching or selling themselves.
- These applicants had to compete for spaces to attend.
- They worked day and night for three months to come up with a winning idea to get additional funding and survive.
- They had to survive rigorous scrutiny and interviews conducted by Graham, who gave them tough-love feedback.
- He pushed the students to undertake the deliberate or deep practice that all high performers must undergo, which included selling themselves and selling peers, who gave them input on the merits of the Idea, Design, Discovery, and Development (steps in the Seven Step Process) or prototype.
- The apprenticeship culminated in Demo Day in front of hundreds of venture capitalists and angel investors, where they pitched for potential millions.

Through this rigorous Y Combinator program, a few companies have become blockbusters. One immense success is Dropbox, a file storage company used by tens of millions. Another big hit is Airhnb, which offers an online marketplace for home owners or apartment dwellers who want to rent out a spare room to travelers. Heroku, which has software that helps run the cloud, is the Y Combinator's biggest unknown success.

In order to be successful, though, you first need to understand what makes you tick inside. The world's oldest self-help book, *The Art of War*, by Sun Tzu, emphasizes is that your success stems from who you are: the inner you. You can fake who you are with some difficulty in the short run, but over time who you are will come out. Who you are transcends the ups and downs of your life. To get from here to where you want to be rests upon who you are.

What you want to achieve is a *pleasing personality* to get others to cooperate with you. It may seem contradictory comparing the world of business to war and then speaking about cooperation, but in sports, team members cooperate among each other, yet they compete against other teams.

You need to do more than put on a smile, though. To truly succeed, I advocate an approach used by peak performers in sports and in the arts called deliberate or deep practice. This is a disciplined approach to achieving both inner and outer success.

You can apply deliberate practice to improve the *inner you*, which in turn will lead to exterior success.

This is especially important during the Discovery step of the 7 Step process. You have to compare yourself to others in your field. Through this process you can create your personal look or brand or overall personality—the personal prototype that you constantly test. You may be introverted or extroverted. You may stay to yourself or cultivate a few friends or be a social butterfly. You can win without being popular—but not if you constantly try to pretend to be someone you are not.

For instance, David Ogilvy was expelled from Oxford University, and then he went on to fail as a tobacco farmer in Pennsylvania. Yet Ogilvy became one of the most important figures in modern advertising, co-founding the Ogilvy & Mather advertising agency. He found himself and then he found success.

Your personal values and biases often are reflected in your pitch. You must understand that others will perceive you differently than you perceive yourself. For this reason, you need to deeply practice your pitch and get feedback so you know how you appear to others. Then make a decision as to whether what you are saying reflects who your company and you are.

Within yourself, you must develop an ability to think critically and not be swayed by your emotions and fears to make impulsive decisions or statements you will regret.

Outside, your success rests on your ability to listen to others and emulate successful models that motivate people to cooperate to reach a common goal.

In crowdfunding, you have to build a platform or crowd following that wants to donate money to your cause or project. To accomplish this, you have to take a disciplined and creative approach to how you will pitch your idea and company to the crowd. Just like trying to achieve anything first class, you have to work hard at it and stretch yourself beyond your comfort zone. You make mistakes and learn what to do from your mistakes.

This is a key point. Deliberate practice involves doing over and over what you are not good at. No one likes to fail over and over at something. People like doing what they do well. But learning both to invest and to build companies involves testing, failing, getting feedback, refining your approach, and trying again.

In effect, deliberate practice is a trial and error approach. You set up a scientific approach—a hypothesis—and test it. You practice pitching your ideas and products over and over. You get rejected constantly. But over time, you see what resonates with others and what does not. Then you have to make the crucial decision what to invest in or bet on since the market may not know what it wants. You have to take the leap of faith because you will never have all the information that guarantees a successful outcome.

In this chapter we have examined the basic fundamentals of a successful pitch. In the next chapter I am going to drill down. What are the specifics of a pitch that you should know? Or, to be more precise, what are the specifics of several different types of pitches? Once you're in the know, crowdfunding could lead the way to your millions.

To understand and execute a successful pitch for money, I constantly look at the big picture and what is going to motivate someone to invest with my client or my own transaction.

I ask myself over and over: where is the market I am presenting to investors going and how does my specific project or company related to that trend?

It's easier to sell a deal where investors feel there is a potential for a lot of growth, since there is more room to make errors and have the market erase them.

View investors as customers who have certain wants and needs specific to them. As you will see, they are similar to any buyer who has a defined shopping list.

## TAKEAWAYS AND INSIGHTS

- To understand and execute a successful pitch, I constantly look at the big picture and what is going to motivate someone to invest with my client or my own transaction.
- I ask myself over and over where is the market I am presenting to investors going, and how does my specific project or company related to that trend.
- It's easier to sell a deal when investors feel there is a potential for a lot of growth, since there is more room to make errors and have the market surge erase them.
- View investors as customers who have certain wants and needs specific to them. As you will see, they are similar to any buyer who has a defined shopping list or criteria study to whom you are pitching to understand their shopping list.
- View raising money like creating a Hollywood movie. When you pitch, you have a short time to sell the concept and grab the investor's interest and emotions. If your story doesn't click, it's over. You don't get a second chance to make a good impression.
- Another way to look at a successful pitch is to analyze successful reality TV programs such as *American Idol* or *Shark Tank*. Whether they are singing or presenting a deal, they are pitching to judges or investors and a viewing audience. Although in *Shark Tank*, the viewing audience doesn't vote on the deal, they often vote with their money. The result can be skyrocketing sales for a company that pitches on *Shark Tank*.

- Arrogance (ego + ignorance) and over confidence can turn investors and customers off. The danger of these traits is a blindness to reality—and investors suffer from the same trait. The result is dismissing signs that indicate things are not working and the investment in a product or deal should be reviewed carefully on its merits by the entrepreneur and the investor.
- To succeed, a pitch must show that the innovation solves a real problem or pain and that there is a focus on how to develop and sell the solution.
- According to Jim Collins' research, he concludes that success comes from leaders and companies being more disciplined, more empirical, and more paranoid. There has to be the right blend of creativity with discipline and the ability to scale the innovation.
- By deliberately practicing a constant iteration and testing, the company prepares itself to recognize a turning point advantage and act upon it. This recognition of the opportunity and how to take advantage of it is the core of a successful pitch.

Click here for additional resources: http://bit.ly/16Ggxsk

## CHAPTER 7

# THE PITCH: GETTING TO YES

We have reached the point where you know enough about what a business looks like in its formative stages to determine how to evaluate what will happen once it goes public. A key part of this process is getting the seed money to launch the business. That is the all-important pitch. Yet because this stage has several parts, I am going to break it into several chapters. In this chapter, I want to cover the opening steps of a successful pitch. Like the Development Step in the 7 Step System, this chapter shows you what makes up an actual pitch. Once you understand why each step is important, you'll be able to take the first steps in creating or evaluating pitches for yourself.

Even though an entrepreneur may not be pitching an early-stage deal to venture capitalists or super angels or angel investors, she can learn a lot about pitching anything, especially when it involves money. From learning the process of how big deals are put together, the entrepreneur can get great insights into how the best financial investment minds evaluate early-stage investments.

To start off, you should realize that people often forget the basic fundamentals of business itself. Both small businesses and large businesses must generate cash flow to survive. Here are a few questions you must consider:

1. How will the business make money?
2. How much money will the business make?
3. Will the money the business makes keep growing?
4. Is making the money and/or the growth of the business sustainable?

The key point to remember is that you have to remind yourself over and over that you are in business to deliver a solution to others' problems and in return make a profit and positive cash flow. Profits allow you to deliver your solution to help more and more people. There's nothing wrong with making the world a better place to live and being paid handsomely for your team's and your stakeholders' efforts.

Crowdfunding donations and crowdfunding donations with rewards normally involve raising small amounts of money—$5,000 to $10,000—for causes and projects. Reviewing how the biggest and brightest invest in companies puts a magnifying glass on the fundamentals of business and pitching to attract money and generate sales, growth, free cash flow, and value that can lead to financial independence.

## DEFINING PITCHING SUCCESS

Before we plunge into the different pitches, it's very important to know what outcome you are seeking. In other words, how do you define success?

Assume you want to build an apartment building like the 23-story tower they are building adjacent to me in Austin, Texas. Someone had a vision or solution (Idea) of what the land could be used for. They tied up the land and created a Design. They looked at the market competition versus this specific location and decided whether they had a competitive advantage (Discovery). They purchased the land, staked it out, cleared it, excavated it, and started putting in the foundation (Development/Implementation/ Execution). When the building is further along, they will start pre-marketing the building (Pre-launch). When the building is built, they will lease out the apartments and retail space on the first level (Launch). They will get feedback from the market and keep leasing and manage the building (Post-Launch). Those are the 7 Steps.

Let's assume the developer pitched investors to invest in the land and then pitched the bank to give him a construction loan and later a permanent loan when the building was completed and a certain number of tenants were leasing space.

The question for you becomes: Where in the process of building the apartment building would you say the developer's success occurred?

1. Was it coming up with the Idea for building an apartment building (product/solution)?
2. Was it getting an experienced team together to develop the building (people)?
3. Was it showing the potential—the profitability and competitive advantage—of the building (potential)?
4. Was it the ability to pitch investors and get the money?
5. Was it building the apartment building?
6. Leasing space in the building to the tenants?
7. Generating a sustained positive cash flow?
8. Selling the building for a sizable profit within five to ten years?

Let's compare a successful business to the proposed successful apartment building:

1. A business has an Idea/*solution* to a problem, similar to the apartment building, which provides affordable, competitive rents by building smaller units (less absolute rent in dollars per month) in a top, normally high-rent downtown location in Austin.
2. It has a *successful* business model: it makes a positive cash flow.
3. The cash flow grows and is *sustainable* because it has a competitive advantage: the apartment building's location and its ability by its zoning and land size to offer many small units at a low rental.
4. The business is *scalable* or can be *leveraged* in that it can grow in size and value by bringing in new customers (tenants) and getting old customers (tenants) to buy more frequently and pay on average more and more without more proportionate input (investment) or effort by you or your team. The apartment building can keep its existing tenants or attract new tenants;

can increase its rent over time; and its profits and its value can go up without expending more effort. Because the building was financed with debt and is making money, the increase in cash flow makes the building's return to the investor higher and higher.

5. The business can be *sold* in part (*shares*) or whole, just as the apartment building can sell part of its equity to new investors or sell the entire building.

You must understand what success looks like and how the different pitches help you articulate that potential success. As I will emphasize, pitching to get the money is only the beginning—not the end goal, unless your business is raising money. But even as a money raiser, if you want to keep your clients, then your goal is to give them a business that is strategically designed to succeed.

Understanding what success looks like is important because your goal is to get investors to say "I'm in!"

Let's look at another example. Entrepreneurs go onto *Shark Tank* to get desperately needed funding for their ideas. If the Sharks say "I'm in," the entrepreneur stands to make a million-dollar deal. But often the budding entrepreneurs are literally eaten alive if their pitch is poor and unprepared. The Shark simply says, "I'm out."

How about the Living Christmas Tree Company, which "rents living Christmas trees as an alternative to a cut or artificial one"? You can see their pitch on the *Shark Tank* website. "Scotty Claus and his elves deliver the trees to your home before the holidays and pick them back up after Christmas. The trees grow at his nursery and return again the following year!"

All the Sharks said, "I'm out." Why is that? What makes one pitch an "I'm all in" and another "I'm out"? In this case, the Sharks voiced concerns about the fundamental business model, such as the business being seasonal. How do you make money for the other months? Plus, shopping for a Christmas tree is a ritual for many families. Would they give up this family event? The business model did not appear to have large profit margins. Besides, to the Sharks, the Living Christmas Tree appeared difficult to scale. So given our definition for business success, the Living Christmas Tree failed on its business model or how the business would make money; its ability to sustain itself; and its ability to scale, which would make it difficult to sell in part or whole.

## MY CONFESSION ON PITCHING FOR MILLIONS

Candidly, I don't like the term "pitching"—never did. But that's the world of marketing, advertising, and e-commerce. You are not going to change the world.

Virtually anyone can improve the way he presents himself and network. Back at the beginning of my career I was terribly shy and still am. I realized that to succeed, I had to push myself to relate to others. To this day, it's hard for me to get up and shout at football games.

Yet I like to speak to audiences because my passion is teaching and patterns and connecting dots. I have little training in speaking techniques or closing tactics, but I do well by being sincere and knowing my subject.

If "pitching" sounds crass and manipulative, then you are right. In some ways, you are selling. But even in your personal life, you are always selling or expressing yourself and your desires, wants, or needs. Just try to focus upon helping others solve their needs. Then you will feel that you are making an equitable exchange.

By now I am an experienced investor and presenter, but even after all that experience, I'll be honest. Providing you a simple checklist of dos and don'ts about different types of pitches won't really help you with making one or evaluating one, nor guarantee you success.

You need to understand that pitching is both a science and an art. When I say *science*, I mean that you can measure results, such as the number of conversions (sales/unique visitors to a web page), in direct marketing on the Internet. When I say *art*, I mean pitching has various intangible aspects, such as personality, appearance, voice tone, and passion, that can make a difference between a successful pitch and a failure. That's because pitching is *complex*. It involves a lot of skill sets that can differ from one pitch type to another and one personality type to another.

Most people seek simple formulas—magic bullets—that do not work in real life. People think they can pitch an idea that sounds grand and get the money or sell out quickly for a big sum, like Instagram. If success rested merely upon pitching and getting the money, you would see a lot more successful companies, millionaires, and billionaires. Yet it isn't just luck either, since Richard Branson, Jack Dorsey, Mark Cuban, and others like them have succeeded too many times just to be rolling the dice.

Then why are some people successful while most are not in pitching and business? The answer is that someone in business has to know the art and science of pitching. From my experience in real estate, coal, oil and gas, film, publishing, food, and software companies—mostly in early-stage start-ups—I know pitches have common patterns, processes, and sequences. For example, a pitch always pinpoints the core elements that make all businesses successful—such as people, products, and potential (the Magical Ps)—and addresses the large amount of hard work already invested to get the company off the ground and the milestones to get it to the next level.

The 7 Steps System, the Magical P's, and others can be used for developing pitches, getting the money, and knowing what to do with the money once you get it. That's because most of the time pitching and getting the money is more the beginning than the end.

## THE LOWDOWN ON THE EXPERTS

The truth is: the so-called experts don't know much more than you do. This is a recurrent theme of mine. Many so-called *experts* are phonies with big fronts and little success. Or maybe they had one success where they made some money and blew it. They need you to pay for their lifestyle they can no longer afford. Their pitch is designed to inflate themselves and deflate you.

Be aware that most pitching/selling focuses on people's inadequacies and tells you to buy something in order to make you adequate. Day after day you are told you are too fat; you smell; you're dumb; you are financially illiterate. Whatever your circumstances, don't let the pitch people manipulate you into buying their products. Make a decision to not allow yourself to be sucked into today's inadequacy marketing, aimed at preying on your struggles and failures.

To the contrary, I am trying to help you see that with the right mind-set and the correct understanding of the different pitch types and business models and patterns, you can successfully learn to pitch, or evaluate a pitch or business, and feel empowered. Like legitimate experts, you can develop a certain mind-set, know-how, and process to create and evaluate pitches and deals.

## THE CRITICAL ELEMENTS FOR ALL PITCHES

What do all pitches have in common? They are structured to fulfill the classic advertising formula AIDA:

A: Attention
I: Interest
D: Desire
A: Action

Here's how to apply AIDA to the different pitch types. Start with the Emotional Grab. The first lines of a pitch should grab your *attention* emotionally and pull you into the pitch. *Attention* is key in today's fast-paced world, because tied to attention is *time.*

What's one of the biggest barriers to sales? I don't have the time! Your number one task is immediately to make the reader or listener or watcher feel you are offering something so important or engaging that it's worth her investment of time. Call it TIME ROI.

A good pitch needs to neutralize the part of the brain called the gatekeeper. It asks, "Should I worry?" "Is this a survival, fight-or-flight issue?" In other words, "Should I invest my time, which is very limited, on this issue?" If this part of the brain does not *tag* or *label* the pitch as something seen before or as boring, then it will take notice. In effect, the emotional grab breaks a pattern—called a pattern interrupt—to get attention. Pattern interrupts can be gruesome or unexpected. Put another way, why do you rubberneck on a highway even if the accident is minor?

A second key element is a story. Explicit or implicit in the headline, tag line, and the remaining parts of the pitch has to be a story. In *Winning the Story Wars*, Jonah Sachs writes, "Human beings share stories to remind each other who they are and how they should act. These stories are deeply ingrained in the DNA.... So many of the stories that have really stuck, that have shaped culture, are about one thing: people reaching for their highest potential and struggling to create a better world. If the test of time is any judge, stories with this formula have a near monopoly on greatness."

Stories grab *attention*, can evoke *interest* and *desire*, and motivate *action*.

Say you are an entrepreneur. When you write about your Idea, Design, and Discovery, you are writing about your story—your myth—your heroic efforts. This is how you are going to achieve AIDA in your pitch. You establish simple, not simplistic, rules for the complex processes of raising money for early-stage companies.

You might say to yourself: "Here's the Idea I came up with. Here's my Design for my product and business. Here's how I went out into the world and, in my exploration and Discovery, I found this unfair advantage. Here's my team that's going to support me in my journey to slay the dragons of competition and implementation—Development—so I can find the Holy Grail, the blockbuster solution. I will return to the community and make the world better with my Holy Grail solution—and make tons of money."

In creating a pitch, you must convey the emotion of your story. As an exercise, write out how the Idea came to you. What frustration, pain, or struggle prompted you to become an entrepreneur? Then transfer your myth and its appeal to your products and your company as part of its culture.

Why does this method work? Let's look at the issue this way. If you went on Match.com, looking for love, you'd get lots of rejections. To get chosen, you work on your profile—your pitch, your first impression. You want to connect emotionally with someone. You also want to avoid being predictable or boring.

If your goal is to actually attract and meet investors, this initial phase is a screening process. You want to move from attention to interest to desire and to, hopefully, a date or a meeting with investors. That's right: you're doing all this just to set up the initial meeting. According to the Angel Capital Education Foundation, 75% of entrepreneurs get rejected at the pre-screening stage by angel investors. They never get to meet the investor at all. By the time the investment process is done, only one deal out of a hundred or less may be funded by angel investors and even less by venture capitalists.

In crowdfunding donations with rewards, sometimes you will meet with backers or donators, but most of the time you won't. This may surprise you, as most backers or entrepreneurs, creative types, or small businesses believe you go onto Kickstarter or RocketHub and you get the money. As I will show you later, the successful crowdfunding campaigns start with friends, families, and fools, similar to raising equity. This is the reason for most failed crowdfunding projects or for raising much less money than could have been gotten. Those seeking capital must establish a core group of backers before they seek capital. Like most things in life, people want to see proof of concept. How many times have you walked away from an empty restaurant?

## THE DIFFERENT TYPES OF PITCHES

As you review the different type of pitches, keep in mind that a pitch does not occur in a vacuum of some spic-and-span corporate conference room. Pitches occur everywhere in every aspect of life. They are how we often communicate, selling ourselves and others on ideas and opinions on virtually any topic.

In business, successful pitches evolve from understanding the mind-sets of the investors, the entrepreneurs, and the crowd (different groups such as prospects, customers, and employees). What makes investors like the Sharks say "I'm out" or "I'm in"?

They look for certain patterns and formats in a pitch that indicate to them that an investment is viable. They want to know if the person is a true expert. Does the product have a competitive advantage? Does the company have a patent or other protection against competition?

Does the product have measurable sales, and over what period of time? Does the presenter/pitcher indicate an entrepreneurial leverage mindset? Is he confident? Does he have a genuine passion?

Here is a list of pitches and the typical order in which they are given:

1. Headline
2. Tag Line
3. Elevator Speech—Short
4. Elevator Speech—Long
5. Executive Summary
6. Slide Presentation
7. Business Plan

## HEADLINE PITCH

Even though you might not think of a headline as a pitch, it conveys an instant message. A headline is the main lure in a print (newspaper, blog, magazine) or web page advertisement, usually the first and largest words. You can have multiple headlines in an article or ad campaign. Headlines should be aimed at your target audience. Because your pitch or presentation will most likely consist of print text or slides or videos, you will need attention-grabbing headlines. Some copywriters believe 80% of the success of the copy comes from the headline itself.

Here are some crowdfunding examples of headlines, names, images, and descriptions from successful crowdfunding projects:

(shows image with the name as a headline and description below)
**Heaven's Hell - The Art Book The Art of Anthony Jones**

An 128-page art book of a wildly weird and dangerously interesting world from my imagination. Heaven's Hell.

- **377%** funded
- **$34,004** pledged
- **21** days to go

**Rivet Wars by CoolMiniOrNot (image with title acting as headline)**

A new miniatures RTS inspired board game. Walking tanks, crazy artillery, and cool characters battle in the trenches!

- Atlanta, Georgia
- **671%** funded
- **$167,842** pledged
- **25** days to go

**CST-01: The World's Thinnest Watch by Central Standard Timing (image with what it is as the headline)**

A 0.80 mm thin, flexible wristwatch with an E Ink display housed in a single piece of stainless steel.

- Chicago, Illinois
- **56%** funded
- **$113,050** pledged
- **44** days to go

Notice a similar format on a successful RocketHub project:

**Amal Women's Training Center and Moroccan Restaurant By Rachel Mead**

- Social 128% funded

## TAG LINE PITCH

A tag line can be defined as a business or product slogan or benefit phrase that you tag to the business or product name. Product designer Katy Dwyer advises: "A tag line is one short phrase (usually no more than eight words) that describes the purpose, product, service, or philosophy of your company. The tone of the tag line sets the voice for your business, and should appeal directly to the type of client/customer you are trying to attract." The tag line should become as recognizable as a company's name. She goes on to say, "It's a phrase that's meant to be repeated over and over throughout advertising, websites, even corporate stationery or business cards, building recognition for both your business's name and personality. Tag lines can change over time, but they don't (and shouldn't) change frequently."

You can think of a pitch as if it is an ad campaign. Think of tag lines you know, like Nike's "Just Do It" or Wheaties' "The Breakfast of Champions." That sort of instant identification not only attracts customers; it attracts investors, who know a good one when they see one.

Here's an example on Kickstarter of a headline with a tag line:

**GameStick: The Most Portable TV Games Console Ever Created, by GameStick (headline)**

Putting Big Screen Gaming In Your Pocket. (tag line)

- Santa Clara, California
- **280%** funded
- **$280,334** pledged
- **22** days to go

**Indiegogo example:**
**iLumi—The World's Most Intelligent Light Bulbs (headline)**
Bring your light to life with iLumi. (tag line)
Energy efficient multicolor LED lights you control and program through a convenient mobile app to do amazing things. (description)
Technology—Dallas, Texas, United States

Now you might be wondering: how can a headline or tag line attract an investor? It's because potential investors go to your website to review your product. The first thing they see is your headline and tag line. Eighty percent of the time, someone reading your headline or headline combined with your tag line makes a go or no-go decision. If the investor likes what he/she sees, then they will search your name on the web, including your LinkedIn profile. These pages all have headlines and tag lines, which contribute to the first impressions of your company and you.

If you can get past these first impressions (headlines, tag lines), then you have the chance to tell more of your story during a meeting with potential investors. That's where the Elevator Speech becomes vital.

## ELEVATOR SPEECH—SHORT

The elevator speech is the first step in speaking at greater length with the person to whom you are pitching your deal. The *short* elevator speech comes from the following situation. You enter an elevator on the ground floor, and you recognize a top venture capitalist who walks into the elevator at the same time. You have 30 seconds plus to pique his interest enough to want to hear more about your deal. The parallel with crowdfunding is obvious. If someone is reading your copy, she is going to spend about thirty seconds on you to see what you;ve got. If she is not sold in that short block of time she gives you, she will move on to the next deal.

Your objective is to hone your short elevator speech to no more than 35 words. Guy R. Powell, in *3 Steps to a Great Elevator Speech,* makes the following points, which he calls the "five Ws." You should develop answers to the following questions:

1. What does your company do? For example, "we provide…."
2. Whom does your company do it for? "For small and midsized health-care providers."
3. Why do they care? (What's in it for them?) For example, "So that they can…."
4. Why is your company different? For example, "As opposed to…" or "Unlike…."
5. What is your company? For example, "My company is an insurance company."

Using that as a guideline, let's look at a typical elevator speech:

Trey Research: "For restaurants that need to measure and improve customer satisfaction, Trey Research provides answers you need in half the time through its proprietary combination of online and offline survey techniques." (30 words)

This speech looks simple, but it's not. Do you really understand what "proprietary combination of online and offline survey techniques" means? I don't. Above all else, you want to pick simple versus complicated. You need to hone your elevator speech by deliberate practice: repeating over and over to anyone who will listen, such as a spouse, friends, or business associates. Like an actor in your own movie, you have to know your part as if it's second nature. Get feedback and refine it. And smile when those listening to you ask for clarification—they are trying to help you.

After you have tested it out a few times, you might find that refining the pitch produces something like this:

Trey Research: "If you're a restaurateur and can't keep your regulars coming back, you're lost. Using proprietary online and offline techniques, Trey Research will find out how you can stop the losses and start generating profits." (35 words)

OK, that is clearer. Now the meaning of "proprietary" can be understood by a businessperson. Yet how about some regular Joe visiting a crowdfunding website? You also have to adjust the pitch to your audience. Every audience is different, so make sure you speak their language. You might prepare an alternate speech that runs like this:

Trey Research: "Trey Research helps restaurants improve customer satisfaction so that people keep coming back. Nobody else does it the way Trey Research does it—with combined telephone and internet contacts." (29 words)

How about that? I understand what the pitch is now. I might want to investigate this idea further.

You should keep one important point in mind. View your elevator speeches—short and long—as verbal expressions of your written executive summary pitch. They are *not the same* but have similar elements or parts.

All of these pitches, however seemingly simple and stripped down on the surface, have a significant impact on the first impression your company and you make on an investor. Remember, Peter Guber said in *Tell to Win* you rarely get a second chance to make a first impression.

## ELEVATOR SPEECH—LONG

The long-form elevator speech runs from 150 to 225 words and is given in 60 seconds. If you like, imagine you're in one of those old New York City office buildings, where the elevator takes forever to get to your floor. Here's what you need to cover for the long-form elevator speech, which is very similar to the short-form elevator speech:

1. The emotional hook
2. Show passion and enthusiasm; be likable, persuasive, compelling, and credible (believable)
3. Ask for something: the meeting

Startupnation.com provides a more elaborate list of what you can cover in the long-form elevator speech:

1. What's the Idea (product/solution)?
2. What's the status of the idea or business (product/solution)?
3. What market or markets does the business address, and are there any testimonials or customer feedback (message; market; measurement)?
4. Why do you believe you have the advantage in the marketplace relative to the market needs (potential)?
5. What's the competition in the marketplace (marketplace)?
6. What's the revenue model (potential)?
7. Who is the team that's going to make the business a success (people)?

As an entrepreneur or an investor on a crowd-funding portal, you need to consider these factors in evaluating whether the idea succeeds or not. For an example, let's go back to iLumi light bulbs.

The following description comes off their pitch page on Indiegogo:

> Create Amazing Lighting Experiences with iLumi
>
> Enjoy the convenience of complete wireless control, create beautiful personalized atmospheres, and even program your lighting to do amazing things! iLumi is a series of customizable and energy-efficient LED light bulbs controlled wirelessly an easy to Android or iOS mobile app. After two years of research, design and development, we are ready to manufacture iLumi, and we want you to be a part of it. Support our campaign and help bring the world's most intelligent light bulbs to the world, and in return be some of the first to receive iLumi.

Now, you can turn this into a long-form elevator speech with a "headline" and "tag line":

> Hi, I'm Gary Spirer with iLumi light bulbs. We create Amazing Lighting Experiences with iLumi. On your iPhone

> or Android, you can program your lighting to do amazing things! You can create beautiful, personalized atmospheres. After two years of research, design, and development, we are ready to manufacture iLumi. I just want to mention also that we have patent-pending HyperLux LED technology making iLumi the brightest and most efficient multicolor light bulbs We'd love the opportunity to meet with you and show you how you can help bring the world's most intelligent light bulbs to the world and in return be the first to receive and enjoy the iLumi experience.

As I hope you are realizing, the same questions and patterns repeat over and over in the elevator speech—short and long—as well as the executive summary, the slide show, and the business plan pitches.

By seeing what is common among the pitches, you can incorporate into them what is most important to investors. As a result, both investors and entrepreneurs can benefit because they more clearly know what each expects.

As you can see, crowdfunding uses the same pitch strategies and techniques: images, headlines, tag lines, and elevator speeches that are used for any type of fund raising. The main point is that we are in a multimedia world. To get the money, you must paint like an artist an emotional story that appeals to all the senses and clearly states why you are doing what you are doing, how it can work for them, and what it is. Why, how, and what, in this order, rather than the reverse what, how, and why. People buy your why before your how or what. So let's now turn to the pre-launch phase, where you can see how all of this fits in action.

## TAKEAWAYS AND INSIGHTS

- Over the last 30 years, your stage or platform has expanded immensely. When you communicate with someone, you are evaluated on many levels—in person, on the web, mobile, and social.
- Each of the different pitches you use combine to tell a story of who you are: your company, your status, your relationships, your appearance, your track record, your reputation.
- Any one of the different pitches you use can turn an investor or others potential stakeholders on or off
- Knowing the various pitches gives you a starting point. You should view the pitches as part of your own canvas. You are the artist that must paint the picture which tells your story and that of your company in an impactful way.
- The question you may have: how can I do all this stuff? The answer: you first have to understand what Shakespeare said—we are all players—so are investors.
- Investors are just like you. You can be an investor with $100, $1,000, $10,000, $100,000 and more.
- Investing is a game—although a serious one when it comes to your own career and business.
- Since we are all actors on a stage, we are all artists. In the world of art, there is no paint-by-the-numbers solution if you want to make meaning and excel.
- Ralph Waldo Emerson said, "To be yourself in a world that is constantly trying to make you something else is the greatest accomplishment."

- Take the pitches and study them. Know the fundamentals and deliberately practice them until you understand them.
- You can get today a lot of people to assist you: copywriters, editors, speech writers, executive summary and business plan writers, private placement memo writers, lawyers, accountants, etc.
- You can find lots of mechanics, but what makes you different is you and your solution to someone's pain or satisfying their need.
- In this fast-paced world, we seek safely, security, a reliable future, a nest or a retreat from the world. The irony is that you achieve that by being an artist and a scientist—being different, unique, and vulnerable and proving your uniqueness can be a solution which betters the world and attracts money.
- Tell your story: reach for your highest potential and create a better world.

Click here for additional resources: http://bit.ly/19IzAad

CHAPTER 8

# THE PITCH: LAYING IT ALL OUT

The opening salvo has been fired. The headline, the tag line, and the elevator speeches have been crafted with the idea of grabbing an investor's or crowd funder's initial attention. An entrepreneur's initial role is that of a marketer. Unless you are profiled on the front page of a crowdfunding portal, you have to pull the investor or crowd funder to your site or crowdfunding page. Unless investors know of you, they are not going to troll the Internet or crowdfunding portals, seeking to give you money.

Once they arrive, an entrepreneur has a few seconds to grab and hold their attention. The headline and the description paragraph—which could be the tag line or could contain the tag line (sometimes called the deck copy)—are the opening conversation or door opener (called in copywriting "the lead").

The next part of the presentation must keep the story going. Where's the beef inside all these come-ons? The next stage is describing in depth what a start-up and the related new product or service are really about. You are expressing your WHY. Ultimately, you are showing what's different for the investor or backer. This more detailed process breaks out into three steps: the executive summary, the slide deck, and the business plan. Each one has its own purpose, and each one can be powerful if you know which components determine the difference between success and failure.

Caution: Don't get caught up in the details and lose sight of the overriding purpose of most pitches: to "sell" a meeting with an investor or backer, not to educate or merely describe what a company is doing or what a project is about. To reiterate, the best-kept secret of crowdfunding is that the initial money comes from friends, family, and fools, just as it does for any type of early-stage company or project.

The key to getting the money is constantly reminding yourself that an investor or backer is like any potential buyer or customer. In the case of money raising, the investor *purchase* can be in the form of donating or investing money into a project or company. The investor in a company can (1) buy shares or an ownership interest, (2) make a loan (or guarantee a loan or line of credit), or (3) a combination of a loan and a purchase of shares in the company.

At the outset I will deliver a warning. Even though you are learning what issues investors and backers want to see presented and in what format and sequence, don't ever fall into the trap that you are learning a cookie-cutter formula to getting the money. You must be who you are and, above all, have integrity. As an entrepreneur, creative type, or a small businessperson, you should study but not copy other pitches or say what you think investors want to hear.

Your biggest asset is your uniqueness as a person. Investors are looking for extraordinary stories that narrate the WHY, HOW, and WHAT of extraordinary products and people (your team and you) that have the potential to make lots of money and/or change the world for the better.

I am going to discuss pitches in terms of venture capitalists or angel investors, but keep in mind that you can use these principles to pitch on a crowdfunding portal page in a format which typically includes a video and offers different rewards for different pledge amounts from backers.

Here is a crucial insight. Each type of pitch gives you another insight into the mind of your potential customer—the investor or backer. Getting the money involves the same strategies and tactics used by top marketers and salespeople. Ultimately, people who get the money learn to understand what moves people: the importance of first impressions, social proof, competence, and trust.

## THE DIRTY SECRET OF RAISING MONEY: THE CONVERSATION

Before turning to the executive summary pitch, I'd like to share with you the best-kept secret about getting the money. Despite all of the digital connectivity, venture capitalists, angel investors, and many initial crowdfunding backers meet entrepreneurs *in person.* They pitch each other back and forth, depending upon who wants to make a deal more. Max Chafkin describes in a *Fast Company* magazine article, "The Zen of Silicon Valley Chatter," how Kevin Rose, the founder of Digg and now a company picker for Google Ventures, spends his days looking for deals in which to invest. "At ground zero of the information revolution, pickers like Rose make most of their discoveries in person. For them, the important currency of our digital world is not code, it's conversation." Rose has invested in Twitter, Square, Fab, Facebook, Path, and other unheralded companies, producing a return of 22 times his initial investment, Chafkin reports. Not bad for chitchatting about deals in coffee houses and burning up cell phone minutes.

## THE EXECUTIVE SUMMARY

Wow! Cool! Awesome! Intriguing!

That's what you want the potential investor to say to himself or herself after reading the first few sentences of your executive summary. That's the internal conversation you want investors and backers to have about your company so that it leads to a face-to-face conversation (presentation and pitch) where you can persuade them to move forward and ultimately invest.

That's why executive summaries are so crucial to getting the money. They are your written story and opening conversation rolled into one short typed document. My own feeling is that you need a good two to three pages to explain your company. One page is too short. Two to three pages is long enough that you can give a pretty comprehensive view of what you are planning. Just as an example, I normally sold my deals solely off the executive summary. Many times I did not create a business plan—the final step—for an investor.

Similar to other pitch types, you must grab the reader's attention in the first few sentences. Otherwise, your executive summary will become part of the 75% of all executive summaries that are rejected. That means right out of the gate you only have a 25% chance of moving to the next step in getting the money! Think of initially scanning an unknown blog or novel. What percentage do you really read? The same holds for your executive summary. If you don't get the reader's attention and emotionally grab the reader, then you are immediately a no-go.

What gets attention and grabs a reader emotionally in an executive summary? First, tell the reader what product or service you are providing, so there is a context to what you are presenting. Then weave your "what" (product or service) into your story or script and arouse excitement by demonstrating traction (noteworthy accomplishments or milestones) or social proof. For example, show that you already have current paying customers or a significant accomplishment like a known strategic partner.

As a sample, I have provided the points I covered for the pitch for my company, Questionmine:

Questionmine is an interactive choose-your-own adventure video platform where viewers answer questions and get back immediate real-time personalized responses in the form of videos, email, mobile texts, voice messages or live calls.

It has integrated its interactive video and mobile video Q&A proprietary technology (overlays questions and answers such as surveys and quizzes on videos) with IBM's Connections Platform. Connections is the largest enterprise social media platform in the world and exposes Questionmine to 90,000 companies and potential customers. As an IBM Global Partner and World Entrepreneurial Partner, Questionmine receives free marketing assistance, direct introductions to potential customers, technical support, and certain IBM technology.

Questionmine's strategy is to integrate with and enhance CRM and CMS systems including Oracle's Eloqua, Infusionsoft and Kentico by offering video engagement and analytics across social mobile and the web.

Our management team...

Our sales to date...

Our strategic partners are...

Other milestones and successes...

What I am doing is grabbing attention in 30 seconds (similar to the time you have in the short elevator speech) and establishing credibility by mentioning:

- Recognized names
- Strong management and advisory team
- Existing sales

I am going to continue with the Questionmine model, not because I'm trying to sell it to you, but so that you will see why and how the different pieces of an executive summary fit together. The next step is laying out for the investor what the problem is that a company will solve.

## PROBLEM

Like many marketers, I struggled with how to get to know my customer. With the rise of social media, customers now have access to unparalleled amounts of information, and they control the *conversation* that affects the buying decision. Studies show eight out of ten consumers want to engage with and help brands they support, but only 16% of all companies allow them to help in any meaningful way.

Demanding, empowered consumers want to be engaged, listened to, rewarded, and responded to in real-time *two-way conversations*—otherwise, they are gone.

As a result of the shift in consumer power, a major problem for Enterprise companies is how to retain their key customers (and their best employees as well).

Companies have attempted to use videos to engagement their customers but the videos they produce are *not* designed to be conversational. Instead, virtually all video material is static, one-way broadcasts, and offers no effective and efficient way for companies to determine real-time customer likes and dislikes, wants, needs, and purchase intent. This has led to low marketing and video return on investment.

The video problem will only get worse, as video growth is exploding and companies know they must invest more and more in video marketing advertising, e-commerce, training and education. Cisco estimates that by 2016, 1.2 million minutes of video content will cross the network every second, and 90% of web traffic will be video!

## SOLUTION

Now comes the next critical part of an executive summary: the solution. Questionmine increases marketing and video return on investment by creating a real-time dynamic two-way conversation between the customer and the company. Based upon custom or employee answers to survey, polls, quizzes, and assessments, Questionmine's proprietary video branching technology feeds different videos in real-time while measuring the entire interaction. Prospects and customers can be rewarded with coupons discounts or loyalty points to answer questions, comment, or review the video content.

Questionmine's automated, personalized, precision marketing increases engagement, generates sales-ready leads, grows sales, and maintains customers.

## MARKET SIZE

I say, "Forrester reports that by 2016 marketers will spend $77 billion on interactive marketing, as much as they do on television today... Or, other studies show that mobile commerce will increase from $3 billion in 2010 to $31 billion by 2016. Forrester projects by 2015 smartphone adoption will grow 150% and 82 million consumers will own a tablet."

This only shows that there is a large market. What you want to demonstrate is what slice of the market or niche you are going to dominate. For example, Questionmine has an interactive mobile video advertising solution for advertisers seeking to know who their customers are and what they are buying in real time in retail locations.

Investors want to know:

- The breakdown of the market segments, such as their size in dollars or customers or users, growth rates, and what is the impetus behind the growth.
- How to define a growing rather than a maturing niche and what percentage of this niche a company is targeting to capture.
- Whether you can demonstrate a bottom-up approach to market size by evaluating for example the number of potential users, your projected share of those users and your average charge per user based upon your business model.
- Note: This avoids the to-down approach telling investors our market size is 10 billion and if we can capture only 1% of the market, our revenue will be $100 million.

## COMPETITIVE ADVANTAGE

Let's extend this example to show another essential element of a good executive summary: the competitive advantage.

Questionmine has developed a two-way conversation feedback and measurement software platform. It has provisional patents that include an admin; create the interactive videos and mobile videos that capture, filter, and measure this real-time interactive data and key performance indicators, including video metrics; and send real-time responses based upon this data.

At all times, you need to consider the competition. In this case, Questionmine is located in a competitive environment that includes traditional survey, poll, and quiz companies and a number of other established video platform companies. Which have degrees of interactivity such as lead generation forms and call-to-action buttons (Questionmine has these as well). The same is true with every company. You typically have direct competitors and indirect competitors. A company should never say it has no competition, since everyone has competition, even if customers are doing what they do without your product. Also be on guard against the argument that "if we are half as good as the competition, we'll make a fortune." Instead, of this negative-comparison argument, an executive summary should state how a company *positively* compares to the competition and what percentage of the market it can capture and why.

Let's take as an example a new supersized truck to carry goods. What is the competition—railroads, planes, cars, boats, tankers, barges, motorized carts, and even people with carts or bags. How does that big truck fit into this very crowded marketplace? An investor is going to ask you that question. What is the advantage over these other modes of transportation? Are you going to be able to sustain that advantage?

## BUSINESS MODEL

The next question an entrepreneur needs to answer is: How will the company make money? For example, Questionmine provides a software service (SaaS) or "on-demand software," where the software and associated data are centrally hosted on the cloud. Questionmine charges a monthly subscription fee based upon video usage and other criteria.

Every business has a key metric that indicates a successful business model, such as revenue generated per square foot in retail. Others might be the number of customers or number of franchises. For some businesses, your key metric may be gross margin (sales minus cost of goods).

Secret: It may take years to figure out the key number or metrics that you must achieve to optimize your business model. For example, you may wrongly focus on how many new customers you can get when your highest return would be on a much smaller subset of repeat customers—your ideal highly profitable customer—who you are ignoring and soon leave.

In reviewing your financials, the investor wants to look at the business model and whether it seems plausible. What the investor wants to see is the growth in revenues and the net profits and cash flow you can achieve with your business model and his or her money over a three- to five-year period.

## THE TEAM

Your team is a critical part of your story that tells the investor who is going to implement your plan. Using the running example for the executive summary, Questionmine team is outlined

An executive summary shouldn't be merely a list of resumes. It also wants to highlight the team's backgrounds as to why these people can execute the business's specific plan. In other words, why is this team qualified specifically for the type of product and service the company is bringing to market? Does it have the experience to scale the business?

An investor also wants to know: Do the entrepreneurs have any of their own capital at risk? How much money and time has been invested in the venture? Are the entrepreneurs engaged full-time in the company? After all, businesses need full-time, dedicated people to succeed. As for the advisers, are they window dressing or are they really active? Are they investing their money and/or bringing investors to the table?

In addition, an executive summary should provide the company's strategic partners. Included among these are joint ventures, affiliates, large corporations or organizations, as well as value-added resellers (a company that adds features or services to an existing product). For example, IBM has given Questionmine numerous free resources, instant credibility, validation of its technology, new ideas for products and services, and access to many potential clients.

## FINANCIALS

The numbers should show over five years what the revenues and expenses are—the profits, losses, cash flow, and staffing needs. The numbers reveal how an entrepreneur breaks down the business into its components, such as salary levels, pricing, sales commissions, marketing budget, gross margins, number of customers, repeat customers, payment terms, head count, when hired.

The numbers should calculate in a bottoms-up approach where sales will come from in the first year, month by month—from salespeople, Internet/inbound marketing, affiliates/joint ventures, etc. How much cash is needed for the business to break even? What multiple on investment is being offered?

At this point the pitch should ask for money needed to reach the goals and milestones that have been laid out in the financials. It may want to indicate if the company anticipates a future round of financing.

## EXECUTIVE SUMMARY TIPS

Finally, any entrepreneur should consider some smaller points that can add up to a big difference in whether you get the money or not. Here is a list of guidelines that will help:

1. Do not start your executive summary with a mission statement—it's boring, and who really cares? Your goal is to state your why or your purpose, your passion, and the magic you are bringing to the world.
2. Use short paragraphs, short sentences, and bullet points.
3. Do not use empty clichés, such as "revolutionary," "dynamic," "groundbreaking," "intelligent," "easy to use."
4. Have a summary graph or table that sums up the opportunity.
5. Be careful not to exaggerate when comparing yourself to successful companies. Exaggeration: "We are the next Instagram or Google. Thus, give us the big bucks now why you have the chance." Compare and contrast: "We enhance Google's organic search or SEO by doing…."
6. Do not say your financials are "conservative."
7. Do not use the 1% argument: "If we only get 1% of a $100 billion market, then we can do such and such…," or "Our market size is $50 billion" when your market is a small part of this market.
8. Make sure you have a clear call to action, such as a certain number to call or email address where you can be contacted or a website to visit. A common mistake is to omit this information and the ability to act right away and move the investment screening process forward to the next step, such as a face-to-face meeting.

## SLIDE DECK PITCH

The investor slide deck represents the next step in the venture capitalist and angel investor screening process. If you are seeking crowdfunding money or to invest in crowdfunding, you might be wondering how knowing how to execute an in-person slide presentation will help you. First, let's define a slide deck pitch:

It's a slide presentation in person, normally by the CEO of the company (sometimes other members of his team as well), to one or more sophisticated investors. I should point out right away that having more than one person pitching can be distracting and break the emotional momentum of the pitch. Also, it's harder to tell one cohesive story in a short amount of time with two or more speakers.

Here's what is critical to understand. The most successful crowdfunding sites have videos at the top of their page. The videos are used to present and pitch their projects and products. The video pitch can be very similar to a recorded elevator speech or a short slide show presentation, covering some of the main points of the project or product, such as: What is it? Why are you doing this? What's unique about it? What's in it for the audience or crowd? How can they get it? At what price? Why should they believe you? In other words, you are spelling out an irresistible offer similar to what you want to achieve in a slide deck pitch.

Back to the slide deck pitch: since this is an in-person presentation, this pitch is similar to the elevator speech. The slide presentation differs, however, in its length and purpose. The elevator speech's goal is merely to induce the potential investor to hear more. The slide presentation is a big leap forward in the screening process. If you are invited to a slide deck presentation, this means a venture capitalist angel investor is definitely interested in your deal. For that reason the slide presentation becomes about you, the person, your character, your skill set, your ability to pitch, and how you respond to criticism if you are challenged with tough questions.

Keep in mind, this does not mean they want chapter and verse on your life story. They just want to learn how you will lead your company. Let's take a look at the personal traits that investors evaluate. As a crowd-funding investor, you should also be looking for these essential qualities as well:

1. Integrity: This tops the list, since without integrity little else about the pitch is believable. You can't teach integrity.
2. Passion: You are looking for enthusiasm and excitement. If the entrepreneur is not excited about his company, then why should you be excited?
3. Resourcefulness: Does the entrepreneur demonstrate from her story a desire to find a way to get things done when the odds seem slim?
4. Resilience: Tied closely to resourcefulness is the ability to be knocked down and bounce up and move forward.
5. Persistence: That also is tied to the ability to stick to things and move forward, no matter what the obstacles.
6. Experience: Has the CEO and/or his team been involved in starting up other businesses? Have they been able to take a business from beginning to end, whether successful or not?
7. Knowledge: Does the CEO have specific knowledge and experience in the industry and specific business product she is promoting? Do any members of the team possess this knowledge?
8. Skill set: What specific skill set do the CEO and his team bring to the business: sales, marketing, technical, management, finance?
9. Humility: Is the CEO or other presenter humble or arrogant (ignorance plus ego)?
10. Leadership skills: Does the CEO demonstrate the ability to motivate, inspire, and lead a team—critical to the business's success?
11. Coachable: Does the entrepreneur seem to be open to advice from experienced and knowledgeable investors who were or still are entrepreneurs?
12. Commitment: Is the person *totally* committed to the venture, or does she have a side job? Or, is she involved in other ventures? Do the CEO and other key team members have their

own money invested in the company and that of their family or close friends, so the entrepreneur stands to lose a lot too?

13. Vision: Are they trying to be the best and change the world with their product or just be another me-too product?
14. Realism: Are they so in love with their vision that they are unrealistic about the ups and downs of business or the challenges to implement a business plan and achieve profitability? Or, can they deal with obstacles and reality when things go badly?

In an article in the *Upstart Business Journal* titled "What Do Venture Capitalists Want?," Tarang and Sheetal Shah write: "Venture capitalists look for a very specific entrepreneurial profile. Most first-time entrepreneurs believe that successful entrepreneurs must have high IQs, high tolerance for ambiguity and risk-taking, dogged persistence, nimbleness, and the drive to succeed. These are all necessary, but they are neither sufficient nor primary success factors. Venture capitalists are really looking for entrepreneurial leadership, which includes missionary passion, balanced ego, transparency, trust and integrity, and objectivity. Authenticity combined with entrepreneurial leadership creates a talent magnet necessary to build an awesome startup team."

When you describe your team, your goal is to highlight their experience and how it will contribute specifically to the success of the business or project for which you are seeking funding. You can state where you have holes in the management team and how you are going to fill them. Also, point out key advisers or consultants with expertise and connections. Remember, above all, sophisticated investors know you need a solid team to execute your plan, compete, and make money.

Beyond the characteristics they are looking for, they want to see professionalism. Every slide show has a basic format with the same elements, such as "the problem," "the solution," and "the competitive advantage." These elements are expected by investors but not necessarily in the same order. This basic format makes it easier for them to follow and evaluate key issues they want answered in your pitch. It also indicates that you know what your customer-buyer or customer-investor wants.

The following are the usual slide headings or elements:

1. Title
2. Business Overview
3. Management Team
4. Problem/Pain
5. Product/Solution
6. Market
7. Business Model
8. Secret Sauce/Barriers to Entry
9. Competition
10. Strategic Partnerships
11. Financial Overview
12. Capital and Valuation

## THE FINANCING

Of course, the whole point of all this hard work is the financing. How much do the owners of the company want as an equity investment from the investors in their company? What ownership percentage of the company will the owners give to the investors?

I want to emphasize the inherent conflict between the investor and the entrepreneur. The investor is seeking to get at the facts of the deal. The entrepreneur is trying to weave a story that combines certain facts and assumptions and attempts to persuade the investors that her truth is worth investing in.

The investor's fear is that the entrepreneur will steal his money or the investor is incompetent. The investor knows that his chances of getting his money back or losing it all are maybe fifty-fifty or even worse in early-stage companies, depending upon what stage of development and how he invested his money As a result, the investor tries to protect herself. The bottom line is: the key motivation for a venture capitalist is to find the Next Big Thing. This is what keeps her taking meetings at coffee shops, like Kevin Rose, and watching slide show after slide show on iPads in conference rooms.

According to one benchmark, a venture capitalist will look at 2,000 deals, evaluate 200, do due diligence on 40, and fund 10. That's 1 out of 200! Venture Capitalist David Rose says 1 out of 400. Angel investors will fund on average one out of ten deals David Rose says 1 out of 40. In other words, the odds are very low that an entrepreneur will succeed. So how can he tip the odds in his favor to get the money he is seeking?

At the risk of being repetitious, an entrepreneur has to tell a good story. To create a great script for your crowdfunding project or your slide show or other pitches, you need keep in mind several cardinal points. The first is one that Robert McKee points out in his book *Story*: "Story is about principles, not rules. A rule says: 'You must do it my way.' A principle says, 'This works…and has through all remembered time.' "

Ronald Tobias, in *20 Master Plots: And How to Build Them*, states, "Years of schooling have conditioned us to think about fiction as something either on the page or on the screen, so we overlook the fact that our everyday lives are steeped in stories." When you pitch a deal, you are a storyteller. The repeating parts of the pitch are similar to the repeating elements or themes or plots in a work of fiction, such as underdog, riddle, discovery, quest, sacrifice, adventure, rivalry and pursuit, transformation, and love.

In writing your executive summary, you are choosing a plot. "I was an *underdog*, but I surprised everyone and here's what I invented." Or, "I knew there was this problem and through years of *sacrifice*, I discovered this very lucrative solution."

An entrepreneur can't wander, though. He also needs to remember to stick to the point. Famous venture capitalist Guy Kawasaki has what he calls the 20/10/30 rule. A slide presentation should be:

1. No longer than 20 minutes, leaving 40 minutes for discussion
2. No more than 10 slides
3. The font size should be no smaller than 30

The next must is that the slide show has a logical progression. Venture capitalist David Rose emphasizes, "You must start like a rocket and grab their attention in 10 to 30 seconds with some fact or story. From there, you got to get them on a very solid upward path from beginning to end.... Every part of your story reinforces the other part. Your story gets better and better and better and at the very end, you knock them out of the park. You get them in such an emotional high, they are ready to write you a check."

That is not achieved just by good acting skills, though. Investors are seeking proof or evidence—the FACTS—that prove your story has real traction. They want to see proof such as:

1. A beta test going well: a customer-paying beta test is better.
2. Some reports or statistics that say what you are doing makes sense.
3. A large strategic partner.
4. The product received a prestigious reward.
5. A growing customer base—paying more.
6. The company reached the break-even point.

Among the facts they really want to see are financials. An entrepreneur needs to show a significant sample, such as five years of revenue and expenses. He needs to emphasize some key metrics and assumptions, such as the average sale cycle, the average sale amount, and current monthly/quarterly sales. What are the number of products to support those sales levels—now and in the future? How many people are needed to support each level of sales—now and in the future? What are the salary levels for you and other key people?

## SLIDE DECK SUMMARY

Here are some extra pointers just on the presentation side. The idea is to keep the show as visual as possible. This is a pitch, not a lecture.

1. Don't be too technical—don't try to explain how the motor works.
2. Mostly try for photos, images, diagrams, and graphs. You can show product photos. You can use diagrams to show how the

business works. You can use graphs to show trends and financial outcomes.
3. Don't use a lot of text.
4. In the end, a slide deck pitch needs to bring back the key points in a quick summary.

## THE BUSINESS PLAN

To start off, let me make a critical point: the Executive Summary Pitch and Slide Deck Pitch are more important than the business plan. The world has changed in 30 years. It's more fast paced, more uncertain, more competitive, and more risky. Here's the process I use to sell every deal nowadays. First, I call up an investor I know or am referred to. I pitch her on the deal. The investor is instructed to go on the web to check me out on LinkedIn and Facebook and see my blog or company website. I set up a meeting to show my product and how it works if I have a working prototype. I send her an executive summary or meet with her and explain the deal, using a slide deck. If the investor is a lead angel investor, then she will arrange for me to meet other angel investors. If she is a venture capitalist investor, then I am merely invited to present a pitch deck.

Notice how many steps have taken place without a business plan. By this time, the investor has made up his mind about his level of interest. Usually he wants to use the business plan for more limited reasons. He may want to confirm a decision he is leaning toward already. He may want to have a backup in his/her files for the positive decision. If he/she is on the fence, he may want to peruse the business plan to see if there is anything that would change his decision. I should note that if the investor is leaning negatively, then the plan will most likely not change his mind.

There is a common myth about a business plan: if it is well written, the reader will be so taken that she will write the check or wire the money. But the business plan is preceded by so many steps these days that in some cases, as has been my experience, you may never write a formal business plan.

Nonetheless, in most cases investors do expect business plans. Potential advisers and board members often do require one to move forward. Plus, whether you are seeking capital from crowdfunding donations, product launches on the Internet, crowdfunding equity, or traditional venture capitalist or angel investors, there are reasons to have a written plan.

Here are some of the reasons for writing down your plan:

1. It makes you think about what you are doing in a more focused way.
2. It demonstrates if you have a team that can work together or not.
3. You start to see the holes in your team and business—who can implement what.
4. It exposes whether you have a pricing strategy or business model that works.
5. What number of customers do you need to be paying what amount to break even?
6. Do you have a true competitive advantage? Is it sustainable?
7. Do you have the experience to scale a company?
8. You see the intangible dreams in a much rawer, more tangible light that shows your company's warts after the romance has worn off.

From the very moment you start a business, start to pitch your Idea to yourself and those who want you to succeed. A good pitch is the basis for a solid business plan. If you get the elements of your pitch down correctly, then you can get your business plan right as well. The reverse is not true, since the business plan comes later in the investment screening process. It may never get read and you will not get any feedback.

The slides that you used to create your pitch deck become the framework for your business plan. As with the executive summary, the first paragraphs are key in the screening process. These initial paragraphs dictate whether you will clinch the deal.

The business plan is also important for crowdfunding donations with rewards or for product/business launches on the Internet. The objective is to understand your goals for your project and business. Do you have a true company and asset? Big or small, you want to evaluate what your purpose is? What does success look like for you? How much do you have to work to achieve your idea of success? What can go wrong? What are your backup plans?

## THE KEY POINTS FOR WRITING A BUSINESS PLAN

The first point is simple: one person should write the plan so that you have one voice. Think of reading a novel or listening to someone tell you a story around a fire on an eerie night. One person can build the intrigue and suspense. More than one voice may break the rhythm of the presentation. You get the point, I'm sure.

Second, you should expand directly from the executive summary, covering the same topics or headings. You don't have to get too elaborate. You are better off keeping it short. I believe a good business plan should be ten pages, although you should keep in mind that some experts say up to twenty pages. For ease of sending it among the possible interested parties, provide the plan in a PDF or Word document.

Make sure you spell out your assumptions. You need to lay out what cash you need to generate a certain level of proceeds with a certain number of products, people, and publicity. Tie your financials and your key metrics to the following four Magical Ps:

- Proceeds
- Product(s)
- People
- Publicity

Top investors do not believe your financial projections will become reality. They want to see:

- Your reasoning
- Your business model
- What the company looks like if it could scale

- What money is needed (the cost) to achieve your projections
- What is the total market and what share of the market is needed to achieve the projections
- The initial years' revenue, expenses, and cash flows, shown monthly since the first two years are most critical; then quarterly; sometimes annually in the last two years
- Your gross margins, pricing strategy, and distribution channels
- People or capital intensity to achieve the revenues

Keep in mind that investors want you to write logically about the future. They know you don't know any more about the future than they do. Humans are not good predictors. In reality, as Andy Grove of Intel said, your real skill is how well you react to daily occurrences, rather than how proactive you can be. For start-ups, you create a minimum viable product, or MVP. This means the product works enough to bring it to the market and get customer feedback. You test the MVP, which represents your hypothesis or Idea for a solution to a problem. You get feedback and keep adjusting your hypothesis and MVP as if you were undertaking a scientific experiment, plus using your intuition, to make certain entrepreneurial leaps of faith.

Investors want to see well-written, logically thought-out business plans written in a confident but not arrogant voice. Even though the business plan is purely a guess at the future, investors don't want to hear that. You employ the willing suspension of disbelief that the poet Samuel Taylor Coleridge pointed out is essential for storytelling. We know it's a story, but we suspend our disbelief to enjoy it and become immersed in it. Venture capitalist Fred Wilson has pointed out that many of his investments became successful only after companies changed their original plans.

## PITCHING FOR MILLIONS

The last few chapters have tried to make you aware of what type of issues your pitch has to address. The topics I have listed are not necessarily checked off by investors on a piece of paper. But they are investor concerns (and an entrepreneur's concerns) in one way or another that your pitch is addressing.

In other words, the investor is constantly asking: What's the downside risk of your deal? Is there a sustainable competitive advantage here? What's the upside or potential? Could this deal be the blockbuster I'm looking for? Is there enough staying power? Is the entrepreneur likable or arrogant? Is she coachable or a know-it-all? What do I feel on a gut level—an emotional level—about this deal?

If you want to have pitches that make you millions of dollars, you have to see both the investors' side and your side of the deal. Investors can be angels or devils. As angels, many investors can add value. Some are successful entrepreneurs who have faced, and may still be facing, the same issues in other deals in which they are involved. As devils, they can look to steal your idea and compete against you or wrest control of your company.

When you present your company to venture capitalists, an angel network or crowdfunding investors in person, you have to anticipate what can go wrong with your pitch:

1. What if they tell you your idea is unclear?
2. What if the time you have to present is reduced or lengthened?
3. What if you are interrupted by an impatient investor?
4. What if a prior presentation was extraordinary?

The point is that the process of pitching is fluid. You have to know your subject so well that you can adjust on the fly. Recently, I prepared for days to speak at a conference on our software company, Questionmine. I crafted a solid 25-minute pitch. Yet just as I was about to go on stage, I was informed that prior speakers had gone over their allotted time. I had to cut five minutes from my presentation. That's 20% suddenly lopped off my speech!

Since I had rehearsed my presentation over and over, I shortened certain explanations and finished at 20 minutes on the dot. The event planner was very happy. Candidly, I wasn't. But the audience liked my presentation and I made some valuable business connections as a result.

In crowdfunding, you have to build a platform or crowd following that wants to donate money to your cause or project. To accomplish this, you have to take a disciplined and creative approach to how you will pitch your idea and company to the crowd. Just like trying to achieve anything first-class, you have to work hard at it and stretch yourself beyond your comfort zone. You make mistakes and learn what to do from your mistakes.

## SIMPLE VS. COMPLICATED VS. COMPLEX VS. CHAOTIC?

Make no mistake: the Pitch is complex. If I started out saying, here are five basic rules that govern the different pitches and do this and that, I wouldn't be telling you the truth. The same is true of building a software or technology company, which venture capitalists like because of the upside potential. Trying to invest in or pitch this type of early-stage company is *complex*.

Compare investing in or pitching early-stage companies to developing software, which also can be complex. You have to know the difference between simple, complicated, complex, and chaotic. Otherwise, you may be seduced by people hawking investments or ways to pitch or write executive summaries or plans by telling you they are simple when they know they're not. You can get very frustrated in trying to accomplish the impossible. Here's some definitions, provided by LoopNL:

**Simple** = easily knowable.
**Complicated** = not simple, but still knowable.
**Complex** = not fully knowable, but reasonably predictable.
**Anarchy**= neither knowable nor predictable.

*"My computer is complicated. My software project is complex. My house is complicated. My household is complex. My blog is complicated. My thoughts are complex. Your dinner is complicated. Your dog is complex."*

You can't invest in or pitch early-stage companies by just breaking down the parts and analyzing them as if it were simple or complicated.

You must gain and understand the entire process by watching and studying how the whole early-stage investment and pitching process works.

The Loop NL article goes on: "We create complicated systems by first designing the parts, and then putting them together. This works well for mechanical things, like buildings, watches, and Quattro Stagioni pizzas. But it doesn't work for complex systems, like brains, software development teams, and the local pizzeria. We cannot build a system from scratch and expect it to become complex in the way that we intended. Complex systems defy attempts to be created in an engineering effort.

"Some people picture complexity as a state that somehow surpasses that of complicatedness (see next picture). But this view is incorrect."

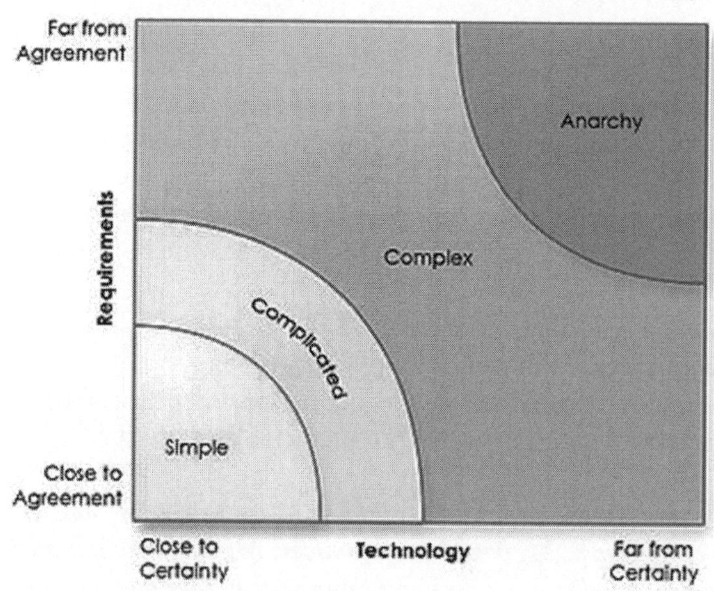


(From: Managing Game Design Risk: Part I)

## SIMPLIFY YOUR STRATEGY

If you want to find great investment ideas and pitch them well in a complex investment and entrepreneurial early-start-up world, then you have to *simplify* your approach. Paradoxically, come up with simple rules to address complex undertakings such as early stage investing and pitching. But know a pitch or the process of pitching or investing itself is not simple.

Donald Sull and Kathleen M. Eisenhardt, in the article "Simple Rules for a Complex World," published in the *Harvard Business Review*, tell how Ideo did it:

"In IDEO's early days, clients often wanted to rush through the brainstorming process and jump into prototyping." But the founders of Ideo discovered that they could come up with more great ideas (a complex process) if they did more brainstorming (a complex process) up front and didn't rush to create prototypes. The "strategic bottleneck" they concluded, was brainstorming. The article goes on: "The simple rules they wrote to address it, which are stenciled on the walls in IDEO's conference rooms, include 'Defer judgment,' 'Encourage wild ideas,' and 'Go for quantity.' "

To create simple rules to simplify your pitch, know the following:

- Simple rules match or beat more complicated analyses.
- Companies must balance efficiency and flexibility.
- Use checklists to perform a process repeatedly and efficiently.
- Use simple rules to adapt quickly to changing circumstances.

## SEVEN RULES FOR DEVELOPING SIMPLE RULES

1. Identify a bottleneck that is specific and strategic. Ask, where are opportunities or resources to address the bottleneck? Focus on one or two bottlenecks that, if resolved, would have the greatest impact on ROI.
2. Rely upon data and facts rather than opinions, which can be biased. Again, you will have to use your intuition, as testing

can't always give you absolute answers. Make sure to test your hunches.

3. Have the people who are going to use the simple rules create the rules, and get different opinions from different members of your team.
4. Make sure your rules are concrete and easy to understand and call for a simple yes/no answer.
5. Rules are made to evolve with changing circumstances and market conditions. Too often you can get stuck following what worked before in an up market, which may not work in a down market.

In the end, you have to keep stuff simple so you keep clearly in sight your milestones and goals you are seeking to accomplish. Make sure you do not have too many rules, and prioritize the ones you do have.

Simplify Your Strategy:

Clarify the key drivers behind value creation
Identify critical challenges
Determine your must-win battles

Now think of the investment or pitch process. You need simple but concrete rules to identify the key points that frame your value proposition, your positioning, and why investors should believe in your team and you.

My simple rules in looking at projects or deals are:

1. Look at the Three Magical Ps: People, Product, and Potential.
2. Evaluate the 7 Step Process: How can an Idea be created, implemented, marketed, launched, delivered, serviced, and refined based upon feedback?
3. Business model: Understand the Money Machine or Golden Goose: How do you make money?
4. Measure everything possible: Break things down into numbers and analyze the assumptions.

5. Review carefully the Magical Ms: the message, market (Are you listening, targeting the right audience? Do you know who they are? What they do and why?), and the metrics (the market timing of your message and measurement of their responses for insights and patterns to increase quality leads, sales, and customer engagement and maintenance).

As you move forward, you will see that complex processes such as investing, marketing, and selling have simple principles, patterns, and rules that repeat over and over. Nobody knows for sure what will happen to investments in companies or to pledges in crowdfunding projects. This is what makes the investment and crowdfunding world so challenging and fascinating, with stories of successes and failures that inspire us and make us pause and reflect.

An entrepreneur can take strategic steps, however, to avoid failure. All that is needed is an open ear when testing out a potential Idea. In this age of social media, there is no excuse for failing to pretest a product. If there is any doubt about whether customers want what you have to offer, then be smart. Start a conversation and ask them.

## TAKEAWAYS AND INSIGHTS

- In the reality TV talent shows we watch part the screening process, and with *Shark Tank* the producers screen the applicants to decide who can pitch the sharks.
- What you want to understand is that all these shows have their pitch formats: how much time you get to pitch, to whom, when and how. On *Shark Tank*, entrepreneurs are invited to pitch venture capitalists or angel investors in a presentation without the more formal slide deck presentation. The Sharks ask the same questions a venture capitalist, super angel investors (which they are), or experienced angel investors would ask.
- In all the shows, we learn the story of the contestants, their struggles, challenges, obstacles, visions, dream, and purposes.
- In the beginning, the judges as the sharks decide who moves forward or who gets the sharks' money respectively.
- In *Shark Tank* the audience never votes directly but often buys the products shown. These product purchases are similar to crowdfunding audiences but differ in that crowdfunding donations with rewards buy presales of products at a discount.
- Raising capital today is very similar to these reality TV shows. It's a multimedia show with pitches, auditions, screenings, narrowing down the contestants, and getting the final yes or no. The size of the audience a company has or its current customers or users and its potential audience size (called by some investors the amount of traction) has never been so important.

- Just like contestants (individuals or companies) and the TV shows themselves, everyone is being rated within the contents of the show by the pitch format. This is why I call the world in which we compete the Performance Economy.
- The CEO pitching his or her deal is a performer in front of their specific audience of VC, super angels, angels, or the general crowd.
- You are at the same time an actor, artist, visionary, creator, producer and director of your own multimedia (combining text, video, audio image animation) show to achieve high ratings.
- To achieve high ratings from your audience and beat out the competition, you must understand. First you must know how to build an audience and grow it using social, mobile, and the web.
- This means you have to not only perform as an actor/ artist but also as a scientist/ experimenter to build a remarkable product which solves the audience's problem or satisfies its needs.
- For early-stage companies to attract investor financing from VCs, angels, or the crowd, they must understand and assemble a team which can be artistic and scientific at the same time. They need to use multimedia across social, mobile and the web to engage, generate key analytics and metrics to know their customer. From listening and entertaining their audience, they can increase the quality of their leads, increase sales, and increase repeat sales.
- Go through the criteria I've presented so far, and rate your company with a point score of system where 1 is the worst and 10 is the best. Pick 10 key criteria,

assign each criteria 10 points, and see out of 100 where would you rate yourself, e.g., problem (pain); strength of team; market size and potential; presentation and overall marketing ability online; analytic and metrics tracking.

- Then define your key weaknesses or bottlenecks which if resolved would give you the highest ROI and best chance of getting funding.

Click here for additional resources: http://bit.ly/1aJxQ3m

## CHAPTER 9

# PRE-LAUNCH: ACCELERATING THE CONVERSATION

Here's where the fun really begins. We've examined the various types of pitches: headlines, tag lines, elevator speeches, executive summaries, slide decks, and business plans. Once upon a time these were presented to a limited pool of investors, mainly venture capitalists and wealthy angels. In those days of factories and mass advertising on TV, starting up a business normally required a lot of capital. Entrepreneurs relied upon friends and families. For example, Sam Walton of Wal-Mart went to his wife's family for initial funding. All of that has changed. In this era of mass communications, you can talk to all sorts of people.

The revolution began with the rise of the personal computer. Malcolm Gladwell wrote in his famous book *The Outliers*: "The most important date in the personal computer revolution according to Silicon Valley veterans was 1975, when *Popular Electronics* ran a front-page article on the Altair8800: 'World's First Minicomputer Kit to Rival Commercial Models.' Ideally, you wanted to be 20 or 21 or born in 1954 or 1955. Bill Gates (1955), Paul Allen (1953), Steve Ballmer (1956), Steve Jobs (1955), and Eric Schmidt (1955). Their success was not just of their own making. It was a product of the world in which they grew up."

With the advent of PCs and the Internet, Bill Gates and Steve Jobs ushered in a world which required less capital, faster growth, and scaling of businesses. But most of all, they opened up new ways to access information, communicate, conduct business, and have conversations.

The world of crowdfunding is an extension of the movement in which a start-up business needs less money and more conversations with its potential backers or investors. The first perfect wave was the combination of the Internet, direct marketing, and information. The next perfect wave is the combination of social media, information, video, and mobile.

This is the age of the dialogue and collaboration internally and externally among numerous businesses, organizations, groups, and tribes.

## DITCH THE MONOLOGUE AND JOIN THE DIALOGUE

This is Questionmine's tag line. The new era of two-way real-time conversations via video, mobile, and social is still in its infancy. I cover this topic in detail in a later chapter. The key takeaway here is that a company's presentations must be given within this context. With any type of pitch, it is entering a two-way dialogue among an enormous number of conversations competing for potential investors' or backers' attention.

The Pre-launch phase, fifth of the 7 Steps, entails a running dialogue that must begin with the entrepreneur the moment an idea for a business or product arises in his mind. The entire 7 Step process, from Idea to Launch and Post-launch, is all part of an ongoing conversation. The entrepreneur learns and tests his assumptions mostly by engaging in dialogues and then studying markets and customers and refining his product and business based upon feedback from the various relationships that he grows and improves by expanding his network.

Marketing is essentially a conversation. Go back to Bill Gates of Microsoft, Sam Walton of Wal-Mart, and Michael Eisner of Disney. What did they have in common? They were all voted marketer of the year by *Advertising Age* magazine.

Companies such as IBM and Oracle are now listening to the chief marketing officer more than the head of IT. Why? Because marketing departments must find ways to engage prospects and keep preferred customers. In addition, many of these companies—used to a one-way company sales pitch—must get back into conversations with their customers who have tuned them out. To do this, marketing needs data that is personal and precise so prospects and customers are made to feel cared for and participate in a genuine two-way dialogue that is relevant.

What does this have to do with raising money for a company or project?

Everything! To build a company, an entrepreneur must know how to carry on numerous online and offline conversations on many different stages. The power of the individual and the power of the crowd are evolving forces touching every part of an entrepreneur's life, career, and business. Young and old, experienced and inexperienced, are thrown together with different perspectives about the world and business.

A younger person may run a large tech company like Facebook and communicate in ways alien to older businesspeople. Presentations and pitches must match different companies, departments, and investor types. Skype, GoToMeeting, and texting are becoming the norm for meetings. Whatever age you are, you had better start communicating.

## TWO MODELS TO WATCH

The Development Step transitioned a business into the stage of creating a product and moving the business Design, or business model itself, forward. The Pre-launch step is the second major reality check for a project or business. This is where testing the minimal viable product, or MVP, and the business model with prospects and customers occurs.

What makes one business stand out over another is the focus of its conversation and how clear its message is and how well it's matched with the right audience at the right time.

That's what makes the Pre-launch step so important. Here the conversation with prospects and customers becomes more vocal. That's because the company is expanding its conversation beyond its insiders and most ardent supporters.

Unless an entrepreneur, creative type, or small businessperson is known to investors, the Pre-launch step is pivotal. It provides the first clues about customers' interest in the product or its perceived value in alleviating some pain. Will the prospect be willing to pay for the solution where a profit can be made, and will the customer keep buying? For example, so many webinars are free that few people will pay to attend one even if the information is valuable.

All too often the entrepreneur is too focused on building the product that she believes is the Next Big Thing. But she avoids building the other, equally important product, which must be part of the conversation in order to satisfy all the stakeholders, including customers and investors.

To pitch successfully and get the money, the reader must understand the distinction I made when I used the difference between the Golden Goose (the money machine) and the Golden Eggs, the income from the sale of the product/solution. In the Pre-launch step you are testing two products, not one:

1. The product or solution created (Golden Eggs/Income)
2. The business or business model itself (the Golden Goose/Money Machine)

According to the *E-Myth Enterprise*, by Michael Gerber, "a business exists only because people want them to and is a *mechanism* designed to produce more for the continually rising expectations of people in a free market system." He goes on to describe three types of preferences which must be tested in the Pre-launch stage: "(1)Visual Preferences, such as form, color, attention to detail, order or neatness, e.g., a logo; (2) Emotional Preferences that evoke positive feelings by giving purpose, make prospects and customers feel listened to, being cared for and loved, important and relevant, a sense of partaking in something bigger than them; (3) Functional Preferences or being a process-oriented company answering the question of 'What's the best way to do this?,' 'What's the cost?,' and 'Is it worth it?' "

The people listening to a pitch have the same preferences themselves. Think of the different pitches: they are based upon first impressions of the *visual* look and *emotional* feel that come from a company's materials or the entrepreneur in person, such as his voice tone, body language, or the specific words he chooses. Those listening or reviewing the pitch will evaluate the company's website, their profile on

LinkedIn and Facebook, as well as the design of the product, how it functions, and the *functional* processes it demonstrates to create a product/solution.

The key point is that if you want to get the money, from day one you must build two products for a targeted group of customers and stakeholders: (1) the business itself/business model and (2) the product(s)/solution.

*Inc.* magazine, in its article "The Rules," asked John Mackey, cofounder and CEO of Whole Foods, about his approach. "You have to stop thinking about yourself and use a systems intelligence approach he calls SyO. It's the ability to see the big picture and how the different parts of the system interconnect. With a high SyO, you can see how a decision you made had an impact on your stakeholders. His advice to entrepreneurs is to think about your business and all the relationships it has. You have to develop a feeling for who your stakeholders are and figure out how to make them all winners."

Each pitch type you have learned is a road map spelling out the elements that investors are expecting you to address so that they can evaluate quickly whether they feel strongly enough about your product and your business model to invest.

Presenting and pitching success depends upon your target audience of investors or backers, similar to selling a product to any customer. Your pitch tells your story, your stage of product and business development, and how you, your team, your product, and your business model are positioned differently than others in the market.

Pitching a business plan to investors or lenders can't provide the real-world test a product needs. An entrepreneur has to learn by doing! She must create an MVP and test it—not by studying and analyzing hypothetical potential markets and customers. One of the biggest errors in business is convincing yourself and your team that everyone wants your product and *then* "doing" by leaping blindly into the market—only to discover too few customers want the product or won't pay the price.

Make no mistake: all businesses require, especially at every stage of development of a start-up company, a leap of faith. The difference is whether it takes a totally blind leap of faith or assesses the height of the jump, the depth of the water, and whether there are any rocks below. An entrepreneur needs to think in advance about what type of funding he will need and how long he can carry himself. Use a rule of thumb of tripling the costs and time to market and cutting the revenue projections by at least 75%.

Testing products during the Pre-launch step can save a lot of time and money as well as answer key investor questions related to how viable a product and business model is (pricing; gross margins; can cover costs when everyone is being paid a fair amount for the stage of that business) and if it is sustainable and can scale.

## THREE ADDITIONAL MAGICAL PS

During the Pre-launch, three other critical variables come into play and combine with the basic Three Magical Ps:

- Proceeds
- Publicity
- Proposition

To build a business that will attract customers, investors, and other stakeholders, you have to coordinate and balance the proceeds, the publicity, and the proposition or offer with the people or staff, the product(s), and the potential, such as profitability and scalability.

Take, for example, what happens to a small massage business when it offers 75% off on an hour massage (*proposition*) using Groupon. Its *proceeds* spike, but its share is less than 10% after splitting with Groupon and the associated credit card and other processing costs. The *publicity* overwhelms the staff and the number of *people*. The *product* or service and its delivery time may suffer. The proposition rarely gets enough repeat customers.

A Pre-launch testing of their proposition before trying Groupon might have indicated this highly discounted Groupon-type offer would not be profitable or sustainable as a business model. Or, using Groupon, the company might test its assumptions on how much staff it would need to grow rapidly and scale in one or more markets. For the business model to work, the company might evaluate a franchise model which has been used for massage companies, along with the systems and training that would have to be in place for the business to scale.

The massage business normally would not appeal to venture capitalists, but it might appeal to local angel investors who like massages, their stress reduction, and other health benefits, and they might know the talents of the specific massage therapists. They might see ways to add other products, such as unique nutritional supplements or exercises. But this is a highly competitive field with a very low cost of entry. The Pre-launch step would test the business model and product assumptions in light of the various Magical Ps I have enumerated.

## JOIN THE CONVERSATION AND GET THE MONEY

Here's a powerful insight: whatever you are marketing or selling, especially in the world of social media, video, and mobile, winning comes down to owning a share of the conversation. Think back to high school. Unless you were part of the most popular group, you felt left out of the conversation. Even in the most popular group, competition arose about who would control the conversation.

Food companies, for example, fight for a share of your stomach. Kraft and Hershey want young kids to get hooked on their products so when they grow up, they keep buying their products for their kids as well as themselves. The *Wall Street Journal* and the *Economist* compete for a share of your conversation about economic and financial news.

Facebook is essentially a high school scrapbook talk, or conversation platform, that dominates where conversations take place. Twitter dominates instant short- conversation bites. YouTube rules the video conversations. LinkedIn controls the professional networking conversations.

Presentations and pitches are ways to open up conversations and begin an ongoing dialogue to get the money. But a successful presentation or pitch rests upon the delivery and the content. If you are an entrepreneur, the content depends upon ongoing conversations, first with yourself about your Idea and then with others close to you. Call them your internal group. As you proceed with the Seven Steps, you begin mapping out a product and hopefully a business model in the Design step. You do your research and due diligence in Discovery and begin your product creation in the Development step. During this entire time you have certain conversations.

What conversations and with whom are the secret to moving the odds in your favor to get the money and build a successful business. Tony Hsieh of Zappos relates his fascination with serendipity and meeting people, or collisions where you converse and exchange ideas. As Hsieh told *Inc.* magazine, "it's all about maximizing collisions and accelerating serendipity...maybe the chance of one of these collisions being meaningful is one in 1,000. But if you do it 100 times more, your odds go up...Meet lots of people without trying to extract value from them. You don't need to connect the dots right away. But if you think about each person as a new dot on your canvas, over time, you'll see the full picture."

Serendipity means a "happy accident" or "pleasant surprise"—specifically, the accident of finding something good or useful while not specifically searching for it. Serendipity is the way I have developed my pitches and gotten the money.

Collisions and serendipitous conversations work hand-in-hand with another valuable tool called the buy-in strategy.

## THE BUY-IN STRATEGY

In the 7 Step process, the Pre-launch step occurs in a linear progression and follows the Development or implementation step. But the real conversation started in your mind when you imagined an Idea. You could call this the pre-Pre-launch or the opening conversations, which can go on for years within you or among others until you decide to act.

The way I discovered to get a project in motion is what I call the buy-in conversations. They can be collisions and serendipitous or not. The key is that you consciously seek to have buy-in conversations while hoping that the serendipitous conversations come along sooner rather than later.

I define buy-in as a process of having lots of conversations with people during each of the 7 Steps and getting their feedback. Even more important, I get people to buy in to the project or business as partners, consultants, advisers, suppliers, customers, lenders, and investors. In other words, you make from the very start of your project or business a conscious effort to recruit your partners, team, and the rest of your stakeholders. This strategy mirrors the lean start-up strategy in that you begin testing your Idea or hypothesis for a product (MVP) and a business model and the underlying assumptions from the very beginning.

Over 30 years ago, I stumbled upon the buy-in strategy. I realized that investors and customers would tell me in conversations over the phone or in person what they wanted and didn't want. With all the changes that have occurred with the Internet, social media, and numerous ways to connect, the phone and the face-to-face meeting still remain the most valuable ways to get the money, build companies, find investment opportunities, and establish meaningful relationships.

The three critical parties that must buy in and stay engaged positively to win at investing or raising capital are the following:

Customer (crowd/audience)
Investor
Entrepreneur/small business/creative type

Each of the three participants has to buy-in. "Buy in" has two meanings: buy into the concept/idea/USP and buy in by purchasing or investing money, time, and resources.

Your biggest obstacle to buy-in is the status quo, i.e., people you want to buy in don't do anything. They wait. They kick the can down the road. Remember, most people like the status quo. It's familiar. If people do something different, then they go into new territory, the unfamiliar, and they can make mistakes and fail. People want to avoid failure. In business, investment, and relationships, there is a high probability of failure.

For most people, the best strategy is to resist change. Change threatens habits. People are, as the cliché states, creatures of habits (patterns). When you approach most investors or other potential stakeholders, they associate your desire for them to buy in with asking them to take a risk on you. You are asking them to trust you as a person and trust your competence and your willingness to give them a big enough payoff emotionally and/or financially for helping you.

Contradictorily, people also want novelty, since they get bored. They search for what's new. The key to getting others to buy in is to understand human nature. Most people will resist your new idea, especially if it's a radical idea or change.

When Coke tried New Coke, for instance, consumers rebelled. Traditional Coke represents a belief—almost a religion. Diet Coke or other variations of Coke or different ads about Coke are OK. They are familiar. Incremental changes to a brand or a person are easier to accept than radical change.

Research on habits confirms that to change yourself or to get others to buy in or change, you want to deploy the strategy of continual incremental or tiny changes called kaizen. Why does this work? Because new things evoke the reptilian brain's fight-or-flight mechanism. We are wired to see new things as the saber-toothed tiger of caveman times.

The good news is that showing something new is a technique to get attention. That's the concept that all good pitches deploy. Get attention. The emotional grab. Then you have to keep the listeners' attention and show them what's in it for them and why they should trust you.

The challenge to achieving buy-in is that an entrepreneur has to first change her own mind-set or paradigm. She has to be open to creativity and innovation. Most important, she has to realize that she will constantly face rejection, betrayal, and the chance of being cheated or defrauded.

Why?

Early-stage companies can potentially represent a big payoff. Greed and envy are evoked in others along with your threat to their status quo. What if you succeed and they remain stuck? What if they take a chance on you and you fail? How can they get a piece of the action if you succeed? Can they get a bigger piece than they deserve because you don't have the money or resources to protect yourself or get the project off the ground?

To create a new habit, you cannot override in your brain the old habit you want to get rid of. Picture that the old habit is like an old road you have traveled for many years. To build a new habit or road, you can't replace the old one. You have to create a separate new road in your brain, and, by repetition, the new road or pattern becomes the one more traveled and takes over.

To accomplish this, you have to step out of your comfort zone, even though doing so creates discomfort and stress. One of the secrets of success—and buy-in—is to become comfortable with your discomfort. An entrepreneur has to go through the process of *deliberate practice.* You do what others don't want to do. You practice the hard, uncomfortable stuff until it becomes comfortable. You model and apprentice under those who already have succeeded at what you want to achieve.

An entrepreneur should not lose sight, however, of the fact that other people out there may also be willing to move out of their comfort zones. Buy-in represents a testing of the marketplace's and a company's customers' conversations for its product and a business model. What's in the news affects people's decisions. With instant coverage on start-ups, you are confronted with a rapidly changing competitive environment. Every second some genius is working in a start-up incubator to come up with a similar but better product than yours. The rule: if you are thinking about it, so are a lot of others. If not, then you should wonder why not.

It may seem paradoxical and contradictory. You want to be different and appear to be a first mover, but really you may be better off being a fast mover. Will you be in the 50% of first movers that fail or succeed?

## BUY-IN AND FIRST MOVER ADVANTAGE

What does being a first mover mean? First mover advantage is often extolled in the buy-in process. It means a form of competitive advantage that a company earns by being the first to enter a specific market or industry. Being the first allows a company to acquire superior brand recognition and customer loyalty. The company also has more time to perfect its product or service.

According to Investopedia, "First movers are often followed by competitors that try to capitalize on the original company's success. By this time, however, the first mover has usually accumulated enough market share, expertise, and customer loyalty to remain on top."

Yet using the argument that you have a first mover advantage when trying to pitch investors and achieve buy-in can be dangerous. Here's what venture capitalist Steve Blank points out in his blog "Why Pioneers Have Arrows in Their Backs": "Fast Followers are a better idea. In a 1993 paper Peter N. Golder and Gerard J. Tellis had a much more accurate description of what happens to startup companies entering new markets. In their analysis Golder and Tellis found almost half of the market pioneers (First Movers) in their sample of 500 brands in 50 product categories failed. Even worse, the survivors' mean market share was lower than found in other studies. Further, their study shows early market leaders (Fast Followers) have much greater long-term success."

Often, the first to market—the pioneer—gets killed. What you want is who gets it right first, like Google. In technology, you can die if you are too early or too late. You have to time the market just right. You have to be clear on your customers' problems and what features your products possess to solve them.

Yet here is the counter argument of why being a first mover can be an advantage. The first company to launch a new type of product should have a competitive advantage over those that start later. Before competitors get started, the first mover should have been able to:

- Build a customer base
- Build a strong brand
- Develop economies of scale
- Develop distribution channels

This should mean that a first mover has a good chance of remaining the market leader. Moneyterms.co.uk points out: "The usefulness of the first mover advantage needs to be judged in the context of the product, the industry concerned, and the actual and potential competition. Points to consider include how much of an advantage is conferred by having an established customer base; whether there are any advantages in distribution or economies of scale that competitors will find hard to replicate."

If you as an entrepreneur feel you can maintain these advantages, then you're on solid ground. If you are a crowdfunding investor, try to judge a project you're interested in with these parameters.

## IDEA TO IMPLEMENTATION

I have tried to give you a sense of the uncertainty of the marketplace. There are no clear road signs that guide a start-up to success. An entrepreneur needs to network to find an Idea, test it, implement it, and then test the product and business model in the real world and get feedback. In order for an entrepreneur, creative type, or small business to raise money, it has to persuade and convince others to follow and overcome their own habits, concerns, and fears.

Let's go through my 7 Steps and examine how the buy-in process I have been describing works:

The entrepreneur comes up with an idea. Often, the idea comes from a personal frustration—"I can do this better than anyone else": Create a quality coffee in an Italian-type café (Starbucks). Make consistent hamburgers and fries for families on the go (McDonald's). Most business and scientific ideas are built off what others have done in the past, such as Steve Jobs improving upon the Sony Walkman with the Apple iPod.

Given the idea, the next step is the Design. There are two broad parts of the Design step: Design a business such as Southwest Airlines and sketch it on a napkin—it will fly to Dallas, Houston, and San Antonio. Low-budget, no frills but fun. Or, Design a product—an airline that will fly from Point A to Point B to Point C but not from one hub out to different spokes. The entrepreneur has to begin the conversation and tell his "story" to the other(s). That starts the buy-in process.

The "others" can be biased: spouse, children, friends. Others can try to kill the Idea and Design—for many reasons good or bad—such as the Idea and Design stink because of these reasons. If the small businessperson is not dissuaded, then she should—but often doesn't or doesn't thoroughly enough—research the market carefully to see what the competition is doing (Discovery). Does the entrepreneur's Idea/ Design have a competitive or unfair advantage? If the entrepreneur is still convinced it does, then she must get more and more people—including potential investors—to buy in.

The entrepreneur's biggest challenges: are time, money, and resources. How can he get his Idea to be Designed and proven? How can he get investors and potential customers and other stakeholders to buy in? The entrepreneur looks at his own resources. What money, time, talent, skills, know-how can he pull together to make his conversations—pitches—more exciting and persuasive?

The entrepreneur has to be all at once a juggler, magician, alchemist, artist, scientists, marketer, salesperson and resource to keep the process going. This is where you, the investor or backer, come into the conversation. Your question: How early in the process will I be able to accept the unknown (uncertainty and risk) in return for my greed (high rate of return? And how much will I be willing to invest and what do I get?

You as an investor start to ask more questions as the entrepreneur tries to persuade you to get involved with her project or company. Is there even a prototype in development or just some design sketches or a working prototype? Does the start-up have any paying customers at all?

As you will see, you as the money raiser will have different questions to answer if you are seeking a backer using a crowdfunding donations strategy versus selling ownership in your company or project. For example, the small businessperson selling a certain ownership percentage in her company must ask the investor for a certain amount of money at a certain price per share.

As an entrepreneur moves through the 7 Steps, you begin combining your Pre-launch marketing step with your buy-in networking strategy. Once you get into the actual Development of your product, you can start hinting to others that your product is coming to market. Call this hinting the pre-pre-launch. Then the buy-in face-to-face networking and the pre-launch work hand in hand as you recruit partners and stakeholders. At times the buy-in strategy and the pre-launch strategy can be identical when you are networking. But the Pre-launch marketing and testing of your MVP and your business model as a product can expand out to a much wider circle by using the Internet or other distribution channels such as radio and TV. For example, in Pre-launch, you could email someone for his list of customers has. He could endorse your product and give them a free trial for their feedback via a survey.

All along the way, throughout all these steps, the conversations that you are having help to shape how the product will appeal to your customers and investors. It is a dynamic process, ever changing—because when you initiate a dialogue, guess what? People tell you what they want.

## NETWORKING BUY-IN SECRETS

Over the years my personal money-raising and business success has been a result of face-to-face networking and buy-in strategy. As the Internet has created new options for conversations, I have found that these core ideas work even better. Here are my networking secrets:

**#1 Secret of Networking**

Listening is the key. Too often people think networking is rushing up to others to tell them about your stuff. Wrong! You must listen openly, with no agenda, to what others are trying to accomplish. Genuinely try to help them get the answers they need. Just listening often creates a valuable bond that may pay off later. If not, then feel good. You created goodwill and good karma. Good will follow when you least expect it—the serendipitous meetings that happen when someone does for you what you did for others.

**#2 Secret of Networking**

You only need one great relationship to move closer to your vision and goals. At most events you collect a lot of names and few—maybe one—leads. So you want to meet as many people as you can. Your goal is to exchange your feedback and help with others. You want to find those that potentially may buy in to what you are doing. Often, mutual buy-in occurs where each can help the other.

**#3 Secret of Networking**

Sometimes, one person points you in the right direction of a key person. This can be someone you considered a weak link in your network—someone you hardly know who can turn out to be a key person for your future success. Most of the time it's not the person you meet or know well but someone they know—a referral—that opens the door to your success.

**#4 Secret of Networking**

Act immediately. Plan your next steps with the person you met that appears to be a buy-in candidate. Or, call the weak link to whom you were referred to maintain momentum. Leads go cold very fast, and emotions die out once events are over.

**#5 Secret of Networking: Target Marketing**

**Step 1:** Your aim is to target groups online and offline that have similar interests and emotional needs. Then see what events they attend and go to these events. See if you can befriend someone who already is a member of these groups who can show you the ropes. Most groups always want more members. Make sure you have a genuine interest.

**Step 2:** The key to networking is going beyond niches or affinity groups with which you have something in common. You must get more individualized. In the Starbucks example, your aim is much broader than the general niche of coffee drinkers. Think also of espresso, latte, and added flavors, such as vanilla or hazelnut.

**#6 Secret of Networking: Respected Names**

Who can endorse you and your deal? In the venture capital world, Sequoia Capital or Draper Richards or a superangel like Marc Andressen as your lead investor brings other investors to your deal. Every industry has respected names—advisers, customers, investors—who give you credibility. It takes a lot of time to get to them and get their attention, interest, and desire. See with whom they network and get to know them. If the people with whom they network like you, then in time you will be introduced. Your first move should be to befriend them. Then you may get a chance to do your elevator speech. After that, you never know.

**#7 Secret of Networking: Visibility and Influence**

The right visibility is associated with influence and prestige. In Internet marketing niche, certain players have large lists. When they mail to their list endorsing you, their list buys. Others follow. Successful product launches gross millions in days.

In social networking, Facebook experts and companies build large fan bases of 50,000 to 100,000—even of fans. Being endorsed is huge. Every industry online has influencers who will promote you online for money—most have to believe in you. Some will promote but want no money. They just have to believe in your product and company.

**#8 Secret of Networking: Pay to Pay**

The fastest way to meet and to work with influencers is go to their paid events, buy their products, and join their mastermind groups. I know that sounds crazy, but the right person and connections can save you years of heartache. If they believe in you, they will find a way to help you by endorsing you to their followers and selling your stuff. I will cover this more under the product launch/business launch money-raising strategy.

**#9 Secret of Networking: Create Your Web Presence**

Think of yourself in a game called connections and networks. Everything you do on the web builds your visibility and credibility. Your web presence is like an extended business card and bio. People will check you out. They will ask what value you can bring them. When you network, they will buy in if they like you, your story, and how you can tell them what's in it for them.

**#10 Secret of Networking: Bring Real Value and Meaning**

You can let people know you are looking to invest in deals or assist others in growing their business. Let them know that you want to create a great product. Assess whether they can help you as you listen carefully to what they are saying about their business or project. Be candid about whether you can help them and/or they can help you.

But when you are networking and seeking buy-in, also keep in mind what I am sharing with you: Why do people and companies fail?

As you have seen, most have little value to offer. They are unaware of the 7 Steps and how to turn a company into a Golden Goose money machine. They have no clue of the difference between a product and a company. They do not understand the different pitch types.

Most ideas or products you will be pitched are me-too ideas and companies. Very few investment opportunities meet the basic criteria of the Magical Ps. People or the team are weak. The Product is not remarkable and has no competitive advantage Potential, or the ability to scale is limited because of the People and the Product. The Proposition, or the deal, the project, or the company itself, is overpriced.

In this book you have seen certain themes pop up over and over again. If you take away nothing else, remember this key principle of conversation. Conversation means a dialogue, not a monologue. Employ the "social" in social media. People will tell you what they want. You merely have to listen—and then act on what you have learned is the Next Big Thing.

## TAKEAWAYS AND INSIGHTS

- Marketing is a conversation. The new currency is relationships.
- Another way to frame what is going on in your head is what I call the Conversation Economy.
- Everyone has their own self-talk made up of fears, desires, and beliefs which create their motivations, biases, and overall world view.
- In effect, you are competing for your conversation time with others. For example, the giants of the conversation economy are your large social networks—Facebook, Twitter, YouTube, LinkedIn—as well as Amazon and the TV networks.
- Thus, your goal to succeed involves building relationships to become a top marketer.
- As a top marketer, you are an artist and scientist designing and experimenting with the three types of preferences Michael Gerber outlined: Visual, Emotional, and Functional.
- John Mackey of Whole Foods uses a system intelligence approach that looks at the big picture and how things interconnect within his organization. In other words, how do all the conversations connect up internally and externally?
- The goal is, how do you influence and dominate as a company the conversation so customers and other stakeholders are excited to tell your story and share their experiences with peers via their conversations?
- In the Performance Economy you are seeking to become conversation-worthy. You don't want just your 15 minutes of fame, but you want to dominate the ongoing conversations.

- When investors evaluate your pitch and deal, they are weighting the risk and reward of investing in your conversation and whether it solves a problem or satisfies a need.
- When you use a product or service, you are using it to meet some conversation going on in your mind consciously or unconsciously. If it fulfills that conversation, you tell others.
- Marketing accelerates that conversation when you use it across multi-channels—inbound and outbound.
- Tony Hsich says to succeed you need to maximize collisions or conversation to find the serendipitous relationship which gives you the resources and relationships which you need to get the sales or funding you are seeking.
- Buy-in is a marketing process of getting others to support your conversation. Buy-in takes a lot of collisions or conversations. You help others with their conversations so they will help you and expand your network. Buy-in is the secret behind success since it brings you the time, money, and resources you need.

Click here for additional resources: http://bit.ly/16Ghbq3

# CHAPTER 10

## CROWDFUNDING DONATIONS

In William Shakespeare's play *As You Like It* is the famous line: "All the world's a stage, and all the men and women merely players." Each page on a crowdfunding portal like Kickstarter is a stage on which players (those pitching their projects or companies) make their "exits and entrances," presenting deals for financing. Think of each deal with its own story, history, and age of development as similar to a human life. Shakespeare said that a person aged in seven acts from "infant, whining school boy to maturity, second childishness, and oblivion." Crowdfunding donations with rewards mostly cover projects and companies at the seed (infant) and start-up (whining school boy) age.

In today's fast-moving environment, the entire world is now a fierce, globally competitive stage with the Internet, instant connection, search, communications, and e-commerce made easy by companies such as Google, Facebook, Twitter, YouTube, LinkedIn, Amazon, and Apple. To succeed in today's real-time environment, you have to play many parts on many stages, switching costumes and roles at a moment's notice. Each day you have to pitch or present to numerous people and organizations offline and online. Each type of pitch has to address the need, pain, or problem of the specific person or organization by offering a promise or solution.

By engaging, entertaining, educating, and evaluating your prospects and customers, a company can build relationships that translate into sales and growth. The key is interactivity, and the largest trend is interactive marketing. A multimedia company has to create meaningful experiences for its prospects and customers by using blogs, white papers, video, games, photographs, audio, images, social media, and mobile.

For a young company, the real-time environment is a double-edged sword. Properly positioned and prepared, the company can catapult into the news, attract a large following quickly, like Instagram, and be valued at a billion dollars. On the other hand, most young companies can get lost in the tremendous static of the marketplace, as every second new players can make their entrances as others who fail make their exits.

Likewise, crowdfunding is a double-edged sword, as it too is a real-time stage for start-up companies. The advantage of crowdfunding is that it provides a relatively low-cost platform on which to test a company's ability to pitch a crowd, get feedback, and build a product and a relationship that the crowd likes.

"As you like it" is ironically a term that captures the gist of crowdfunding and social media. To win backing, an entrepreneur has to make the crowd "like" (just as Facebook's Like button is a yes vote) the deal and the entrepreneur's pitch and presentation. Crowdfunding presents projects and businesses to the crowd—donors, investors, fans, and customers.

What does "like" mean? Of course, there are degrees of "likes." In crowdfunding a like translates into a backer pledging money to your project or company. That pledge is an exchange. A key insight with all pitching is that you are seeking an *exchange* of something for something else, monetary or nonmonetary.

Exchanges are motivated. At the lowest level of motivation, according to psychologist Abraham Maslow's hierarchy of needs, you are trying to survive, and at the highest levels you are trying to self-actualize. Without getting into the pros and cons of Maslow's theory of motivation, the important point is that we have different levels of motivation or needs we seek to meet through exchanges. Once basic needs are met, we seek things that are not necessary for survival.

Think of Mally Beauty, QVC, and the entire home shopping phenomenon. How much of this stuff is actually needed? Yet home shopping is now a huge platform, like crowdfunding, where individuals vote with their dollars to buy stuff available in limited supply for a very limited period of time. During the allotted segment of time, the entrepreneur and a QVC pitch person pitch over and over the merits and benefits of the stuff. People call in to tell the potential buying audience—the crowd—how much they enjoyed the widget or gadget to give social proof. Meanwhile, potential buyers are shown the retail price, the QVC discounted price, whether shipping and handling are included or not, and the number of units being purchased in real time. The pitch is made on QVC's stage, where everything is carefully laid out to optimize an emotional connection to the stuff being presented.

One could call this phenomenon social or crowd buying. We are intrigued with what others are saying and doing. By nature, we want to be part of the group. No matter how much we see ourselves as rebels, we still want to belong.

Because of human social needs, we can be influenced by crowds and individuals that crowds score high. With the Internet, mobile, and social media revolutions, the power of the crowd is growing. At the same time, though, so is the power of personal influence. In the book *Return on Influence*, Mark Schaefer states, "Companies such as Disney, Nike, and Microsoft are creating successful marketing efforts centered on people's social influence scores...We are at the dawn of the creation of a new social media caste system determined by how and when you tweet, connect, share, and comment...You no longer have to win an election, be an elite athlete, or possess movie star looks to have power. We are entering the age of the Citizen Influencer, in which every person has a chance to get behind the velvet rope and be treated like a rock star."

All of the influences on the Internet form the context for the crowdfunding revolution that's under way. Crowdfunding portals themselves are new and emerging to cater to different marketing segments with different needs, such as microloans.

Because of all these dynamics, a lot of needs as well as fears and uncertainties come together and are magnified in crowdfunding. It represents public pitching. If the crowd likes a company's offering, it can attract money, sometimes lots of it, as the Pebble watch example to follow shortly demonstrates.

But if the crowd rejects the product or company, the entrepreneur will fail to attract the money. This can be a crushing blow to some creative types, nonprofits, and small businesses. What is even more disconcerting is that the company could have a very good project or product, but it didn't pitch or communicate the product's advantages well.

How do you make sense of so much uncertainty and increase the odds of your success in crowdfunding?

## HOW TO SUCCEED AT CROWDFUNDING DONATIONS WITH REWARDS

To win in the fierce, globally competitive marketplace, you must understand the paradox of chance. Little is left to chance, and yet a lot is. This is not meant to be a Zen statement. It goes back to one of the main premises I have been reiterating. You can't overplan. No business plan, no matter how long, can cover a fraction of the variables I just enumerated. The key is to create a minimum viable product or project (MVP). Then launch. Get feedback. Learn. Adjust. Learn by doing—not by overlearning, then doing. Interactivity and feedback in real time are key variables to success in pitching, getting the money, and building a sound project or business.

Creating an MVP does not mean throwing some crap together and winging it. No one should be seduced by the simplicity of a single page upon which a crowdfunding project is pitched. Much time, effort, and money goes into a successful crowdfunding presentation, pitch, and MVP.

You need to be conversant with each type of pitch—elevator pitch, executive summary pitch, slide deck pitch, and even a short business plan pitch—and how it can apply to a crowdfunding campaign.

Keep this in mind: even if an entrepreneur is not raising capital for the business and giving away ownership, as with crowdfunding donations with rewards, the same principles of getting the money apply.

In crowdfunding donations with rewards, an entrepreneur still needs to address on its crowdfunding page on a portal such as Kickstarter, Indiegogo, or RocketHub the same elements that investors seek in the executive summary and slide deck pitches:

1. An emotional grab (*story*).
2. What do you do (*project; product*)?

3. Who is on your team (*people*)?
4. What *pain* or *problem* are you addressing (need a game to play, I'm bored, or I'd love a coffee table book on the best women singers ever)?
5. What is your *product/solution*? How do you alleviate the pain, entertain, educate, engage, make the world better?
6. What is your *business model* if you are for profit (for example, sell cool watches at varying prices and gross margins; sell movies, music, art, food, books, technology, games, or photography)?
7. What's the market *potential* (how many people will you sell or affect; what niche or slice of the market)?
8. What's your *proposal* to have your project featured on the portal site?
9. What's your value *proposition* or *your different rewards* for different pledge amounts that you will give backers to donate money to your project or company/product?
10. What's the amount of money you are seeking within what period of time (the minimum threshold you must meet to get on Kickstarter to get any money differs from Indiegogo, where you keep any money you raise)?
11. What will you do with the money, such as produce the different products to sell in advance at a discount, such as a Pebble smart watch or Seth Godin's *Icarus Paradox* book at a pre-publication price? Plus, you have to produce the rewards as well.

Although crowdfunding with rewards does not give the backer any ownership in the project or company, the backer gets some reward in the *exchange*:

- Emotionally becomes a crowd member for a certain project
- Buys a new product at a discount—first on the block to get it
- Receives a *reward* that can be fun or commemorates a contribution to a good cause
- Gets an education regarding a specific crowdfunding topic, cause, or product and how the deal succeeded or not

## HOW DOES A CROWDFUNDING PORTAL WORK?

Here is how one of the major sites, Kickstarter, works:

1. Entrepreneurs and project creators submit a *proposal* to have their *project* featured on Kickstarter. The project must have a *clear goal*, like making a movie. Kickstarter staffers then briefly review the project.
2. Kickstarter puts the project proposal on its website. A *funding goal* is stated.
3. The fund-raising period can be set by the project creator for between one and 60 days. If the project meets its funding goal, Kickstarter charges a 5% fee on the total amount raised.

Entrepreneurs, creative types, and small businesses go onto portals (stages) like Kickstarter not only to pitch their ideas for the chance to attract millions of dollars. They also want to attract a *fan base that spreads the word* about the project or company like evangelists. Crowdfunding donations with rewards/perks are essentially raising money by *selling stuff*:

- No ownership stakes are given up!
- Imagine, backers give you money *in advance* of your having an existing product to sell.
- You have *Proof of Concept*, i.e., presales: you sold your stuff to buyers at a discount.
- Backers become your customers and evangelists.
- You get *critical feedback* before you create the actual product and after you get more feedback, similar to crowd sourcing.
- You can test new ideas with your crowd and get the wisdom of the crowd.
- You get the feedback in REAL TIME.

In effect, you create your MVP. You have made certain assumptions about your project or product that you need to test, such as:

- Your Market/*People*/Customer Assumptions:
  a. Who is your potential customer?
  b. What is their pain or problem?
  c. What is the niche or slice of the market in which you will find them?
  d. What channels of distribution will you use to reach them—crowdfunding being one of them?
- Your *Product* Assumptions:
  a. Will your product solve/alleviate the pain or create the pleasure?
  b. What is your unique value proposition?
  c. Will they pay for it at a price at which you can make money?
  d. What is your unique competitive or unfair advantage?
- Your Marketing and Sales Assumptions
  a. How will you reach your prospects and customers—the channels, such as crowdfunding?
  b. How will you get your prospects to buy from you?
  c. What metrics will define whether you have succeeded, such as how many prospects who come to your web page actually buy?

## A GLOBAL BUSINESS LABORATORY

Crowdfunding has become a global Internet-based laboratory for investors and entrepreneurs to learn and perfect more efficient ways to match investors and entrepreneurs with capital and ideas that can make the world a better place to live.

This new world is not only more democratic. In many cases it shows the way to the future of investing. Most of us believe that intelligence and expertise are concentrated in the hands of the few. But under certain conditions, the crowd is smarter than the expert. Many people chase after experts when in fact they should be running from them. Take the story of the story of the U.S. submarine *Scorpion* that disappeared in May 1968 in the North Atlantic.

No one had a clue where the submarine was in a stretch twenty miles wide and thousands of feet deep. The rescue mission seemed hopeless. The first inclination was to turn to a few experts on submarines and water currents. But the naval officer in charge, John Craven, had a different plan. He came up with a series of different scenarios and then assembled a group with a broad range of knowledge, including mathematicians, salvage men, and submarine specialists. He asked each for his best guess of the scenarios he put forth. Instead of using any one piece of information, Craven's solution rested on compiling a composite picture of what happened to the Scorpio when he put all the answers together.

Five months later the Scorpion was found by a navy ship 220 yards from where the group had estimated it was.

How does this idea apply to picking winners? When you apply for crowdfunding with rewards, you are seeking the same wisdom of the crowd to select your project or product from the numerous possibilities. Like the Scorpion project, the entrepreneur is asking individuals who are part of a crowd to make their best guess of all the different projects and their chances for success to choose hers.

As I've stated, if the crowd becomes excited about a project or a product, an entrepreneur can raise an impressive amount of cash. That's what happened to Pebble's Eric Migicovsky, the entrepreneur who came up with the idea of an e-Paper smart watch that can display messages on it from an iPhone and Android. Pebble created a prototype and set up a campaign on Kickstarter. The amount of money initially sought by Pebble was $100,000. Instead it caught the crowd's fancy. Within the first six days, Pebble raised $4.7 million, the most ever in Kickstarter's history. With 30 days remaining, Pebble had attracted 68,929 backers. Instead of $100,000, Pebble raised $10,266,844.

As you review Pebble's Kickstarter site, you see all the signs of a crowd gone wild. They earned 115,221 Facebook likes. Those who pledged $1 for exclusive updates had 2,615 backers. Pledging $99 or more as Early Birds earned a Jet Black Pebble watch, retailing for more than $150. That offer sold out at 200 backers. Same deal for non early birds who pledged $115 or more. That gained 40,799 backers. For a pledge of $125 you got colors like Arctic White, Cherry Red, voter's choice, or Jet Black. That offer sold out at 14,350 backers. Beyond that 31 pledges ranged from $220, $235, $550, $1,000, and $1,250 to $10,000.

The owner, Eric Migicovsky, had successfully taken his idea through Y Combinator's business incubator program. He was able to raise $375,000 from investors, including VC Tim Draper of Draper, Fisher, Jurvetson, but Migicovsky could not raise any more money from venture capitalists or angel investors. Instead, he raised it from a crowd of almost 69,000 backers.

Yet what does all this mean to you as a Pebble *backer*? I noted some of the benefits above. As a Pebble backer, you receive a watch at a pre-production discount that has no value as an investment. It's only a prototype. The entrepreneur collects your money in advance and you have no ownership in his company. As an *investor* looking for upside, you gain nothing.

## PRE-LAUNCHING A BRICK AND MORTAR BUSINESS

Keep in mind that money fuels your project or business. Money launches your business and grows your business. No matter how much you dream of innovative ideas, you need money at some point to implement them. The Idea, Design, Discovery, Development, and Pre-launch steps of the 7 Steps system are mainly preparation and practice steps to start up a product, project, and business to get the money. Yet that is just the beginning. Growing a business is the next step.

You need to know how to navigate in today's world of business. You might start by learning from companies like Project Grow, which interviewed entrepreneurs at New York's In Good Company co-working space and asked them how they meet the challenges of starting up and growing a business. For instance, Colleen De Baise of Project Grow interviewed Marissa Lippert, who for six years has run a nutritional consulting business called Nourish. At the beginning Lippert decided to open a brick-and-mortar shop selling prepared food. She used various Pre-launch strategies to build buzz about the store before it opened in order to create a future customer base and to raise additional funding.

Here are the Pre-launch strategies she employed to set up her product launch:

- She created a profile on crowdfunding portal site Kickstarter.
- Knowing the importance of a good presentation, she paid $1,000 for a high-quality video that captured the look and feel of her yet-to-be-built store.
- She also began a social media campaign, updating fans and followers on the progress of her space.
- She's also doing "content marketing," or positioning herself as an expert: writing a book called *The Cheater's Diet* as well as blogging and speaking about nutritional topics—all ways to keep her store's name trending.

Lippert points out that her Pre-launch strategies enabled her to raise $20,000 and keep up the "momentum." Creating positive momentum, or an upward trajectory of awareness, interest, and desire that leads to sales becomes critical to attracting money and investors. You want to orchestrate the people, products, and publicity to create a critical mass of activity and buzz which says to the world: this project, event, or business is happening. Get aboard this rocket ship or you will miss out.

Think of your crowdfunding campaign or product launch as a process of getting a heavy truck to move faster and faster. At first you need a lot of effort to get the truck moving. As the truck gathers momentum, it starts to move more and more on its own. To carry the metaphor further, the truck needs money or fuel to keep moving faster and faster. That's the kind of force a business wants to build for its project. Now you are ready for the sixth phase of the 7 Steps system: the launch.

## WHO SUCCEEDS THE MOST?

Creative types such as artists, game developers, and musicians succeed the most. Who succeeds the least? Entrepreneurs.

This is critical to understanding how to pick the winners in crowdfunding. Backers of crowdfunding donations receive no ownership and upside. This is not an investment in an early stage company. It's a pre-purchase of product or service.

Entrepreneurs and small businesses would love to attract capital as advance sales for a product that at best is a prototype! The problem is that entrepreneurs are not the best suited for crowdfunding.

Why can't the entrepreneur succeed very well at crowdfunding donations with rewards, but creative artists, game developers and musicians can?

The reason is that the creative types have learned how to build audiences and fans. They know how to entertain. They know how to appeal to the emotions. They know how to tell compelling stories.

This is nothing new. Wealthy patrons have supported artists throughout history. Artists such as Leonardo da Vinci and Michelangelo, William Shakespeare and Ben Jonson, all enjoyed the support of patrons. In crowdfunding, you can be a patron/donor on a small scale, support an artist, or help an entrepreneur like Migicovsky lift off the ground.

The problem remains that not nearly as many as entrepreneurs succeed in getting the money in crowdfunding with donations. The Pebble watch is clearly an exception.

Stepping back, let's look at how crowdfunding fits into a money-raising strategy and what makes up a successful crowdfunding donation with rewards project or campaign.

Brian Meese, co-founder of another crowdfunding portal RocketHub, says crowdfunding relies on three pillars:

1. The project or campaign
2. The network
3. The rewards

In looking at Pebble, you see as an investor, or an entrepreneur, the elements that make for success:

1. An attractive, appealing product.

2. A network of friends and family who start the ball rolling. They attract their friends and then friends of friends. You have to build a fan base through social media marketing.
3. It offers different tiers of rewards.
4. It has an emotional story.
5. Its campaign has clean, well-written copy, and its video gets twice the donations.

If the pitch doesn't generate interest, then it should raise a red flag to the entrepreneur or creator/artist that something is off. For example, the right audience or market is not being addressed. A business or project's success rests upon targeting the right audience, which means the right niche or slice of the market that would want a product or cause to back if they became aware of it.

Even if a product has the right audience, it needs to have the right message crafted to arouse their interest. A businessperson has to get the conversation going on in the mind of the audience he is trying to reach. This could mean the copy is weak, such as the Headline Pitch. Or, the offer itself is underwhelming. The price or terms may be too high, or the company doesn't give a strong enough warranty or money-back offer.

If you analyze what makes up an ideal crowdfunding campaign, you will find the same elements that make up ideal pitches and investments. The right audience is being addressed with the right message, the right story, the right solution to their problem, a compelling emotion-evoking offer that is timed at the right time. The right time can be when they are searching for your solution or made aware of it and realize they need it.

## PROS TO ENTREPRENEURS

Other pros of crowdfunding donations with rewards/perks for entrepreneurs are:

- Seed funding a company: sometimes getting much more than you anticipated

- Source of education on project creation (how do creative-types make their projects more appealing)
- New ideas from looking at other crowdfunding projects
- Competitive analytics from analyzing similar deals; at what did the competition price different products or rewards
- Social media marketing: seeing how others attract and build a crowd or following; communicate with them and keep them engaged

Remember, venture capitalists and most angels invest in people and look for specific knowledge and skills related to the company they are evaluating whether to back. Crowdfunding donations are a training ground (the minor leagues) that can be used to develop and learn a number of entrepreneurial skills that venture capitalists and angels seek, such as how to:

- Create a project/campaign/
- Define a vision/goal financially
- Set a deadline and meet it
- Get the project or company up and running
- Meet milestones that show traction
- Build a fan/customer base that buys your product shows traction
- Motivating with different rewards and succeeding shows the ability to market and make converting offers and sales
- Learn your real costs of marketing/sales campaign-very important
- Demonstrate that you can communicate with your fan base and keep them engaged
- Pre-sell the products to reduce risk
- Get constant feedback as to how to better your products

## CONS FOR ENTREPRENEURS

Let's look at the cons of crowdfunding donations with rewards/perks:

To repeat, for an investor looking for the upside from an investment in an early-stage company, crowdfunding donations with rewards/perks don't give the true bang for the buck unless you are a creator/investor or an investor/donor with close ties to the company, or you can offer your products and services to the project creator.

It's very time-consuming both for the creator, and she may see little for her efforts and even lose money after producing the products and rewards and paying the portal fees and all the other parties involved in the campaign

Another problem is that the offer is very public. An entrepreneur is in a fish bowl with a lot of donors who will watch his every move. They may voice opinions he doesn't want to follow. They may ultimately turn on him and become as much or more of a critic as they were originally a backer and a fan

Whether online or offline (brick and mortar), companies from start-ups to multinational grants are under immense scrutiny from citizen journalists to citizen donators or investors. The crowd can arise at any moment to vote yes or no—go viral on YouTube, Twitter, or Facebook. In effect, the crowd giveth and the crowd taketh away. The crowd can evangelize in your favor or tear you down. Today, you can pitch, but the crowd can catch on and throw the ball back.

Large companies like Dell and United saw how single incidents could materially affect their brands within hours of occurring. United and Dell both failed to respond quickly to customer complaints and take responsibility for their actions. Songwriter Dave Carroll, on a United flight from Nova Scotia to Nebraska with other members of a Canadian pop folk band, had his $3,500 guitar crushed by baggage handlers. The repair bill was $1,200. United gave him the run-around, hoping he'd give up his claim. Dave threatened to write three songs and post them on YouTube. The video "United Breaks Guitars" went from six views on July 6, 2009, to two million by July 12 to three million by July 23. On July 19, Dave had a website up for Dave Carroll's Traveler's Edition Guitar Case. "Note how quickly the new product is developed and launched," remarked David Meerman Scott in his book *Real-Time Marketing & PR*.

Another con is that what you receive has no investment value—you are a glorified consumer. Plus, often your product will be shipped late. Pebble is months late on its delivery of the watches to 85,000 total buyers. That's not to mention the obvious: You may be disappointed in what you actually purchased

You should also keep in mind that almost 50% of Kickstarter campaigns fail. Remember, you have to hit a certain target, or you lose it all. Even when creators hit the target, the average amount raised is less than $10,000. When you factor in the costs of the campaign, the project creator doesn't get much money. For the investor, you should be aware that a site like Kickstarter doesn't keep track of whether projects funded through its site are delivered. It relies on the project's creators to fulfill their promise. That's not to mention that some of the products can take time to reach completion.

Another con is that a project is not a company. Many entrepreneurs confuse running a project or creating a product with building a sound business that makes money, is sustainable, can scale, and can be sold in part or whole. To be clear, a project/campaign is more an event with a defined scope, such as a given amount of a product such as Pebble watches.

## CAREFULLY STUDY CROWDFUNDING DONATIONS WITH REWARDS

Crowdfunding donations with rewards/perks are a microcosm of the current global stage upon which companies small and large must compete. As with the example of "United Breaks Guitars," crowdfunding emphasizes your need to understand the power of crowds, inbound marketing, direct marketing, and interactive marketing, including video marketing, social media marketing, and, more and more, mobile marketing. Crowdfunding donations bring attention to this new world of social and mobile marketing at a time when relationship and peer-to-peer marketing and sales are taking on more and more importance for small and large companies.

In the beginning, most start-ups are seen as outsiders, interlopers, who are saying things should be different from the status quo. Naturally, people don't like change, especially those in power, i.e., competitors. This brings the power of persuasion—marketing and sales—full center. With all the noise and clutter, all companies, especially start-ups, must clearly make their case to investors, stakeholders, and customers. This makes marketing and sales skills vital. Crowdfunding provides a needed and valuable platform where new ideas are welcome, can be marketed and sold, and can receive invaluable feedback.

However, you could use the following investment strategies. Remember, venture capitalists want proof of concept. Crowdfunding donations can be used to develop and learn a number of investment skills, such as how to:

- Create a project/campaign/
- Define a vision/goal financially
- Set a deadline
- Build a fan base
- Motivate with different rewards
- Learn your real costs of marketing/sales campaign
- Communicate with your fan base and keep them engaged
- Pre-sell the products to reduce risk
- Get constant feedback as to how to better your products

Let's turn away from how crowdfunding originally started and move into how you can use the lessons that this type of raising money has to offer for both the entrepreneur and the investor. If you're putting in your hard-earned cash, you need to know about all how the world of marketing has evolved over the last decade. Just as a product can become a hit on Kickstarter, Internet marketing can achieve rewards that are so colossal, they could only come from a viral product spreading globally.

## TAKEAWAYS AND INSIGHTS

- Crowdfunding donations with rewards have ushered in an awareness of how the Internet, social, and mobile can be used to fund projects, especially those of creative types. In addition, crowdfunding can be used to inject capital as well as small businesses and some entrepreneurial companies which have to the potential to grow and scale.
- Crowdfunding donations with rewards requires using many of the pitch components we have been reviewing. The main exception is that the funders or backers receive no equity ownership or upside in the project or entity in which they put money.
- Crowdfunding is a grand experiment which allows ideas to be tested and funded that traditional investors would typically reject for being too small in potential or run by creative types rather than the more traditional entrepreneurs who want to build the next Google, Instagram, or Facebook. Even so, products like the Pebble watch can attract significant sums of money.
- Staying with the concepts of Performance and Conversation Economy, crowdfunding represents a new stage or platform where pitches can be honed, products tested, and audiences built.
- On average, crowdfunding donations with rewards is a means to get seed funding for causes, products, and projects which can provide the sales and social proof to attract additional rounds of financing.

- The key to succeeding in crowdfunding relies upon getting a core group of backers to get the project off the ground. Many groups seeking crowdfunding fail to realize how much work goes into attracting the core donor or backer group, laying out the crowdfunding portal page and designing the rewards for different levels or donor price points.
- Crowdfunding donations with rewards can be amplified by tying the campaign to social network sites and creating links back to the specific campaign.
- Crowdfunding donations with rewards is a way to raise money by selling or pre-selling stuff. Another way to do this is product launches.

Click here for additional resources: http://bit.ly/19VljKO

CHAPTER 11

# THE PRODUCT LAUNCH

There are two types of product launches. The first is a Steve Jobs of Apple-type launch, where a new product such as an iPad or iPhone is designed to capture the public's attention and drive sales. All types of media, online and offline, are used. The second type of product launch mainly is conducted online by Internet or online marketers.

Product launches, whether massive like an Apple product launch, which can run up to $50 million or more, or much smaller online product launches that promote a book or a coaching or training course, possess many similarities in goals and follow the 7 Steps system.

The goals of product launches can vary, but some key ones are creating and building:

- Awareness: visibility and capturing attention for promoter and/or brand
- Reputation/trust
- A sense of community: belonging
- Community engagement in conversations among themselves as well as with the promoting person and/or company
- An event with a beginning, middle, and end (from pre-pre-launch to pre-launch to launch to post-launch) that leads to defined actions such as buying the promoted products
- A list of prospects and qualified leads that can turn into customers and repeat customers
- Up sells and cross sells to increase the amount each customer buys

A product launch can take advantage of a common human problem. Customers and investors, like all people, want excitement in their lives. Properly orchestrated events excite them and get them to take action.

Why is this? No matter how rich or poor people are, they have similar desires. People want to feel good, look good, and find purpose and meaning. Many people are bored. They are stuck in habits and ruts. They seek to be entertained and wowed. Events such as product launches create a feeling of common interest and belonging. Customers tell others about good deals or new products. Investors tell other investors about good, exciting deals.

Like stories, product launches have a beginning, middle, and an end. A good model is a movie launch. Movie launches seek to build suspense, anticipation, buzz, or word of mouth so that people's desires are so aroused that they line up to buy tickets. Actors in the movie being launched do appearances on TV and radio shows to promote the movie, and allow magazines and the press to interview them. Movie posters appear in stores and movie theaters under "coming soon." Behind-the-scenes interviews and clips of the director shooting the movie are released. Stories appear in the media about conflicts among the actors or affairs or director/actor conflicts or cost overruns. The purpose: to generate a conversation about the coming attraction. From a dead start, the movie takes on a life of its own. Ultimately, on sites such as Fandango, moviegoers look up whether critics say "go" or "no go" and fans say "go" or "no go."

The world of start-ups and raising capital is very similar. The benefits of a successful product launch go beyond just making a lot of money and creating a list that keeps buying the product. An entrepreneur can gain great influence and visibility. That in turn not only generates lots of PR, but he or she can generate a large income from high-end, high-margin consulting, coaching, and mentoring programs in his field of expertise. He can become a paid speaker or a speaker who sells onstage high end/high margin products. You can even earn equity in other businesses if you reach the status of an expert. In turn, the publicity and the influence gained increase your power to do more product launches with more and more joint venture partners and affiliates.

Product launches provide great insights on how to build visibility, influence, and star power, which can be turned into winning products and very successful businesses. Remember that underlying crowdfunding and product launches is event marketing. Event marketing can be online via product launches or offline in such activities as attending seminars. On the next page is an example of event marketing by Constant Contact to attend offline seminars.

Note the headline, the personalized use of my name, the free offer to learn about email marketing (direct marketing), and combining this strategy with content marketing from experts (indirect marketing).

**Upcoming Events to Help Build Your Business or Nonprofit!**

Hi Gray

Constant Contact is doing all that we can to help nonprofits succeed with online marketing tools. To get a better idea of best practices specifically for the nonprofit community, please join Mike Neuendorff at the first of a three-part series on February 27. Whether you are fund raising, looking for more volunteers, or staying in contact with your current participants, email marketing should be driving all of your communications. Come find out how and why, as Mike discusses best practices for email marketing for your organization. Join us for tips, resources, ideas, networking, and a light breakfast.

Have you heard the phrase "content is king"? Come hear why as Ann Gusiff talks about email marketing and the importance of a strong content on Tuesday, February 26.

See below for more upcoming events brought to you by Constant Contact and our team of Authorized Local Experts.

**Looking forward to seeing you!**

## THE VALUE OF PREPARATION

As mentioned, product launches are used by both large and small companies. The successful ones come about because of careful preparation, not amazing products. According to a *Harvard Business Review* article, "Why Most Product Launches Fail," by Joan Schneider and Julie Hall, "many entrepreneurs and brand managers think they have revolutionary products. Yet most fail upon launch." Why would this be? The article notes, "Marketing consultant Jack Trout says consumers buy the same 150 items, many of their household needs."

If those odds aren't bad enough, even products that start out strong can disappear from the shelves after a few years. Based upon Schneider and Hill's survey of the Most Memorable Product Launches between 2002 and 2008, 12 out of 70 of the initial product successes failed.

The main cause? Lack of preparation. In a nutshell, they fail because of five fatal flaws. The first one is common to small companies: they cannot support fast growth. If you are an entrepreneur, you have to already have a plan to expand quickly if the product takes off.

The second flaw comes about because the company did not do its homework. The product falls short of the claims it makes and it gets bashed by customers. That's why I caution you to delay your launch until the product is really ready.

The third flaw? The new product remains in limbo after it comes out. In other words, its value is not compelling enough for a consumer to tell it apart from the products that are already out there. That's why you have to keep testing a product to make sure its differences are clear and will attract buyers.

Yet flaw number four suffers from the opposite problem. The product may define a new category—and require substantial consumer education in order to use it. Let's face it: if consumers can't quickly grasp how to use the product, it's toast.

The fifth flaw is related to the fourth: the product is revolutionary, but there is no market for it. This is what happens when an entrepreneur gets a "eureka" idea that solves a problem for too few people. You cannot gloss over the basic questions: Who will buy this product, and at what price? You're only as smart as the consumer thinks you are.

A study in Nielsenwire states that millions of dollars are spent developing and launching new products, but only 10% will succeed at all. Nielsen claims its new approach to product launches improves the likelihood of new product launch success to 75%.

Based on tracking 600 product launches and testing 20,000 concepts, Nielsen outlined a 12-step process that predicts success spanning five stages: Salience, Communication, Attraction, Point of Purchase, Endurance.

12 Key Steps to Consumer Adoption

Source:http://blog.nielsen.com/nielsenwire/consumer/countdown-to-product-launch-12-key-steps/

The above wheel of their terrific graphic is focused upon launching a new consumer product mainly offline, but the same principles and guidelines can be applied to online product and business launches. The wheel outlines the basics of an irresistible offer: the right price; the right message as to what is the product and what it does; what's in it for the consumer; and why should they believe you.

Nielsenwire concludes, "Companies need to understand that all 12 steps weight equally on their chances at a successful launch. The age-old saying that you are only as good as your *weakest link* is true. Even one risky area of the launch process can seriously detract from the value of the product."

## PRODUCT LAUNCH—A TO Z

Before I go into more depth regarding online product launches as a sales and money-raising strategy, I want to point out that on the most basic level, product launches appear alluringly simple. They are not. Why? Again I return to the premise that people are creatures of habit. Most people like the familiarity of the status quo. Put another way, most people are risk averse. They don't like or desire to lose. Only 15% of buyers are early adopters.

Seth Godin made a similar comment in his blog post "Understanding Idea Adoption (you're not a slot, you choose a slot)." Some people bought his book *50 Shades* when it was a self-published e-book. Others jumped in when the buzz or word of mouth spread enough for the book to become a best seller. Still others waited until the book was on the best-seller list and in bookstores with positive and negative discussions. And two years later, even another group will buy the book. This is how it will always be. Some may be early adopters of books but not shoes, while early adopters of shoes may be later buyers of books. These groups of book buyers and shoe buyers are "pockets of people or micro markets," where everyone is not the same.

Too many marketers put all their time into obsessing about the first week of the launch and then they are off to the next shiny object. But the mass audience waits beyond the new stage. Today's biggest challenges for any product launch are the amount of noise or static—the global competition where thousands of images and messages overwhelm even the most astute buyers and investors. So a product launch may take time to be successful. In the book and music business the real profits come from the back end—the backlist.

Key Insight: Be aware of time when you plan and prepare for a product launch so that you profit from the back end as well as the initial launch.

## A BRIEF HISTORY OF INTERNET MARKETING

With a little background about direct response marketing and the Internet, you will begin to see how successful product launches have evolved on the web. When I first decided to enter the Internet marketing space, I flew down to an Internet marketing conference at the end of 2006 to listen to a group of self-promoting gurus who explained adeptly how product launches worked. What I heard truly caught my attention. The perfect wave to be ridden: the coming together of information, the Internet, and direct response marketing.

They preached that direct mail tactics could be brought to the Internet. Instead of mailing stuff at 50 cents to a dollar apiece and waiting for results, you could send emails for a fraction of a penny and get immediate responses and metrics which told you whether the campaign had succeeded or not.

But a catch existed on the Internet. To avoid spam laws, you had to get the permission of the person to email her. Put another way, the person had to sign up or opt in with her email or name and email before you could email her. Or, to be even more conservative, you asked for a person's name and email and then asked her to re-confirm them, which was called a double opt-in.

This led to the key idea—why not "bribe" someone to give you her email or name and email? The bribe evolved into free stuff, such as a free e-book or video that made a big promise, such as making $10,000 a month in your pajamas. The sign-up page in Internet marketing was appropriately called a squeeze page, since you literally squeezed the email from the prospect by promising the free stuff that would immediately make her rich or lose weight.

This process is called getting people into the funnel or sales funnel. The top marketers had different strategies, but one company that did over $300 million—90% on the net (and now double that)—would pummel a potential customer with follow-up emails after the person signed up for their free emails. The simple concept—get 'em when they are hot. As they termed it, it's like shooting fish in a barrel. Find the industry (the barrel) and niche (the fish) where they were irrationally biting for your big promise solution.

Many of the gurus came from sales backgrounds, such as stockbrokers, magazine and newsletter subscriptions, even used car and vacuum cleaner salespeople. They had mastered the art of direct selling and studied the legendary direct mail copywriters such as Gary Halbert, Dan Kennedy, Eugene Schwartz, and Jay Abraham.

In reality the top gurus had mastered the psychology of human nature and influence. Ironically, the best practitioners of Internet direct response marketing know their stuff. The problem is, most of what they taught in 2006, as one top Internet marketer confided to me, is the same material sold today repurposed. The rise of social media, social and content marketing, video, and mobile has added many more elements to building a list and selling stuff online. Much of the social, mobile, and video marketing is outside the top Internet marketers' sweet spot. The movement toward greater automated metrics and analytics and the rise of Apple, Amazon, Facebook, You Tube, and LinkedIn now competes with these top marketers for their target audience's attention. In addition, the estimated pool of potential Internet marketing buyers has been shrinking. Buyers bombarded with many similar offers have wised up and are turned off by Internet marketers' overuse of the same psychological gimmicks to get them to buy.

## THE THREE BASIC ELEMENTS OF ALL SUCCESSFUL PRODUCT LAUNCHES

At the root of all product launches, you must satisfy three basic elements:

1. List
2. Offer
3. Copy

From these basic elements, you test your launch product to get the metrics called, in the jargon of Internet marketers, the EPC—or earnings per click. For example, if you generated $3,000 from 1,000 clicks your earning per click would be $3. This tells a marketer of your product that if they offer your product to their list, then 10,000 clicks would generate them $30,000. Most of the elements that surround and support the basics of list, offer, and copy are mainly psychological triggers such as scarcity and reciprocity that have been used for over one hundred years in direct mail and transposed to email marketing and direct marketing in general.

So what do these terms really mean?

**List**. When you first sit down to plan out a product launch, the questions that immediately arise are: Who will we sell this to? Where are we going to find them? Put another way, who has a list we can market to? Unless you have a list yourself or your best buddy or close relative has one, there is usually a dead silence.

This is where an entrepreneur needs to beware of marketing experts. They will rattle off the people they know on lists you can buy. Usually, you'll want to know how much money you want to make on the product launch. They either pull some numbers out of a hat, or they will tell you candidly they don't know and you'll have to test. But to test you need a list. They will point to all those big money product launches. Your greed glands start to pop as they reel you in to the famous monthly retainer.

I don't mean to be facetious, but I've lost enough money going down this road that I hope to save you some. Your chances of getting away with paying no money out to get a good product launch planned, structured, and implemented are slim to none.

The key is to focus your offer to a certain target audience. Without the right promotions and offers, your products sit on the shelf or your website. No one buys.

To succeed in online product launches, you must understand the physical and psychological setup of the industry itself. Similar to Wall Street, the top Internet marketers have formed selling syndicates whose members are called JVs or affiliates. JVs say you sell my product to your list and I will sell your product to my list. In other words, the syndicate sells to each other's list, and they have agreed-upon schedules as to who sells when.

To break into this syndicate is super difficult, since an endorsed mailing—a large product launch—among the syndicate members can bring potentially millions of dollars to you and raise you to Internet marketing stardom. Potentially, you can finance your business without giving up any ownership. Affiliates are more one-way salespeople or organizations that mail to their list for a commission but do not expect you to mail a product they have to your list.

The bottom line is, the world of Internet marketing and product launches rests upon a lot of politics, buddy-buddy relationships, psychology, and self-appointed stars—some who earned their stature and many who have not and are disappearing, as they are not current in the world of social media, video, and mobile marketing.

However you obtain your lists, most marketers will tell you that the list is the most important element to succeed in product launches. But that's only part of the challenge. Clearly, you don't want to offer cat litter to dog owners. You want to know your audience so well that you can target an offer to them that they can't refuse. This is where most product launches fail. Most of the so-called lists are full of phony emails. The people either do not exist or they just want a company's free offer, and to get it they gave you an email to a dummy site they never visit other than to get their freebie.

Even worse, if you persuade someone to mail your offer to their list, they may not mail for many reasons or mail only to a part of their list, which may be the ones that never respond. Here are some reasons those with lists may not mail:

- They scheduled your launch and a buddy's at the same time—too bad, maybe next time.
- A better deal that can make them more money came along.

- They don't want to spend much time on your launch, and you didn't give them the tools to promote you in an easy, spoon-fed way.
- Your metrics suck.
- You failed to put together a product that they feel is remarkable, and they don't want to turn off their list with an inferior product.

In the end, what matters is not so much the quantity of the list but the quality of it. Would you rather have a list of 25,000 people with 100 people buying from you monthly at $100, or a 5,000-person list where 500 people buy from you at $100 per month?

Remember, in crowdfunding the portal brings traffic to your offering page. You want to supplement the portal's traffic by driving traffic from your blog, website, special dedicated page, Facebook fan page, YouTube, Twitter, or other places or sources by having these pages link to your portal page.

**Copy**. The quality of your copy can make or break you during a product launch. Once you get your traffic and list strategies, then you realize how many ways you have to communicate with your potential audience of buyers, backers, and investors. Each of these communications requires copy.

Here's the copy you will need:

- Subject lines of emails sent to prospects. If the email recipient does not open his email, it doesn't matter what you are offering.
- The email itself needs a headline and/or tag line and some copy to lead the reader to click through to a page which has your offer—many times free—to get the person to give you his email or name and email. An offer can be a free e-book, a video with tips on a topic about which people want more info, such as improving their golf driving distance or how to cook romantic meals in fifteen minutes
- Good copy on the page where they land—the landing page. The headline and tag line and rest of the copy needs to be a call

to action—how to give your email or name and email, or more if you are more corporate—and fit with the design and layout of the landing page itself.

- A series of follow-up emails if the person signs up but does not buy.
- Copy for your affiliates and JV partners. If you want affiliates or JV partners to mail to their list. You will need to send copy to get their interest and copy set up for them to mail to their lists.

Here are some copy tips:

- Email marketing in many respects uses direct-response advertising fundamentals.
- To write great copy or hire a great copywriter, you or they have to master the direct response advertising business, which seeks to obtain a very specific response.
- As opposed to ads on TV, radio, or in magazines, direct-response ads are scientific in that they can be tested and measured in terms of the outcomes the ad produces. That's why you test everything in a small way before you go big. This way you keep your investment low until you find a winning offer that converts to sales.
- Ultimately you sell benefits—the "so thats." You buy the drill which makes the holes (feature) *so that* (the benefit follows the "so that") you can hang the beautiful, peaceful landscape picture in your living room
- Like any experiment, you have to show that the promises you make are backed up with some examples. Use cases and statistics, starting with those the prospect knows or can immediately verify.
- You keep backing each of your claims with the reasons why this or that is true.
- Like a story, your copy has a basic structure—a beginning, middle, and end. You have to step back and look at the big picture and see where you are starting and where you want to lead the

prospect. Your copy must have a logical progression to build a belief. Your prospect has to believe you before he or she will buy.

Copy is one of the fastest ways to create leverage (minimal effort, maximum return) and makes lots more money. Just changing a headline or tag line—a few simple words—or a guarantee can increase the leads and sales you generate by ten times or even much more.

Key Insight: Besides guarantees, such as ninety-day money back with no questions asked, bonuses can be the icing on the cake that makes the sale. Some feel bonuses should represent a 50% increase in value to the buyer, while others feel bonuses should represent at least three times the value of your base product or more.

**Offer**. Ideas don't mean much until they are translated into products. The products must address a desire, need, or want. Plus, they must be offered at a price that appears to deliver value. Breakthrough ideas that become breakthrough products don't mean much if they are not couched in a compelling or irresistible offer.

As a pure investor or entrepreneur/investor or creator/artist or small businessperson, you need to recognize the components of a compelling or irresistible offer. Also, you must be able to decipher offers that may be too good to be true.

As I have pointed out, the components of an irresistible offer are:

- Product: What does it do?
- Proposition/proposal: What's in it for me, the buyer (value)?
- Price: What is this going to cost me?
- Proof: Why should I believe you? Who else is using this and is satisfied (peer-to-peer trust and competence)?
- Proprietary: What makes you different—your unique selling proposition?
- Path: How do I get the product? Is it easy to get and use, and to do business with you?
- Protection: What are the guarantees to reduce my risk, such as a return policy—no questions asked?

- Perks: Are there extras or bonuses that sweeten the pie? Another name for crowdfunding donations with rewards is crowdfunding with perks. These are the extras you give to your backers to motivate them to pledge more, such as naming a song after you or signing a copy of a book

The first thing you want is for the product to sell itself. The product has to be buzz-worthy, like a movie that you tell your friends they must see. Where you make the money is when your product is remarkable. It's a must have.

Product launches must be designed and packaged to capture the target audience's attention by drawing them into the uniqueness and value of the product so they have an exciting experience and feel at the same time a solution is being offered for their problem at a reasonable cost with little risk compared to the upside benefits.

Remember, the offer is the final step in the marketing process. It is always is the final step your prospects or customers consider before they purchase your product.

## THE BIG PICTURE

If you want to succeed at launching a product and getting the money on a crowd sourcing portal site or on your own site or via a sign-up page (called an opt-in, squeeze, or landing page) that puts your prospect into a sales or investment funnel, then you must understand that marketing—the conversation—becomes more than a series of features and benefits. Just learning the mechanics of the product launch formula alone does not guarantee success. Above all, you have to make an emotional connection with customers and investors.

Here's an astounding fact that supports the importance of emotional connection, a point which I have made over and over. In 2012, Apple earned $7 billion more than Google, Microsoft, eBay, Facebook, Yahoo, and Amazon combined! Why? Apple uses the same strategies and tactics that blockbuster book, movie, TV, and music launches employ. All of these launch strategies and tactics hold your attention with images, stories, and events that evoke your emotions so you bond and connect with the artist, brand, project, and business.

Steve Jobs' famous product launches made a human connection by evoking our passion to change the world. He told stories and showed products such as the iPod, iPhone, and iPad that made an emotional connection and captured our imagination.

People don't want just to be sold stuff. Instead, they want to be delighted by products and have memorable, life-transforming experiences with them. In a world full of dubious claims and many hucksters, customers and investors crave entertainment, stories, meaning, trust, and emotional connection. You have to convey the same passion and purpose of a Steve Jobs in your crowdfunding or product launches so your customers and investors believe that you truly have created a product and business worth your customers' and investors' time and money. By expressing your passion and purpose for your product and business openly and authentically, you create the means for a conversation to take place, which forms an intimate personal bond with your customers and investors.

When you sit down to lay out a product launch, the key topics will be:

- Will our own list respond to the offer (called an internal launch)?
- Who has lists that will mail for us?
- What product do we have to offer?
- What's the up-front offer: Is it free to get people in the sales funnel or a low-priced SLO, or self-liquidating offer—meaning what they pay covers your cost but you got the person to become a customer?
- Is there an immediate upsell or a more expensive related product after they purchase the lower-priced product (or a product they are sold after they signed up for a free offer)?
- Is there a back-end, more expensive coaching or training product as you move the customer through the sales funnel?

- Who will write the copy for the opt-in or squeeze page; the video offering a free product or the low-end paid product; the video sales letter; the long- or short-form sales letter; the affiliate swipe copy to mail; the numerous emails to get leads to buy or buyers to buy more?
- Who will oversee the entire product launch or be the product launch manager?
- Who will design the different pages in the sales funnel?
- Who will set up the technology—the email system; the shopping cart; the affiliate payment system; the tracking of leads to sales and repeat sales and reporting to and payment to affiliates or JVs?
- Who will solicit the JVs and affiliates to mail?
- Who will test the offers; read the metrics and analytics; calculate EPC (earning per click, or the average amount that an affiliate or JV can earn per visit to a page)? In this case you are using the conversion rate of a product or funnel and the earnings of that product or funnel. Kevin Clayton advises that you take your total amount of money earned by a product or funnel and divide it by the total number of (unique) visitors to your landing page (product page/video sales letter/whatever leads to the checkout page). This can also be deceptive with affiliate sales, since affiliates earn a variable percentage of each sale. This is often clarified by saying "total EPC" or "EPC your way." Earnings/Visitors (clicks) equals EPC.
- Set up more than one merchant account to handle the payments. This is key to a launch, since certain merchant processors that process your credit card orders may shut your launch down if you get too many returns or customer complaints.

## PRODUCT LAUNCH STRUCTURE

Many top Internet marketers acknowledge that Jeff Walker is the inventor of the product launch formula. He has a story of how he sold stock market trading tips. He decided to market a monthly stock market newsletter. He observed that most direct response sales on- or offline used a long-form vertical sales letter, which could be 40 pages long. The weakness of these long sales letters is that people would read the headline and then jump to the bottom to see the offer, price, and bonuses. As a result, the potential buyer or prospect had little emotional connection to the sales copy since she never read it.

He decided to turn the long-form sales letter on its side and called it a horizontal sales letter. The product launch formula was in essence a marketing event that led to a product launch that would engage people so strongly that they stood in line to buy. This marketing and selling event had all the components of a long-form sales letter, but instead of reading it from top to bottom, the sales letter was spread "horizontally" over time. The product launch event had a beginning, middle, and end, like a story, or what he called a story arc. The product launch became a conversation among prospects about the product and its story of struggle to find the solution to the problem, such as how to get more traffic to a site or blog or squeeze page.

Because the product launch had a story and a conversation going about it, you could survey prospects on what they wanted in advance and build suspense and anticipation as the product launch date neared.

The product launch structure could be: pre-pre-launch (hint to others what may be coming in the future to get the buzz, buy-in, and networking strategies under way), pre-launch; launch and post launch like a movie, music or book launch we have discussed. This launch process mirrors in part the 7 Steps system: pre-launch; launch and post-launch. The Idea, Design, Discovery, and Development steps can be used to prepare the content and the offer or even sell a product before it's even developed based upon the pre-launch feedback.

Numerous psychological strategies are used to get people to sign up and or buy, such as reciprocity (I give you a lot of free content and you feel obligated to sign up and buy to reciprocate); use scarcity (such as there are only so many units available); motivation by price (I will be raising the price in the next two days); or taking bonuses back (you get all these bonuses until this date, then you only get these). The end of the product launch also is a natural motivator, since the launch will end on a certain date, which gets as many or more buyers than the initial hours of the launch.

The number of psychological triggers deployed in a product launch to get a person to take action are numerous. One of the most important is different levels of social proof, such as a testimonial where someone says he used the product and it was great, or a case study where the details and the results are carefully laid out, such as someone who used this software, paid this price, and the number of qualified leads doubled and the cost per lead dropped by 70%.

## TWO TYPES OF LAUNCHES

Basically, there are two types of launches:

1. The rolling launch
2. The blockbuster launch

A rolling launch differs from the blockbuster launch in that you market to one or two lists at a time. Instead of one big blast, you roll from one list to another on an ongoing basis. This enables you to create monthly income while avoiding a big boom or big bust. Big launches create tremendous stress on all components of your launch. You can have a technical meltdown, or spikes in income can cause the merchant(s) processing your payments to hold your payments or to shut you down. Why? They fear customer cancellations or charge backs will expose them to liabilities that the banks don't want to underwrite.

The blockbuster product launch normally has a squeeze or opt-in page that gives, in exchange for a potential buyer's email, a free report or a promise of free video instruction on a topic in which the potential buyer is interested. One strategy is to provide three free training videos providing information that gets the potential buyer interested. The fourth video summarizes the first three videos and then makes the offer. Another product launch might use the tactic of getting the potential buyer to give his email and have him sign up for a webinar, which is the selling video. In effect, the product uses one long video to sell the product.

The product launch depends above all on great customer support. This is key to keeping customers happy. A company needs well-written emails to be sent in a certain sequence over a period of days. Yet there must be a motivating reason for the potential buyer to take action. That's why 40% or more of a promotion's sale can come in during the last 48 to 72 hours. An entrepreneur might send five to seven emails to generate excitement. Revenue can double or more using this method. Expert marketer David Bass writes that this surge, called scarcity stacking, is "where you combine different types of real, plausible scarcity (if they don't feel it, they won't respond)." Needless to say, a company must be very skilled in email marketing so it does not overdo sending out emails and get shut down.

As mentioned, another vital aspect of a good product launch is to provide case studies of a product. Showing a before-and-after situation is very important in generating trust and enthusiasm. As part of that effort, a company must make sure that the product appears simple enough to use. As I have pointed out before, complicated and complex products scare potential buyers away.

The Internet marketing gurus often elect the blockbuster launch. All members of the syndicate mail after the guru who is launching his product tests his offer with his own list (called an internal launch). Then, with favorable metrics, (usually an EPC over $2 and preferably $ 4 or more) the launch goes into full gear.

## PRODUCT LAUNCH SUMMARY

Product launches are an excellent list-building and money-attracting strategy. Like crowdfunding for donations rewards, they enable an entrepreneur to test her products and get feedback without giving up ownership.

Product launches take a lot of time to prepare and execute. What I discovered with my own launches was I could get opt-in or sign-up rates of 30% but struggled to convert them to sales. Often, this is a result of messaging and copy. Even with a great offer, the prospect has to get the concept quickly and feel an emotional connection.

Plus, there are a lot more people doing product launches, so the market is tired of them unless they are exceptional on every level. Like any business, it takes time—three to five years on average—to become good at stuff. Even back in 2006, the top Internet marketers had an average of five to eight years' experience. It was much easier in 2006 than it is today with social media, video, and mobile collectively competing for prospects' and customers' attention, as well as Amazon and Apple.

By seeing the entire product launch formula, you can see how all the different attention-getting, traffic, list/audience building, and money-raising strategies differ but mostly complement each other. With careful planning the launch can be a huge success. Now you have to figure out a way to keep the momentum building. That is the last stage of the 7 Steps system, known as the Post-launch.

## TAKEAWAYS AND INSIGHTS

- Along with Jeff Walker, Frank Kern is a master marketer and expert in product launches. Kern advocates the end in mind similar to what is described in Stephen Covey's best-selling book *The Seven Habits of Effective People*. You start with the end or goal in mind and work backward. Kern elaborates on this method by constantly asking what would someone have to do to accomplish each step.
- Another variation of the end in mind Kern calls Results in Advance. Here the person enters at point A, but he or she has to be able to envision point B. The end in mind here is their solution to their pain or need. You have to promise (pitch) them this result in advance where they can envision the result, believe they can accomplish it, and trust you. In effect, you have to build increasingly their desire and trust by moving them through your pitch and content to the point they will take action and buy.
- Like crowdfunding donations with rewards, product launches are a way to generate sales and cash flow for a business without giving up ownership in your company.
- Where crowdfunding donations with rewards may be a one-time event on a crowdfunding site like Kickstarter or RocketHub, product launches can be ongoing.
- Crowdfunding can be a relatively inexpensive way to build a list and social proof. Then you can accelerate cash flow and growth by using follow-up product launches and other sales of higher-end products to your list.

Click here for additional resources: http://bit.ly/178NdB5

CHAPTER 12

# HOW TO GET THE MONEY: CROWDFUNDING WITH EQUITY

Here is the chapter you've all been waiting for. At last you can find out how to mine veins of gold. Plus, each strategy of getting the money such as crowdfunding donations with rewards and product launches can be integrated with the others. There is a reason, however, that I took you through the different stages of pitching crowdfunding donations with rewards and product launches. That's because crowdfunding with equity has parts that are very similar to these other strategies. Only in this case, as an investor you are getting ownership (a piece of the "action") in the company in the hope of seeing your investments grow in value.

The possibilities are revolutionary but also fraught with grave risks. That's because, as we have seen, the chances of hitting a blockbuster deal as an investor and/or entrepreneur are, at best, one out of ten. That's even after rigorous due diligence and tons of hours of genuine well-intentioned efforts. Blockbuster deals are outliers. So are talented individuals whether entrepreneurs, investors or athletes. It takes a lot of hard work, deliberate practice and some luck. Malcolm Gladwell points out in his book *Outliers* that the Outlier has to spend at least 10,000 hours becoming an expert in his field. Think of the deliberate practice of the peak performers who practice 10,000 hours, such as Jack Nicklaus or Tiger Woods in golf.

Yet if you are willing to do your homework and put in the hours, crowdfunding has opened a brand-new way that a person without lots of money can get rich. Equally as exciting, equity crowdfunding opens up a tremendous new source of capital for entrepreneurs and small businesses to get their ideas off the ground.

Why is the promise of crowdfunding so huge? Because it solves a large problem: a lack of seed capital. Small amounts of money—seed capital—can finance start-up businesses at the very beginning. Remember, the JOBS Act's purpose is to spur economic and job growth. This type of funding fills a longstanding gap for entrepreneurs. "Venture capitalists avoid early stages, when the technologies are uncertain and market needs are unknown…venture money is not long-term money," wrote venture capitalist Bob Zider in "How Venture Capital Works" in the November 1998 *Harvard Business Review.*

That risk, though, should make you prudent. Even in small amounts, the money you put down on a loser is still your money that you lost. So you need to learn how to pick the winners.

## WHAT TYPE OF BUSINESS DO YOU WANT?

Since you are venturing where experienced investors do not dare to go, you should know important distinctions as to where you are currently when you assess what is the best place to invest. You need to be clear on the difference among the following: the employee, the small businessperson, the entrepreneurial business, and the investor.

The following grid shows four quadrants popularized in the book *Rich Dad, Poor Dad,* by Robert Kiyosaki.

| $E^{+}$<br>E | $B^{+}$<br>B |
|---|---|
| $S^{+}$<br>S | $I^{+}$<br>I |

The employee (E) trades hours for dollars and has no ownership in the company for which he or she works. The small businessperson (S) can be a store owner, a restaurant owner, a consultant, an agent, a small home builder, a professional such as a lawyer or accountant, or one of thousands of other business owners. Most of them have one thing in common, though. They rest upon one or a few individual's skill sets. Some of these businesses can generate a good or even excellent income. But they are often difficult to sell since the relationships and skills rely upon the small business owner.

On the other side of the quadrant is where the big money is made. Companies (B) that are self-sustaining grow from their sales and capital invested. Typically, the company does not rely upon one individual. If he or she dies, then the company can continue to grow and evolve. Some of these companies can grow fast and become dominant in their industries (B+s).

The investor makes up the last quadrant. He or she can be a venture capitalist, a super angel (I+), a fund such as Fidelity under Jim Lynch in the past or Berkshire Hathaway under Warren Buffet, or an angel.

The bottom line: the key to wealth is ownership. If you want to become wealthy, then you have to own and/or control an asset. Most venture capitalists, super angels, and angel investors want to invest in companies—not operate them. That is the main reason investors focus upon top management, especially in a start-up. Management's "job" is to execute or implement the plan that they pitch to the investors. For this reason, an entrepreneur's presentations and pitches that I have reviewed with you must instill in investors the confidence that the entrepreneur can be trusted to implement the plan.

Let's break the company types into two broad categories so you can see how the sources of capital and the get-the-money strategies match up. Each requires similar common success patterns, such as a great idea and someone or some team to implement it. But look at the differences in uncertainty, risks, and potential. Take the example of two types of companies: a candy store and a software company (entrepreneurial business).

| | **Entrepreneurial Business** | **Small Business** |
|---|---|---|
| People | Different skill sets required at different stages of the business development cycle. | Typically, one skill set to oversee the business from beginning to positive cash flow and some growth unless it expands locally and becomes more entrepreneurial. |
| Product | Remarkable; have national or international sustainable competition advantage. | Averagely good to remarkable depending upon the location of the business and the competition. |
| Potential | Depending on when investors invest in the business development cycle, investors seek typically ten times or more in earlier stages to three to five times in later stages. | Normally, the upside growth potential of the business is limited. Rarely see high growth in absolute dollars of revenue and earnings that you would experience in a high growth entrepreneurial company. |
| Principal | or Investor Types: Venture capitalists, super angels, angels. | Friends, family, fools, some local or regional angels if very strong return on investment and the ability to sell the business or get money out, e.g., loan with interest plus equity percentage or ownership. |
| Job Creation | Top 1% of early-stage high-growth companies contribute 67% of new jobs created. | Contributes much less to net job creation, contrary to popular belief. |

| | **Entrepreneurial Business** | **Small Business** |
|---|---|---|
| Uncertainty | Very high. | Very high when first starting up the business but the variables to succeed or or not succeed are much more defined, such as sell pizza, cut hair |
| Risk | Risk: Very high in seed stage.<br>Very high to high in later stage. | Very high in seed stage.<br>Much lower in later stage. |

Many investors and entrepreneurs, even sophisticated ones, confuse the entrepreneurial business and the small business. As a result, the expectations between the investor and the business can be mismatched.

As you look at the broad comparison between an entrepreneurial business and a small business, you can see that they both normally start out with similar very high risk and uncertainty. But as both businesses evolve, they proceed upon paths that diverge more and more.

Take an entrepreneurial business such as an innovative software company. The entrepreneurial company aspires to be national or global in reach and grow its revenues rapidly to attract venture capitalists, super angels, and most angel investors. The entrepreneurial software company comes up with an untested idea or hypothesis, such as my company, Questionmine. The first challenge is following the 7 Steps system to test a product and see if the Idea or the solutions solves the problem. You have to ask the following questions: Does the product solve a problem the market needs and the market recognizes its needs immediately? You need to educate the market to recognize the problem? Or will you need the problem? If the software solves a problem that the market wants us to solve or a need it wants us to satisfy then the result is called a problem/solution fit. Note that if you have to educate the market, then it will take longer and require more money (almost interchangeable with product/market fit)

The small business, unless mostly or all Internet-based, typically opens up to serve a local area, such as a candy store in our example. The candy store might have more unique offerings if it has to compete in a large city like New York. Or, the candy store could carry known national brands. Most likely, the candy store's success will rest upon the store's location unless it's the only store in town. Most of the other variables for success are pretty clear: parking, traffic, average cash register sale, look of the store on the outside and inside, etc.

Here's a critical distinction: the entrepreneur's vision, ultimate business plan, and financing, on average, will be radically different from the small business. For example, the entrepreneurial software business has enormous continuing uncertainty and risk, even if it achieves fast revenue growth, a large user base, multibillion-dollar valuations, and venture capitalist investors, such as Groupon or Zyna.

The question constantly haunting fast-growth companies remains the ability to have a business model that makes money, is sustainable, and can scale even if the business can sell shares or ownership in its business. For just these reasons, Groupon ousted its co-founder, Andrew Mason. Investors in high growth companies grow more and more impatient when the assumptions in the business plan do not materialize. One fundamental question which will be asked of Groupon: Did they have a business that could make money? If they did, then was it sustainable with the competition. For many companies to succeed over time, they must build and maintain what Buffett calls an economic moat—essentially, a monopoly, duopoly, or oligarchy dominant positioning such as Microsoft, Google, Amazon, or Apple.

The small business, such as a candy store, has a much clearer path to success as the necessary variables are more easily defined.

The investors in the entrepreneurial business often demand a crisp, neatly spelled-out candy store-like plan. They want to see the logic or the thinking processes of the entrepreneur. But in reality, the entrepreneur typically has no idea what will work, when, with which buyers, on which terms, or even what market type are he or she is competing with, such as a new product in a new market or a new product in an existing market. Webvan followed a clean, crisp product development plan and executed extremely well. But they never discovered and developed in advance who their true customers were and whether there were enough repeatable customers as well as new customer demand for their home ordering grocery system. In the dot-com boom and bust, Webvan scaled prematurely and blew through $800 million and went under. The investors assumed they had a could-not-miss, linear, traditional product development, candy-store-type company. Even with a sales track record, the uncertainties remain, as competition is global and fierce just as Groupon discovered with over 500 copycat businesses.

On the other hand, the investors in the candy store are equally unrealistic in their expectations and often expect strategies and business plans with the potential of a fast-growth entrepreneurial business. That doesn't make any sense, because the store has a relatively finite limit to what its traffic can produce in revenues and earnings. If a plan is mapped out for multiple candy stores or a franchise model, then such a plan becomes more the entrepreneurial non-candy-store type of business model. I want to make a third distinction. Starts-up are not small replicas of bigger, existing companies. Bigger existing companies already know their customers and their needs. They can specify in advance to engineering here is the product to build to meet my customers' needs. Start-ups don't know their customers and have no clear customer input as what they want the product to do in order to solve the customers problems. The problem/solution fit is only achieved when the business model—revenue, pricing and customer acquisition—satisfies the customers' needs or solve their pain.

So, the first question you need to be asking yourself as an investor is: What are the future expectations? Are my expectations tied to a true entrepreneurial business model or a true candy store business model or an entrepreneurial business model which I unrealistically want to look like a candy store? Or, are you mistakedly expecting a traditional bigger business linear product development model which focuses on product launch dates, marketing, scaling, and PR before you know your customers well? Are you assuming that the product solves the customer's needs without proof? Why do you and the start up believe it can make money? If the business model is sustainable works, do you believe it is with an unfair or competitive advantage? Once, you focus upon your expectations and how realistic they are, then you are in a better position to assess the following question: How much can my money grow if I invest in this company?

## ENTER THE CROWDFUNDING INVESTOR

With equity-based crowdfunding, investors have the chance to find and invest in the next Apple, Google, or Facebook. All these companies needed investors in their beginning stages. Why not you? One of the purposes of the JOBS Act is to let everyone have an equal opportunity to invest in a blockbuster deal. Why shouldn't you have the same opportunities to strike it rich as a well-connected venture capitalist?

In certain ways, crowdfunding investment reminds me of the growth of blogs. Years ago, certain TV and radio programs, magazines, and newspapers controlled what the public learned. It was mostly a one-way monologue. The same for large advertisers. The public's voice or opinions counted little. Content is often said to be king, and the large media and advertisers controlled its dissemination. But with the Internet, the average person or ordinary citizen could suddenly become a writer or journalist. Just set up a blog and post on it articles and/or videos on virtually any subject. Amateurs can compete with professional reporters in creating content for people.

With crowd fund equity, investing in start-up and later-stage companies has been opened up to what I call micro-angel investors—the average Joe, the general public. Crowdfunding equity provides an opportunity to take a small percentage of your investment portfolio money and attempt to get a very high return on investment. At the very least, it's an inexpensive way to educate yourself about investments, business, finance, and money management.

Once you understand the common fundamentals which underlie successful early-stage companies, you will better be able to spot the winners—companies and people—in other marketplaces. The same fundamentals apply. I have pointed out that as a company grows, each level of revenue triggers different challenges, problems, and solutions. For example, most companies which just start up have no more than an unproven idea. The challenge becomes turning the idea into a physical reality. In the beginning, the solution rests on one or more people to find the resources to create a physical prototype or perform a physical service if it's a service company. Prior to creating the prototype and at the same time, the company has to listen and discover what the customer truly wants and understand if the solution solves the customer's needs and problem. A company generating $10 million in revenue requires more people, more resources, products, publicity and more administrative systems than a company making $1 million in revenue.

Still, a business requires the same basic fundamentals: a sound business model (it makes money)—one that is sustainable and scalable—and a solid marketing and sales plan executable by the right team to keep growing. Plus, winning companies adhere to their core values, such as Zappos, which believes in happiness. Employees derive happiness through focusing upon exceeding customer expectations. Companies which succeed make decisions based upon sticking to their core values.

Southwest Airlines made all its key decisions based upon the core value of being a no-frills airline. If someone internally or externally proposed to management to add unnecessary costs, then the proposal would be rejected as not fitting the no-frills business model. But the no-frills policy did not mean Southwest Airlines' customers would have austere, bland flights. Instead, like Zappos, Southwest Airlines focuses upon the core value of flying being a happy, fun experience. Combining the core values of no frills and customer happiness set Southwest Airlines apart from its competition, besides its untraditional no-spoke-and-hub business model. Planes flew from Dallas to Houston to San Antonio—what Kelleher, the CEO, had written on a napkin as the business model.

When you evaluate a crowdfunding investment, you should assess the core values of the founders and whether they live by them. Look at their actions, not just their words. When you fit together the pieces of what the company is and its products are about, you have to ask yourself whether your crowdfunding investment goals are realistic!

Early-stage company investment remains a high-risk proposition. Many investors wrongly assume that high risk begets high return. In fact, high risk means just that: the chances are very high that you could lose all your money. Neither the amount of regulation nor the wisdom of the crowd will guarantee you that you will pick a winner.

As noted, investing in early-stage companies is complex. You might want to employ the same investment process venture capitalists, super angels, and angel investors use: invest in ten deals and hope one out of ten is a blockbuster hit. Most important, only invest the amount of money you can afford to lose.

## LOW RISK, NOT HIGH

Contrary to most stories on venture capitalists and start-up entrepreneurs as high risk takers, they are in fact the opposite—low risk takers. Entrepreneurs invest their money as well as venture capital. Both try to invest where the downside risk of their investment is minimal and the upside potential is very high.

Fundamental to starting up a business is moving the odds in your favor. As an entrepreneur, the more you lower risk, the more value you create. The more value you create, the easier it is to attract investor money, especially on attractive terms.

Most venture capitalists avoid seed investing in companies. They seek mostly to invest when a company's chances for success are clearer—such as paying customers and a clear demand for the product. On the other extreme is Warren Buffett, who looks for companies that the marketplace has undervalued. Buffett invests where there is a margin of safety between the value and the price of the company as a whole or shares of its stock, i.e., pay as much as possible below the value.

For example, say he assesses a stock's value at $10; he pays $6 for it and he waits for the market to recognize the stock's value and drive it up to the $10 value he calculated it was worth. From my experience, most highly successful investors—and entrepreneurs—find one undervalued deal that succeeds big. This normally gives them the capital and/or credibility to parlay that into more and more money.

Take the example of John Paulson. He was a careful investor, looking for the safest investments. One of Paulson's mentors was an investor, and, as Gregory Zuckerman writes in his book *The Greatest Trade*

*Ever*: "Marty Gruss drilled a maxim into Paulson: 'Watch the downside; the upside will take care of itself.' "

In the mid-2000s, Paulson became very suspicious of the real estate boom. Paulson studied the real estate market carefully. He and his team researched innumerable variables and realized that the market was in a housing bubble. The "crowd," which consisted of most of those on Wall Street, believed that for there to be a widespread mortgage default, a number of factors had to come together: "unemployment rates, interest rates, and regional economic health." The crowd assessed that the chances of these variables all occurring together was slim to none.

Paulson took a contrary position. He made what appeared to virtually everyone to be a crazy bet. He bet homeowners would default on their mortgages. Well, he was crazy like a fox. In 2007 alone, Paulson's company took in $15 billion in profits, of which $4 billion went directly into Paulson's pocket. In 2008, his firm made $5 billion. Rarely in human history has anyone made so much money in so short a time. Yet because he had studied the market thoroughly, he believed he had no downside risk. To Paulson, he had a sure thing. He had the margin of safety that Buffett and other top entrepreneurs seek—the top 1%—which others don't see. And these opportunities do not just fall into their lap. They are discovered by rigorous practice and preparation so that when the market misses value, they see it beneath all the noise of the crowd or the majority's opinion.

Now, if you step back, you can see another trait that lead to Paulson's extreme success. Paulson was an outsider. The outsider will beat the crowd in coming up with creative ideas and new concepts. Paulson saw an opportunity. The maverick entrepreneur or investor sees a perception of value that is a structural hole—the disequilibrium in the market—and seizes a unique opportunity that is much different than what the crowd sees.

You can employ the same strategy too. Think about the things you wish you could buy in your own life. For instance, Apple and other companies will be coming out with the capability to support high-speed 802.11ac networks, which will make the web much faster. The downside is, its speed won't go through walls or floors very well, limiting your router's Wi-Fi range. Will the current router giants be able to adapt, or should you be looking for a new product that does go through walls?

Such an idea may seem far-fetched, but it is ideas that seem improbable or risky to most that possess the makings of extreme success in investments and companies. You would think with so much information and global competition in the marketplace there would be few opportunities. The opposite is true because today entrepreneurs are combining and recombining ideas. For example, what if you discovered a new technology for asking questions while people viewed videos? Then you realized that many companies did not possess the ability to create videos. You might find an excellent video production company and form a partnership so you could offer a fuller solution to a potential user of your new video technology. Everyone wins—the video production house gets more business and you provide your customer the solution it needs. Joint ventures and alliances such as these enable companies to compete where alone they provide only a partial solution. To succeed as an investor or entrepreneur, constantly seek to find new combinations that the crowd does not see.

## INFORMATION YOU CAN TRUST

For the early-stage investor or entrepreneur, one obvious challenge stems from the lack of information (the unknown)—evidence that this deal will be the Next Big Thing. Ironically, the entrepreneur and the investor are both armed with tons of information on any subject or deal, like a car salesperson and a car buyer who researched the car and all its competitors online. The smart entrepreneur should know that technology has changed the investment landscape dramatically.

With the advance of the Internet has come an overwhelming amount of information. Too much information instantly accessed, such as from a Google search, has made investment both easier to research and access but harder to digest. For example, some of the biggest money makers online are video sales letters (slides made into video) and webinars—both virtual presentations and pitches—that are scripted to motivate you to buy stuff, such as how to get more traffic to your website or landing page.

Once you are told this information will give you an edge to get traffic ahead of the pack, you are motivated to buy. Why? Because an expert presenter you trust is endorsing a traffic expert's product, or you search the Internet for traffic solutions and find a video sales letter or webinar by someone who seems to have the traffic expertise. You watch the presentation and the person makes a convincing argument that you need the traffic-getting solution being sold. From either or both traffic presentations, you decide to make a purchase since you need more traffic.

What you are buying in reality is the interpretation of information. The person presenting is saving you the time to filter the numerous traffic—getting solutions in the marketplace.

But when there are too many solutions and you are unsure who to believe and trust, you may not buy any solutions. Paradoxically, even though information, technology, and innovation are moving faster and faster, the result many times is that things move slower. People's attention span and hours in a day are finite. For this reason, appointments, commitments, and decisions on purchases of products and services and investments get pushed out.

Time, speed, and overwhelming amounts of information and choices become the enemy of entrepreneurs and businesses, which require faster decisions from buyers, service providers, and investors. If you seek funding while you are starting up a company, then cash is being burned up waiting for sales to materialize and money to be invested.

Many shrewd venture capitalists and angels use time to their advantage. They drag the deal out for many reasons:

- Practical: They have too much on their plate already to manage their own current investments or businesses, since many angels still run their own companies.
- Wait and see: Do sales projected by the entrepreneur materialize?
- Get better terms: The more desperate the need for funds, the better terms can be negotiated.

The main risk for a venture capitalist is competing offers from other venture capitalists. He may try to counter the threat of competition by having the entrepreneur sign a term sheet which ties up the deal with due diligence contingencies. The due diligence on these deal contingencies can drag on, so time becomes the ally of the investor and the enemy of the entrepreneur, who continues to burn through cash. In addition, the entrepreneur has to juggle many variables, such as hiring key people and suppliers contingent on the money being invested.

To me, one of the key components in most businesses is staying power. Do you have enough money, resources, and information to carry the business and keep learning and implementing? The more you can move forward by bootstrapping your finances, the more you have the opportunity to reduce risk and increase value for yourself and the investor.

Just like the online business seeking traffic-getting secrets, most investors and entrepreneurs alike are seeking specialized or inside information that gives them the edge or Buffett's margin of safety or Paulson's sure thing.

The challenge becomes finding information you can trust. Does it come from your own research, business partners, employees, other stakeholders, advisers, and/or mentors? The challenge and excitement of being an entrepreneur and an investor in early-stage companies is how well you can listen, learn, and experiment in a constantly changing, uncertain environment. How can you find the sure thing? Think about how the press reports almost daily on scandals regarding inside information. Why? Because possessing inside information creates sure-thing opportunities. Who wouldn't want to know about an acquisition by one public company of another at a 50% premium over what the stock currently trades at? Who wouldn't desire to have a special political connection that gives them a way to obtain information and relationships that give a government contract over competitors? Many of the most successful entrepreneurs succeeded because of special knowledge, information, and relationships—not because of being great innovators or pioneers. In the next chapter we'll explore these ideas further—so you can get the money.

## TAKEAWAYS AND INSIGHTS

- The fundamental difference between equity-based crowdfunding versus crowdfunding donations with rewards is that you own a piece of the company and the upside. In equity-based crowdfunding you can lose all your money, some of it, break even, make some or make a lot.
- Investing in early-stage companies is high risk, and high risk does not mean you get high returns. Depending upon which study you read, you can lose all of your money 50% to 75% of the time. Only 10% of the time do you make blockbuster returns.
- The reason for the high losses is that start-ups have very limited knowledge or input from their customers as to what the customers want to solve a problem or satisfy a need. As a result, the start-up is guessing or creating a hypothesis as to whether their Idea or solution is valid.
- To prove their hypothesis or not, the startup should interview potential customers, and from their input build a minimal viable product with the minimum features and test it.
- The confusion for most investors is that they want all pitches and investments to be the entrepreneur high-growth or blockbuster model.
- They expect the executive summary to be written like a traditional large company would, where its customer and market type is known. This is exactly the opposite of a start-up, which does not know either well and is guessing.
- Or, they expect a simplified physical candy-store type pitch where by virtue of the location and the products, the market and customer is better defined. Here is the risk is still high, but the potential to be a blockbuster hit in one location is rare.

- Testing your hypothesis is a process of testing face-to-face the elements of your business model—does the customer want these product or service features, will they pay for it and at what price? With testing, you are seeking evidence as to whether your hypothesis valid.
- You are breaking down each component of the business into elements you can test, such as product, customers revenue models (pricing) cost structures, strategic partners, distribution channels you are testing the value proposition (USP), your unique selling strategy (USS), your market type, and your sales process.
- All these elements make up your various pitches and tell the investor at what stage of development your company is. Clearly, the earlier the stage the more uncertainty and risk for the investor.
- Equity-crowdfunding does not remove the uncertainty or risk of a start-up, but the crowd's feedback may accelerate the testing of the hypotheses or the product.

Click here for additional resources: http://bit.ly/1dJRRq8

CHAPTER 13

# CROWDFUNDING: THE PROMISE OF PUBLIC INFORMATION

Crowdfunding's true promise rests upon the power of the Internet to globally connect people and information related to financing companies in a revolutionary way. Up to now, early-stage companies have had only limited means to expose themselves to pools of investors on the Internet.

Crowdfunding donations with rewards opened up the possibilities of everyday people backing companies and projects in return for getting rewards or products at presale discounts. Likewise, product and business launches revealed how you could market and sell products and services on the Internet directly or through selling groups such as affiliates or joint ventures.

In varying degrees, these selling methods gave a certain amount of information out about the companies and their projects. Still, the standards of disclosure were not fully regulated other than the laws of commerce.

With crowdfunding equity and the ability to advertise and generally solicit private placements, the required level of disclosure of information will be ratcheted up by the Securities and Exchange Commission, since a sale of a security will be available to the public—non-accredited investors and accredited investors alike.

At the heart of the computer, Internet, web social, and mobile evolution is connectivity, the speed of information flow, the relationships which form around the information, and the information's quality, relevance, and transparency.

Although what I just said may sound like a mouthful, you need to realize that at its core, getting money and building businesses rests upon the quality of the relationships and who controls information or content and its distribution and interpretation.

The promise of crowdfunding equity is standardizing and/or mandating as best as possible the disclosure of financial and company information, educating the public about investment risks, compressing time, and avoiding to a degree drag-out investor strategies that force the entrepreneur or small businessperson into a desperate position. With crowdfunding, you can set the terms, including the term of the offer, e.g., 90 days to raise the money. Crowdfunding equity compresses the marketing and selling (presenting and pitching) deals and validates and builds businesses at the same time.

The entrepreneur seeking funding quickly gets feedback on the status of his/her funding and how investors and customers view the products or services being offered.

Along with the disclosure of information, "time" becomes the operative word. Time really is money. Time turns into money in early-stage investing when an entrepreneur earns trust and competence. The way the entrepreneur earns the trust is by how he/she presents and pitches information. What is known about the products and services and the company being offered to investors? How much has the entrepreneur discovered and learned about who his customers are, the problem of his customers, and the solution he provides?

The entrepreneur has to earn the trust of potential investors and customers by demonstrating competence. In turn the trust and competence become the foundations for relationships. Relationships are the new currency. The crowd becomes your relationships. Thus, the crowd becomes your stakeholders: your investors, who often become your customers. Even though what I am stating may seem very general, you can test what I am saying very quickly.

Ask yourself right now: What do you think is holding back financing your business or attracting or growing your customer base? You will find that your stumbling blocks rest upon the trust and competence of your information as reflected in your products and services. Your products and services are a bundle of information stating how they will solve a problem or need of a customer. If you have a valuable solution, then you have to distribute it and create awareness.

This takes time, money, and the right message to the right audience. Crowdfunding's promise is to accelerate your information—your trust and competence—to a larger audience more efficiently and in a resulting lower price.

## THE TIME TO PIVOT

Time also means the ability to change based upon the discovery and learning from the information derived from iterative testing of the ideas, educated guesses, or hypotheses about who customers are, what their needs are, and what solutions you can offer. The first tests are to find if there is a true demand for the company's products and a way to make money profitably. Next, is this business model sustainable against the competition—a sustainable competitive advantage? Then, can the company scale? At every stage of its development, the company and its stakeholders must keep asking these questions.

To succeed, businesses, especially seed, start-up, or early-stage, must or change interatively as they test their hypothesis and sometimes, change dramatically called a pivot, as Eric Ries defines it in *The Lean Startup*. "The pivot—what do successful companies have in common? Pivot is the ability to change direction quickly. The difference between a successful and unsuccessful start-up is the number of pivots a start-up makes before it dies."

Here's the critical point: the crowd—your relationships—have to trust you and your abilities—to allow you to pivot time and time again. Fundamental to the 7 Step process I have been advocating for each stage of your business's development cycle is your ability to go back and forth among the various steps to evaluate whether you should move forward iteratively or dramatically and pivot. For example, does your Discovery step confirm that you know your customers' needs and problems well enough to begin creating a physical prototype? If you are pitching the crowd in crowdfunding, then your learning from your Discovery step becomes part of your hero's journey of searching for a better solution to a problem and your struggle to find it.

When Ash Maurya, in his book *Running Lean*, describes three stages of a start-up, he focuses on a key question: How do I accelerate growth? Here's a critical insight Maurya makes: "Before product/market fit, the focus of a start-up centers on *learning and pivots*. After product/market fit, the focus shifts toward growth and optimization... the best way to differentiate pivots from optimization is that pivots are able finding a plan that works while optimization is about accelerating that plan."

## VENTURE CAPITALISTS, ENTREPRENEURS, AND TRUST

Crowdfunding will change the power structure or control VCs have over early-stage companies. VCs will not be replaced, but they will find themselves to be forced to be more transparent and flexible in their funding approaches since there will be a much larger pool of capital available. By analogy, think of the three major TV networks, the advent of cable TV, and now online TV, such as Hulu. Think of the Internet, music distribution, Apple, and iTunes. Think of local banks to global banks to online banking and the resulting consolidation and efficiencies. As the Internet opens up global connections and a more open flow of information to fund companies, the best of VCs will remain. They will have to adjust to the new environment crowdfunding brings. VCs and angel investors will benefit from the new information disclosed by start-ups and its organization on crowdfunding portals.

Currently, too often venture capitalist or angel investors breed mistrust. They attempt to control the deal with their money and terms. Often, they invest too much money into deals before there is true proof of real demand for a product or whether that demand is sustainable. Part of lacking the proof is the risk they take. But part is a model of investing too much into a business model before it is truly tested. This locks the VC and the entrepreneur into a business model that doesn't work or is not sustainable and/or scalable. The entrepreneur and the VC out of hubris or stupidity refuse to pivot or transform and go under.

In time, new models will evolve from crowdfunding, where there will be more smaller rounds based upon achieving milestones before the larger VC rounds of funding.

In Stephen M. R. Covey's book *The Speed of Trust*, his father, Stephen Covey, in the introduction states that "low trust causes friction, whether it is caused by unethical behavior or by ethical but incompetent behavior (because even good intentions can never take the place of bad judgments)...Low trust slows everything—every decision, every communication, and every relationship...On the other hand, trust produces speed...the greatest trust-building key is results. Results build brand loyalty...cause customers to increase their reorders...compel them to consistently recommend you to others. Thus, your customers become your key promoters, your key sales and marketing people."

This is in essence the promise of crowdfunding. An entrepreneur must build a trusting crowd of investors/customers who will provide the money and latitude to pivot constantly or transform your business.

A major risk of crowdfunding is: How long will the crowd remain supportive of the entrepreneur if they do not see results that meet their expectations? In effect, the entrepreneur fueled by crowd fund investors is running a quasi-public company and is accountable to the "shareholders." One of the key skills to succeed in crowdfunding equity is open communication to all stakeholders. So, as an investor, that's what you're looking for. Are you getting enough information about how the business is growing, or are you getting the equivalent of the bureaucratic run-around?

## RELATIONSHIPS: THE NEW CURRENCY

Marketers have done a lot of research on what's called the stakeholder–focus advantage. This takes customer-focused marketing strategies to another level. Raj Sisodia, Jag Sheth, and David B. Wolfe, in the book *Firms of Endearment*, reveal that if companies want to outperform their competitors, they must understand the demographic shift of baby boomers who want to be treated as *being* customers, not *having* customers. This shift not only addresses how customers (the crowd) will buy in the future, but how products will be designed and how they will be pitched.

As I have been emphasizing, the lines between customers and investors are becoming more and more blurred. Add to the word *customers* the word *investors.*

They write, "Companies that used this *Firms of Endearment* approach by openly communicating with all stakeholders and treating them as human beings more than a means to profits and shareholder value outperformed comparative S&P 500 companies over a ten-year period ending June 30, 2006, 1,026% versus 122%, or eight to one! For a five-year period, the ratio is even higher, 128% for *Firms of Endearment* versus the S&P 500, 13%."

In other words, qualitatively trusting relationships turn into significant profits and ROI. Marketing and truly communicating openly by listening and participating in an active dialogue is the paradigm shift that crowdfunding equity represents. Entrepreneurs must understand that money raising will shift more and more to creative marketers and communicators who can emotionally engage and build relationships with a crowd of stakeholders.

## THE REVOLUTION IN ACTION

With all the hoopla about crowdfunding equity, I decided to examine how crowdfunding equity currently works. I visited the website Crowdcube.com in the United Kingdom, where crowdfunding equity is legal. On the site, you find an infographic with some interesting stats:

- Total amount successfully funded: 5,333,000£ ($8 million plus)
- Number of businesses funded: 39
- Average amount invested: 2,547£ ($3,820)
- Successfully funded businesses—stage of growth

| Funded Pitches | | Average Valuation | Average Equity Offering |
|---|---|---|---|
| 1. Start-up | 30% | $574,095 | 22% |
| 2. Early state | 40% | $1,245,100 | 18% |
| 3. Growth | 30% | $3,774,900 | 10% |

4. Investments by time of day: 8 to 12 p.m., 28%
   12 p.m. to 6 pm, 49%
   6 p.m. to 12 am, 19%
   12 a.m. to 8 am, 4%

- By category: the largest number were in retail, food and drink, professional services, Internet, technology, and health and fitness
- Average investment amount requested: $209,290
- Largest number of investors: 394
- Average number of investors: 66
- Job creation (the number of employees three years after successful funding): 918
- Pitches funded by day: Wednesday 17%, Thursday 23%, Friday 20%, Saturday 17%, Sunday 11%, Monday 6%, Tuesday 6%
- Percentage of investors self–certified as high net worth or sophisticated, 44%
- Entrepreneur Profile: average age, 40. Youngest funded, 20. Oldest funded, 69. Of the 39 funded: male 35, female 4.

These investor and deal statistics reflect the relationship between risk, stage of company development, and valuation, which I have discussed. For example, the earlier the stage in a company's development, the more uncertainty and risk, the lower the valuation, the lower amount of money attracted, and the higher amount of equity ownership given up. In the United Kingdom, the average deal size was not large— $209,290; the average number of investors was 66 and the average investment per investor was $3,820. The largest single investment was $150,000; 22% invested more than once and the largest investment portfolio was 22 deals.

On Crowd Cube the use of the terms "funded pitches" and "total amount invested in pitches" confirms that getting the money relates to the pitch process: how well the deal is presented, by whom, and its terms. In fact, on Crowd Cube's home page, there is a large call-to-action green button with white letters that say "Search Pitches."

If you click on "Case Studies," you find a company such as Escape the City (a website that helps professionals to make a career transition), which raised $900,000 in 14 days from 394 investors for a 24% stake in their company. Even Crowd Cube's videos are labeled "Pitch Video."

In the Escape the City pitch video, you are emotionally drawn immediately into the video (two minutes, twelve seconds) by some cool graphics, a pleasant voice, and the *story* of Dom Jackson and Rob Symington, who quit their management consultancy jobs in order to set up the business. They felt that a lot of people with great skills are stuck in corporate jobs and are seeking something different and better in their lives. Their video shows a slide exactly halfway through (one minute, six seconds) that reads: "Find that job; start that business; go on that big adventure." Escape the City wants "to help ambitious professionals make exciting career transitions...a community of 65,000 escapees...life is too short to do work that doesn't matter to you."

Escape the City underscored another critical insight to build your business: "The alternative to a LinkedIn profile, shifting from being a site that focuses on content to one that focuses upon networking."

An early-stage business must be open constantly to the marketplace's feedback and be nimble and flexible to pivot when necessary. To get critical feedback from customers, suppliers, and other potential stakeholders, the entrepreneur, CEO, other founders, or heads of any organization or project must get out and network. The same holds for investors. To discover and learn, you must incorporate social networking into your personal life to learn about yourself and how to relate to many different types of people and personalities and what makes them tick. Likewise for your business career, you must network online and offline to stay tuned to the marketplace's pulse and find the best opportunities to invest, to drum up business, or to make career changes.

One warning when it comes to networking online or offline. Everyone has an opinion, and many people are conformists and have a crowd or herd mentality. You must refine the ability to look at patterns of behavior or consistent problems beneath the rhetoric, which can spell opportunities for your business or you. By being discerning, you weigh the feedback you receive from potential customers or partners. You don't keep changing your products, business model, or career without any deliberation. But on the other hand, don't get locked into methods or things which are not working. In the end, you must challenge yourself and your assumptions constantly, even daily. You must face the unknowns, test them repeatedly, and make decisions which are not perfect but keep advancing your product, business model, and team to a level which customers will buy and investors will invest.

Escape the City succeeded because it had a good business model that had an emotional appeal: examine your life and career and make sure you live the life you want by choosing a career that excites you. Another emotional hook was mentioned in their story: to gain their own flexibility and better terms, Escape the City raised their $900,000 two weeks after turning down two offers of venture capital funding. They found better terms from the crowd than the VCs. Surely, the crowd emotionally must have liked the courage of the founders.

As I mentioned, this turning away from VCs to crowdfunding equity exhibited by Escape the City is not an isolated occurrence. I believe it foreshadows the coming challenge to the venture capitalist and angel groups whose terms may be too onerous or whose due-diligence process or time to fund may be too lengthy and expensive. VCs and angel capital groups will be forced to change their ways to stay more competitive as alternative sources of capital such as crowdfunding equity emerge. Again, VCs and angel capital groups will not disappear, but their methods will need to be more transparent, and they too, like entrepreneurs, will need to be more agile and flexible in their approaches to business as well.

Another crowdfunding equity site, Funded By Me in Sweden, states it's an "entrepreneur's best friend, connecting entrepreneurs with everyday business angels globally. Entrepreneurs seek guidance and funding for their start-ups and people want to be part of the next big thing.

Crowdfunding equity is bridging the gap between the crowd and a great idea ('start bridging the gap today' is our call to action button)."

Funded By Me, in its "How Does It Work" section, states:

> Entrepreneurs present their start-ups online. It works in two phases, "pre-round" and "open round." Pre-round is where people sign up their interest to be involved in the company.
>
> Entrepreneurs receive all the relevant data to then make educated decisions on how to validate their ideas and what the market is willing to pay.
>
> Going from "pre-round" to "open round" entrepreneurs convert pre round into actual capital."
>
> We believe that 200 people that invest smaller amounts are far better than two to three angels. Mostly because decisions on smaller amounts are easier and faster to make but also because 200 crowd angels can add value to your company and make it grow/spread faster and wider. We see the world moving toward simpler rules to raise capital...Investing in start-up and early stage businesses can be rewarding if you can invest in a start-up before it's well known and profits start to take off.

Under "submitting a start-up," Funded by Me requires the same basic deal elements I have covered: executive summary, business plan, financial projections, presentation of you and your team, how you will make money (business model), and a clear time line: a start and an end.

What Funded by Me points out is that the 90-day period is one of intense marketing where "your job is to talk to everybody, to tell the world about your round and convince them to be part of your idea." In other words network, pitch, and promote your deal to as many people as you can. But remember, the secret of getting the money lies in the preparation, practice, and building of your initial audience or crowd *before you launch your crowdfunding campaign.*

Here's the bottom line from Funded by Me: "A good story, a great team and an active project manager are key!" Plus all the pre-launch preparation I just mentioned and have reiterated throughout the book.

As I review the number of crowdfunding equity projects on Funded by Me in the open round, such as Crowd Murex (an online stock exchange from micro units of real estate) and A Private Story (an international film project—the true story of the largest Adult Entertainment Empire), I quickly realized the dizzying amount of information that companies can provide and investors must sift through. Many of these companies are just seed-idea companies and start-ups.

The problem of crowdfunding will be truly how to get the attention of, engage, and get feedback from investors. For investors the challenge will be how to interact with companies, rate and rank them, and decide which companies in which to invest.

I also noticed that the crowdfunding investor has few means to interact with the management and truly visit with them. For this reason, I believe crowdfunding equity sites will need to provide interactive live and recorded pitches and presentations with the ability for companies to ask questions of investors and investors in turn to respond and ask their own questions of the company's management. By this interactive process online or by mobile phone, companies and investors will give each other immediate feedback and compress the decision-making and investment process. Companies will be able to screen and score which investors are most interested, just as if they'd screened prospects or customers online or via mobile phones using interactive mobile video (see Questionmine.com).

From these few examples of crowdfunding in the United Kingdom and in Sweden, you can see how the new world of crowdfunding equity is unfolding. Changes in technology, the law, and networking will continue to evolve as this source of seed capital becomes more and more available to fledgling companies. Make no mistake. The revolution is under way. The question is: Are you in or are you out? Will you wait or get in ahead of the crowd and ride the massive wave of new sources of capital which soon will be available globally through online, social, and mobile sites?

## HOW TO WIN AT CROWDFUNDING EQUITY

Crowdfunding equity's ultimate purpose is to make raising capital more efficient and effective. As the crowdfunding equity site Funded by Me stated, its role is to close the gap between the investor and the entrepreneur.

When you first think of crowdfunding or any early-stage funding challenges, you might naturally think of the challenges of the entrepreneur, small businessperson, or creative type attempting to raise capital. The VC or the angel investor has the money and, as the saying goes, "He who has the gold rules."

But as you might have seen in *The Voice, Shark Tank*, and *The Taste*, the judges or investors must also pitch the contestants or entrepreneurs—in the case of *Shark Tank*, if more than one judge wants a certain contestant on her team or to invest in the contestant's deal.

Take *The Taste*. The season begins with blind auditions of both professional and amateur cooks during which four judges, who double as mentors, taste one spoonful of food from each contestant prior to knowing who cooked it or what all the ingredients are. Each judge decides whether or not she would like the contestant on her team by pressing a button (green for yes or red for no); the buttons are hidden from the other judges (although some decisions are revealed to the home audience). The four then meet the contestant and press a button to reveal their votes. If exactly one judge votes yes, that contestant automatically joins that judge's four-member team. *If more than one judge votes yes, the contestant chooses between them.* Note my italics. The roles reverse and the contestant listens to the pitch of the judge or Shark.

In today's evolving crowdfunding and private placement world, the investor must not only know how to evaluate an early-stage investment, including how to cut through pitches, but also how to pitch to get the best deals offered.

In crowdfunding equity, the investor must use the Pitch, Pre-Marketing, Social Marketing, and Persuasion to attract deals, get other investors to co-invest, conduct research and due diligence, and understand the strengths and weaknesses of the entrepreneur.

What the investor must know and ask of the entrepreneur, the investor must ask of himself or herself. Does the investor know enough of the investment process to assess the entrepreneur and, in turn, use the process to invest with other investors or get other investors to invest with him or her?

The process of investing in start-ups and early-stage companies is no longer an isolated one. If you as an investor want to increase the odds of making great investments, then you too have to get out, network, observe, and test different investment approaches too.

In evaluating a deal, an investor must ask whether the entrepreneur and he or she, as the investor, have the ability to:

1. Pitch
2. Propose
3. Plan
4. Project numbers
5. Produce on time

You as the investor will see deals offered on a crowdfunding equity portal site. The deals presented will include videos, FAQs, and other deal information. You may see an ad about the deal for private placement or an article or a PR release. But the question arises: How do you find out more about the company and the founders and then interact with them? In which case would you want to pitch them to get more involved with the company as advisers or mentors? Or, how do you determine whether the company or its founders know how to pitch and engage a following or crowd? To do this, you an entrepreneur must know how a person or company builds a platform and spreads the word about itself.

## HOW TO BUILD A PLATFORM

More and more, I believe for companies to succeed, they must view themselves as multimedia companies. They have to know how to engage, entertain, and educate. As an investor, you must understand this new business model where entrepreneurs must be entertainers and educators and crowd pleasers—essentially, have a high social and emotional intelligence. Entrepreneurs or members of their team must be able to relate to people and transfer their story to their company and products. In effect, entrepreneurs are artists and authors.

An instructive guide comes from the world of books, where building customer relations has long been crucial to a book's success, especially a nonfiction book. According to former CEO of Harper Collins Jane Friedman, well known for revolutionizing the book business over the course of her ten years at the top, publishers first look at what is called the author's platform. She writes:

> They're looking for someone with visibility and authority who has proven reach to a target audience.
>
> Let's break this down further.
>
> - **Visibility**. Who knows you? Who is aware of your work? Where does your work regularly appear? How many people see it? How does it spread? Where does it spread? What communities are you a part of? Who do you influence? Where do you make waves?
> - **Proven reach**. It's not enough to *say* you have visibility. You have to show where you make an impact and give proof of engagement. This could be quantitative evidence (e.g., size of your email newsletter list, website traffic, blog comments) or qualitative evidence (high-profile reviews, testimonials from A-listers in your genre).
> - **Target audience**. You should be visible to the most receptive or appropriate audience for the work you're trying to sell.

You can apply these same principles as an entrepreneur or an investor. In today's world of relationships, hard selling does not achieve results. It's more likely to annoy customers. You cannot build relationships overnight, or bank on a one-time event. Relationships come from a company putting in a consistent, focused effort over the course of time. If one of a company's key selling points is that it understands how to build a platform—relationships/customers—like a successful author, then you as an investor have an indication that the company knows part of the process to develop customers and make money.

In the end, all successful companies have the same goal—a happy, growing customer base that loves the company and the brand.

Customer-centric companies like Amazon and Apple create a memorable, delightful experience. In each role that makes up an organization, a company's personnel has different skills, talent, and know-how. But more and more, relationships—and trust—have to be the combined thrust of their efforts. Social media is the new marketing. Pitching, presenting, and networking are the means to building relationships in business, and both the investor and the entrepreneur must master those skills to succeed, make a lot of money, and make the world a better place to live.

## EVALUATE ANY OPPORTUNITY IN MINUTES

How do you figure out what idea is worth investing your money, your time, your sweat equity in? If you are an entrepreneur, how do you road test a product? How do you develop it?

I am going to restate and elaborate more on my Magical Ps formula that eliminates 90% of all opportunities as not worth your while. You just shouldn't waste your time on deals that make no sense, nor get involved as an entrepreneur or small businessperson in ventures that have little chance of succeeding from the very beginning.

I have honed the process to the point that I am typically able to look at and eliminate most opportunities in three minutes or less.

The first thing you are seeking is ownership and control of assets to build wealth. Remember that you build wealth through ownership. You have to have an opportunity to make money—hopefully a lot of money—if you are investing or building a start-up or early-stage company. If you get such an opportunity offered to you, then you want to own as much of that opportunity as possible within your means, abilities, and risk tolerance.

In this age of speed, where time is so valuable, wouldn't you want to be able to look at an opportunity and see quickly whether it makes sense to put your time, money, and resources into it or forget the opportunity?

The Magical Ps is the fastest way I know to evaluate a deal or potentially build wealth. As I have stated, I start out looking at three essential words that begin with the letter P. This may seem simplistic, but when these magical Ps are put together and combined in the right way and made into a reality, they can create lots of value and often fortunes.

The three essential Magical Ps are:

- People
- Product
- Potential

You can eliminate almost every transaction based on just asking if these three P's exist in an opportunity you are reviewing and evaluating.

**People:** A company begins and ends with people, and so I immediately look at who's involved. Who is going to implement the idea? Are they the right people or wrong people? If, for instance, the company founders are not the right people with the right talents, the chances of succeeding are much less.

When I refer to people, though, I don't mean just the founders. Look at the employees; the people in the supply chain; the investors; the customers. You have to access the collective people within or surrounding the organization.

Jim Collins, who wrote the famous business book *Good to Great*, believes that the key to a great company is a great team. In his famous formula, you need the right people in the right place at the right time driving the right bus.

Other business experts believe that a company's success is more a matter of having a great idea, not a great team—that investors ultimately are attracted to the idea, and a hot sector that can make up for many errors.

Under certain circumstances, you could have an average idea and talented team and maybe have a chance of success, especially if the average idea is in a hot sector, such as mobile video. Yes. Why? Answer: a talented team will study the average idea and continually strategize how to better it. They will continue to discover, learn about the idea or concept, talk to potential customers, and pivot or transform the business idea until they find the right customers, the right product, and the right product/market fit, a repeatable business model and one which the team can scale when these key business elements are in place.

But if you have a great idea and poor people, the chances are slim that you'll realize the fortune you're looking to make. Why? Because there are thousands of ideas. Even a great idea has to be implemented by a team of people and stakeholders. Potential customers still must be found and their needs and problems solved by a product. A team which has limited skills will find it very difficult to implement even a great idea.

In sum, the magical P representing people looks for the talented team with the skill sets to implement the idea into a minimal viable product by working from the outset with potential customers to discover and learn what they need and want.

**Product**: The second P is the product or service itself. From the team's customer development process, customer needs and wants are translated to the product developers. The minimal viable product is created, tested, made to work, and then sold.

The Product questions are: What does this product or service do and what are its benefits? Will it attract enough people to buy it? But even more important, will they use the product and become repeat customers and/or refer other customers to you?

I have covered this topic extensively in earlier chapters, but again: Is this something you think a limited niche audience or a mass audience would want to buy? Is the product aimed at the business-to-business market (B2B), and what size businesses? Or, is the product targeting consumers (B2C)? Whether you choose a B2B or B2C strategy greatly affects your marketing, sales, and capital needs. B2B companies normally have much longer sales cycles, since the more people in a company who must decide on a purchase, the larger the cost to the company. B2C requires creating numerous relationships online and offline, which may require very large marketing budgets to educate consumers and more money to service them and maintain their loyalty, building a brand consumers can trust.

**Potential:** The third P is what I call the potential. What's the basic offer and what's the potential? Does the company have the potential for a product or products that can be sold at a profit, sustain its profitability (most want, with few exceptions, high gross margins), get repeat orders, and scale?

The potential is the future stream of cash flow. The question becomes for an investor: How do you evaluate the risk and uncertainty of those projected future cash flows ever becoming a reality? From your evaluation, how do you value the company today, and what percentage of the company should you own to get the rate of return on your capital for putting it at risk?

When evaluating a deal, investors use a quick formula similar to what you hear Kevin O'Leary of *Shark Tank* use. For example, if Ryan, the Rodeo Abs trainer, says he is offering a 25% stake in his company for a $120,000 investment, then he is valuing his company at $120,000/.25 = $480,000, or four times the investment.

Another way of doing this calculation: You can turn the percentage of ownership offered into a fraction, e.g., 25% (ownership offered) equals ¼, or 20% (ownership offered) equals 1/5. Then invert (turn upside down) the fraction so ¼ become 4/1, or 4, and 1/5 becomes 5/1, or 5, which becomes the multiple. Thus, 25% of a company equals four times the investment amount (4 x $120,000) and 20% of the company equals five times the investment amount (5 x 120,000 = $600,000). The less percentage ownership being offered, the higher the company is being valued. For example, if Ryan had offered a 10% interest, or 1/10, or ten times, then he would be valuing his company at $1,200,000 (10 x $120,000).

Next, the investor has to project into the future and predict in three to five years how much the company could be worth. If the company is at the seed stage or just starting up, then the investor may require ten times the return, or $1,200,000. So, if the investor calculates if he owns 25% of the company in five years, then the company would have to be worth $4.8 million (4 x $1,200,000). The investor may feel that in five years the company will be worth $2.4 million and thus ask for 50% ownership (half of $2.4 million gets him his $1.2 million, or ten times the $120,000 investment being asked).

To achieve this, the investor may negotiate for a greater percentage of ownership of the company and/or ask for other terms to protect his investment on the downside and upside. On *Shark Tank*, the Sharks are asking their questions to come to whether they believe in the people, product, and potential. If they do, then they do this math.

All these questions and calculations go into assessing the deal and its potential. As part of potential, they ask often ask what is proprietary—do you have patents? What's the competitive advantage—the economic moat around it that creates the value in the eyes of the customers and stakeholders and protects the value proposition?

To remind you, the value proposition of the product has four components:

1. What does the product do?
2. How much is it?
3. What's in it for the customer?
4. Why should I believe you?

## THE BUY-IN PROCESS AND THE MAGICAL PS

The magical Ps represent and reflect a shorthand formula to evaluate a process that investors, entrepreneurs, and other stakeholders go through to assess the extreme uncertainty and risk of early-stage companies at different points in their life cycle. At each stage from seed investment to an IPO or sale, the investor and entrepreneur are evaluating the people, product, and potential to make a go or no-go decision.

Tied to this evaluation process is another process—the buy-in process, which investors, entrepreneurs, and all other stakeholders constantly weigh. Should I get involved with company and stay involved for monetary or non-monetary reasons or both.

The process of buy-in never stops. A company always wants more and more people (stakeholders) to buy in. Customers, investors, suppliers, the media, even the employees. The buy-in process is ongoing in business and wealth building. Enlisting people is like building the foundation of an asset. To have them buy in, you must make them see the value for their efforts. Everyone (all stakeholders) involved with a company has to buy in to some value proposition the entrepreneur, creative type, or small business has in an offer.

Each stakeholder at the most basic level becomes a buyer of the entrepreneur's, idea, products, and potential. The buyer (the stakeholder) wants a return on investment, and the seller wants a return on investment. Both parties are coming to make an exchange of value. When the customer or stakeholder doesn't get the anticipated return, the customer or stakeholder disappears.

Deals, buy-in, and ongoing relationships depend upon maintaining and increasing buy-in, both face to face and online.

The potential also looks toward the future. This simple sentence contains the essence of what all investment relationships and businesses turn on. Uncertainty and risk virtually always exist in some form, along with change and time. Just because a product delivers value today doesn't mean it's going to deliver the same perceived value in another few years. Competitors come in. Markets change. Customers want change. A company wants its advantage to be sustainable.

When you look to build wealth, you must strategize like a chess player what moves you will make months in advance.

A company has to be flexible. What is the competition today and in the future? Newton's Law says: For every action there's a reaction. When a new product comes into the market, what's the existing competition going to do? They're not going to sit still. If the competition responds, then the new company must respond and keep stakeholders from getting anxious and losing faith as the competitive battles heat up.

The competitive advantage can be eroded. As a result a company's cash flow can decline, its margins can go down, and the money machine shrink—and so does the value of the company, employee stock options, and the investment of the investors.

All these variables affect buy-in, stakeholder morale, and a company's potential. There is no guaranteed way to combat competition or ensure the future that an early-stage company projects. But the best companies, such as Google, Amazon, and Apple, stay tuned to the marketplace and are constantly being innovative by getting out, discovering, listening to customers and stakeholders, keeping them engaged, and constantly buying in to the value proposition the company offers.

## INVEST WHERE YOU ARE

I want to address one last area of crowdfunding equity—local investing. Even though crowdfunding equity opens up money raising on the Internet, the greatest benefit may be to local businesses and communities. Most businesses initially attract local investors, who can visit the small business owner and spend a lot of face-to-face time. The up-close buy-in as well as the Internet and virtual marketing, selling, and capital raising seem to be the best combination for attracting capital and building a business.

The biggest secret to capital raising is very similar to attracting customers. Both investors and customers want social proof that the product works as promised and that others can vouch for this. This requires often an immense amount of time, money, and resources to break through this chicken-and-egg dilemma. Customers want proof, but you need the customers first to give the proof. Investors similarly want proof and often wait to invest until they feel there is enough proof that the product works, can be sold at a profit, and can scale.

That's why most companies can benefit from local input. Local investors and customers are easier to meet, strategize, and assist in getting the company off the ground. Most companies and communities can benefit from local input.

For this reason, crowdfunding equity will not be a get-rich-quick scheme. In the beginning, like other experiments, there may be an initial surge of money until the reality of the risks and rewards of crowdfunding becomes more apparent. To this end, make sure the crowdfunding company—with few exceptions—can demonstrate local investor and community (regional and state as well, depending on the specific business) support and involvement.

## CROWDFUNDING EQUITY AND REGULATION

With all the excitement and buy-in generated by the passage of the JOBS Act, crowdfunding associations, and mostly positive press, there remains, as with early-stage investments, lots of uncertainty and risks.

The positive big promise of crowdfunding is finding lots of exciting opportunities in which to invest and helping entrepreneurs, small businesspeople, and creative types to access a new source of capital and/or be aware of a host of new companies with which to collaborate.

But with all this excitement, you must remember that whatever the government gives, it can take back or convey with many strings attached. It is my fear and concern that the government will decrease the promised value of crowdfunding by imposing overregulation and costs.

My own observation is that the SEC truly does not want crowdfunding equity. It expands what the SEC wants to reduce: investors being defrauded. Additionally, the Internet brings an incredible number of variables that can overwhelm any group of people. There is no way the SEC has the resources and expertise to police crowdfunding equity adequately.

Besides the promoters—the entrepreneurs and the funding portals—the SEC must regulate directly or indirectly the service providers—lawyer, accountants, consultants—who may defraud or take advantage of the entrepreneurs, small businesspeople, and creative types themselves.

Already there are numerous crowdfunding organizations, professionals, and consultants—some very visible—that truly lack the expertise in raising capital up to $1 million for companies.

Because the SEC's lack of trust and the resources required by law to undertake crowdfunding equity, I feel the cost of crowdfunding will be much higher than what it appears. The costs such as accounting reviews and audits, compliance with documents, creating presentations, and social media marketing and will amount to running a quasi-public company. Few entrepreneurs have the experience to handle the demands of running a quasi-public company and building one at the same time by a few that have the expertise—even if experienced entrepreneurs.

In the next chapter we'll cover all of the details that regulate crowdfunding. Smart investing has never been an opportunity to go hog wild. So you should know what the restrictions are. That way you'll be able to match opportunity to reality.

## TAKEAWAYS AND INSIGHTS

- The real connective glue that underlies life and business is information: what, how, when, where, how much, and why. Today, who gets what information when can change lives—save them, injure them or kill them, create fortunes or destroy them.
- Equity-based crowdfunding and advertising private placements offer effectively a new, more open, faster flow of information and money among investors, entrepreneurs, creative types, and small businesses.
- With new pools of money being released by equity-based crowdfunding, combined with great awareness of private placement marketing via advertising and PR, the opportunities are vast for all the participants beyond the investors and entrepreneurs.
- Here's what's really exciting: the crowdfunding and private placement areas will spawn numerous jobs and innovations not only from the companies being financed but from the suppliers and services which will support the flow of information and money.
- To promote private placements entrepreneurs will need to build websites, create sales funnels (business and product launches), create content, generate traffic to their sites, buy media, SEO, social media, content marketing, for JVs. In addition, entrepreneurs will need lawyers, accountants, investment bankers, advisers, and connectors.

- Entrepreneurs, creative types, and small businesses will turn to authors/writers for content; speakers to show them how to present and pitch; copywriters to write their scripts for pitches, and webinars, slide presentation positioning pieces; inbound marketers direct marketers, and PR companies to increase awareness, build trust, and expand their platform seminar, and even creators to give them a stage on which to speak; video experts to create the pitch videos and company explaining the video.
- The world of finance and capital raising will integrate with the Internet, social, and mobile. This will result in reducing costs and squeezing out certain middleman, and transforming the industry in certain ways, as occurred with music and newspapers. For example, documentation of deals will become more electronic and more efficient.

Click here for additional resources: http://bit.ly/17fHA25o

CHAPTER 14

# READING THE FINE PRINT

The last chapter covered the exciting possibilities opened up by the new frontier of crowdfunding equity (and private placements that can be advertised to accredit investors). Yet that also means that the government wants to control that frontier. Part of the reason is that regulation is what the government does. It has the power to prevent its citizens from being abused by flimflam artists. In this particular field, the SEC created all sorts of restrictions before crowdfunding equity ever became available to the public.

Right in the JOBS Act, crowdfunding equity comes with a number of rules, to be enforced by the SEC with the input of the Financial Industry Regulatory Authority (FINRA), the organization that oversees stockbrokers. The SEC requires that any investors must be educated about what they are investing in. This requirement extends to the crowdfunding portals themselves. As for the issuers or seekers of the money, they have to clearly state the risk factors of the deal.

The SEC is worried about more than the fact that most start-ups fail. The agency's job is to protect the general public against being defrauded. Crowdfunding donations with rewards and especially crowdfunding equity are experiments. Experiments are just that. The marketplace must be tested and refined. For example, crowdfunding donations with rewards hinges upon the creative type or gadget maker delivering the pre-sold stuff on time, with the quality promised. Yet already many high-profile crowdfunding deals, like Pebble, have been very late in delivering their products. But with crowdfunding donations with rewards, you are selling stuff, not securities. The laws of commercial commerce and the Internet apply.

In crowdfunding equity, the sale of securities is involved. Hence, the SEC, FINRA, and other governmental agencies and states come into play. Instead of losing your money on getting a gadget or some other product or service in crowdfunding donations with rewards, crowdfunding equity raises the issues of securities fraud and misrepresentation. The losses that could occur via crowdfunding equity portals can be far worse. This new arena of funding exposes the general public to seeing its investments completely wiped out because of the inherent high risk of early-stage companies.

This concern is put forth by Keith Woodwell, Utah Division of Securities director. "We're worried about fraud," Woodall said to the *Salt Lake Tribune*. "Investing in start-ups is the most risky type of investment there is. The problem we fear is there will be a lot of unscrupulous companies out there playing it up to individuals." Woodall said angel investors and venture capitalists do a lot of homework and are aware that the majority of start-ups fail. "Equity crowdfunding essentially democratizes early-stage investing." Woodwell said. "For the most part, small investors are not going to put in the time to read the fine print and look under the hood of a start-up."

Secretary of the Commonwealth for Massachusetts William Galvin sent this letter to the SEC about potential crowdfunding risks:

> While this picture of the potential benefits of crowdfunding is undeniably attractive, as regulators we must be vigilant that the exemption will not become a tool for financial fraud and abuse...Unscrupulous penny stock promoters have used misrepresentations to market obscure and low-value stocks to individuals, often through pump and dump schemes. These kinds of fraud operators have not gone away...The typical crowdfunding offering will be small (many may be far below $1 million), so there is the great risk that these offerings will fly under the radars of many regulators.

On the impact of social networking and potential fraudulent schemes through crowdfunding, Galvin states:

> We expect that various kinds of social media will be used in tandem with crowdfunding. This may involve forums or message sharing through a portal's website; it may involve current social media channels (especially Twitter and Facebook); and is likely to involve new channels and technologies...There is the great risk that pump and dump operators will use social media to improperly promote these offerings.

Crowdfunding investors will be constantly pitched deals, and there is no way the SEC, FINRA, or anyone else can monitor sufficiently all these deals. The SEC and FINRA lack the resources and, in many cases, the expertise. From a practical point of view, the SEC lacks the staff, experience, and even the talent to monitor the raising of capital on the Internet. They cannot prevent all of the con men out there from pitching bogus deals. Once crowdfunding money is entrusted to companies—especially young companies— the SEC, FINRA, and the states believe fraud and misrepresentations will happen over and over.

There are a few observations to be made: the fraud and misrepresentations at the levels feared by the SEC, FINRA, and the states have not materialized in countries such as the United Kingdom and Sweden, where crowdfunding equity is legal.

Nor is fraud and misrepresentation any less where larger companies and SEC, FINRA, and state oversight exists currently for many years and is highly sophisticated. Unfortunately, we see fraud at the largest companies, even with the best accountants and lawyers in the world overseeing them and making very expensive and time-consuming disclosures to the public to protect them.

No amount of securities regulation will be able to protect against the human mind when it seeks to defraud and misrepresent business and financial information.

The answer: there needs to be a practical balance struck between protection and allowing the markets to self-police and work with the SEC to adjust to the marketplace realities, as no amount of regulation can anticipate actual market interactions.

The aim of the SEC and other agencies should be to set out rules that protect but do not overprotect such that the purpose of the JOBS Act to spur innovative company and employment growth is defeated.

## PUTTING NUMBERS ON LIMITS

Let's take a look at a brief summary of the JOBS Act and use its guidelines to help you decide how you can participate as an investor or as an entrepreneur seeking capital (is the risk of being sued as an entrepreneur raising capital via crowdfunding worth it?).

**Illiquidity Risk:** First of all, as an investor, you are restricted to a holding period before you can sell your equity ownership in a business. This means your investment is illiquid for a period of time (which could be years)—you cannot gain access to your invested money. You're not trading in the larger stock exchanges. Whether the company does well or badly, you can't get out. If you have an immediate need for money, then do not invest in a crowdfunding equity deal unless you can draw upon other sources of money.

**Escrow Account and Licensed Intermediaries:** To protect you, portals are required to hold your investment money in an escrow account—where it is safe—until the company in which you are investing meets the minimum or target threshold amount. Then your investment money will be released to the company. You are required to invest through these intermediaries: either an SEC–approved, licensed crowdfunding equity portal or a securities broker.

**Limited Investment Amount:** You can invest the greater of $2,000 or 5% of your annual income or net worth if you earn under $100,000. You can invest 10% of your annual income or net worth, not to exceed in total $100,000, if either your annual income or net worth is equal to or more than $100,000.

**Company Financial Disclosure Required:** What amount of financial disclosure by companies to investors is required? Under Title 111, companies desiring to sell a stock to the public have to give information to the investors and the SEC. A crowdfunding investor must be given more extensive financial disclosures based upon the amount of money being raised by the companies. For example, a company seeking to raise more than $500,000—the maximum amount is $1,000,000 in a 12-month period—is required to give investors an audited financial statement. Note that this seems a costly, onerous provision, especially if the business is new and has no operations history. The SEC has the discretion to change this rule.

Crowdfunding describes various funding relationships between different individuals, groups, and organizations.

Crowdfunding Equity as per section 4 (6) gives a U.S. company seeking to raise money an exemption from the registration requirements of securities under the Securities Act if the securities are offered by an SEC–approved funding portal.

> **Increased Shareholder Threshold:** Effective immediately, the JOBS Act increases the threshold number of record shareholders of a class of equity securities that triggers registration and reporting requirements under Section 12(g) of the Securities Exchange Act of 1934 (the "Exchange Act") for companies with more than $10 million in assets from 500 to 2,000 as of the end of a company's fiscal year, provided that the company also becomes subject to these requirements if it has at least 500 record holders who are not accredited investors.
>
> Bank holding companies with more than $10 million in assets have a similar increased threshold—i.e., 2,000 record holders on their fiscal year end—except that they are not subject to the alternative threshold of 500 record holders who are not accredited investors.
>
> In determining whether the thresholds have been reached, whether by a bank holding company or otherwise, record holders do **not include** holders of shares received through employee compensation plans or **issued under the new "crowdfunding" exemption created by the JOBS Act**,
>
> **Record Holders:** "Record holders" or "shareholders of record" of a company are those listed on its books and records. Many

shareholders of publicly traded companies are not individually counted as record holders, because they may own their shares "in street name" through a broker. The broker would be listed as a single record holder of the issuer, even if many of the broker's clients are beneficial owners of the issuer's shares. Although the JOBS Act increases the record shareholder thresholds, it does not affect the distinction between record holders and beneficial owners who hold their shares "in street name." In other words, the JOBS Act does not "look through" brokers and other record holders to the ultimate beneficial owners of shares for purposes of determining whether the threshold number of shareholders is reached. (Source: LathropGage.com/securities alert)

**Crowdfunding Reg. D:** Under an amended exemption of Rule 506 of Regulation D under the U.S. Securities Act, private equity of U.S. and foreign companies and debt can be raised. All investors must be accredited (see definition below) and sign documents to certify to this. The key provision was the amending of Reg. D by the JOBS Act to permit raising money using publicity and other media such as TV, radio, or the Internet. The accredited investors count toward the new maximum of 2,000 investors allowed under the amended rule 12 (G) under the 1934 U.S. Exchange Act.

## DEFINING TERMS

Here are some crowdfunding equity definitions. First is the accredited investor:

"The federal securities laws define the term *accredited investor* in Rule 501 of Regulation D as:

1. a bank, insurance company, registered investment company, business development company, or small business investment company;
2. an employee benefit plan, within the meaning of the Employee Retirement Income Security Act, if a bank, insurance

company, or registered investment adviser makes the investment decisions, or if the plan has total assets in excess of $5 million;

3. a charitable organization, corporation, or partnership with assets exceeding $5 million;
4. a director, executive officer, or general partner of the company selling the securities;
5. a business in which all the equity owners are accredited investors;
6. a natural person who has individual net worth, or joint net worth with the person's spouse, that exceeds $1 million at the time of the purchase, excluding the value of the primary residence of such person;
7. a natural person with income exceeding $200,000 in each of the two most recent years or joint income with a spouse exceeding $300,000 for those years and a reasonable expectation of the same income level in the current year; or
8. a trust with assets in excess of $5 million, not formed to acquire the business.

Non accredited investor: If you do not fall into one of the categories above, you are considered a non-accredited investor and you cannot currently invest in companies online."

A *security* is a financial instrument such as a stock or bond which gives some person or entity an interest in a company.

*Common equity* is the ownership of a company, and a common (equity) share is the ownership of a unit (fractional percentage). The common share grants ownership in a private company, i.e., not traded on any public market.

When you invest in *private* shares, you can expect to receive a business plan, the company's financial information, and a term sheet that may or may not include more sophisticated documents such as a private placement memo. The term sheet includes the critical terms of the deal—the math, legal protection, and risk factors.

Here are some crowdfunding equity rules which grant to U.S. companies exemption from the U.S. securities offerings:

- An issuer may sell up to $1 million in any 12-month period.
- Offerings under the crowdfunding exemption must be offered through an intermediary registered with the SEC as a broker or "funding portal."

## TOO MUCH REGULATION: TOO MANY COSTS

As I already stated, the crowdfunding laws are attempting to protect mostly unsophisticated investors from mostly inexperienced and, in many cases, unsophisticated funding portals as well as inexperienced issuers—entrepreneurs, small businesses, and creative types. The problem is costly over-regulation that inhibits the potential capital-raising efficiency that is crowdfunding's greatest attraction. How far do state and federal regulators go to protect against fraud and misrepresentation? The crowdfunding industry feels the collective wisdom and scrutiny of the crowd can sort things out and police itself better. For example, the law requires intermediaries "to make such efforts as the commission determines appropriate" to verify that investors have not exceeded their investment limitations covering all stock issuers and intermediaries. The cost to verify independently could be very high if that means a database or checking tax forms.

You want to invest (or, as an entrepreneur, seek) money from the crowdfunding portals that best match up with the type of company, cause, or project you want to fund. Remember, as a seeker of capital, you want to know where you have the best chances of getting the money on the best terms. As an investor, you want to see your money go to the projects that appeal to you the most. For example, you may have a passion for advances in medicine and search for a funding portal that specializes in medical deals.

Let's look at the big picture and the major players in the crowdfunding equity world and what they want to achieve.

The government wants to kick-start a very sluggish economy that has emerged from the Great Recession and generate new jobs in light of the high unemployment rates. As noted, new jobs come mainly from start-ups, especially fast-growing ones.

When Congress passed the JOBS Act and President Obama signed it into law, the interpretation and the implementation of the law came under the auspices of the SEC since it regulates U.S. securities laws. The SEC was given a certain amount of time to issue guidelines. That time period has been far exceeded.

The SEC monitors FINRA—the former National Association of Securities Dealers—of which I've been a member for over 30 years. Even though the proposed crowdfunding laws mandate that transactions occur through a broker or funding portal, the broker will be exposed to significant liability for non-compliance. Since the investment amounts by individuals can be so small, the cost/benefit or risk/reward for a broker/dealer analysis, most likely, will not be attractive. The net effect is that brokers may see money moving away from them, squeezing their income, and to the Internet, which has achieved in industry after industry, such as music and publishing.

As a result of the practical lack of incentives for the SEC and FINRA, there is a strong likelihood that the SEC will over-regulate the industry. The over-regulation will drive up costs for companies (issuers of securities), create uncertainties and greater risks, and decrease the natural flow of capital, which the Internet can potentially provide.

## EXPOSED PORTALS

The SEC–approved funding portals have potentially significant liabilities. The crowdfunding act regulates the sale of securities through a funding portal by restricting the amount of securities an issuer can sell in any 12-month period, plus the amount of securities investors may purchase in any 12-month period. These restrictions impose defined requirements on the intermediary funding portal or crowdfunding site.

The Crowdfunding Act regulates the funding portals in six areas:

1. Anti-fraud protection
2. Disclosure and investor education
3. The manner of sale
4. Conflicts of interest

5. Registration with the SEC and applicable self-regulatory organizations
6. Making available certain information for the investors and SEC

Just look at the obligations intermediaries have under the crowd-funding act to avoid conflicts of interest. Intermediaries cannot:

1. Have officers, directors or partners with any financial interest in the issuer
2. Give advice, solicit or advertise about securities available on their website
3. Compensate any finder or lead generator for bringing investors to their portal

On top of that, the funding portal must by SEC mandate educate investors as well as make certain disclosures about risks associated with (start-up) investments and the potential to lose your entire investment. The funding portal must make sure the investors have read and understand these risks and can afford them. In addition, to avoid fraud, the SEC mandates that anti-fraud mechanisms be in place to include background checks on any director, officer, or holder of more than 20% of the issuer's stock.

The funding portal must make sure no investor has exceeded her 12-month aggregate purchase amounts. It must ensure investor privacy and provide all investors the right to rescind their investment commitments. In addition, the funding portal must file at least annually with the SEC plus provide investors with operational results and financial statements of issuers. Not only is the funding portal under the SEC but it also may be under FINRA.

Note: The practical means to comply with the new law, the SEC mandates, and the associated costs are significant. Many funding portals themselves are new businesses with untrained employees and untested systems. What if portals don't or can't comply? Will the SEC publicize this about the portal, scare away the portal's investors, and shoot the portal's business down or scare investors away from portals and crowdfunding?

## ISSUER BEWARE

When you get to the issuer—the company trying to raise the money—the obligations of the company and its officers are also very far-reaching, costly and risky. Many companies are simply start-ups with inexperienced management who will struggle to get a business up and running even if it raised the money.

When you step back, you realize that the crowdfunding start-up can potentially become an over regulated quasi-public company with reporting requirements and shareholder communications issues that naturally arise from social media, which is a pivotal part of crowdfunding.

The company must provide significant disclosures—many of which start-ups have difficulty creating with any degree of expertise. These disclosure documents must be filed with the SEC, the funding portals, and given to investors who review them. In what period of time? How long does the issuer have to fix them? Disclosures, as mentioned, include the offering and capital structures, such as the amount of existing debt and equity and projected amounts post offering, a business plan, controlling shareholders, management, and potentially a private placement memo with risk factors related to the investment.

One of the areas I have pointed out is the cost of providing audited financial statements when raising over $500,000. Imagine the fears of the auditing firm and its potential liability if its audit of a start-up is inaccurate. The statements—unaudited if below $500,000—must be prepared by an independent public accountant.

Additionally, the issuer must disclose the purpose and use of proceeds, the targeted amount of funds to be raised, the deadline for the targeted funds raised, as well as regular updates as to the progress of the offering. The issuer must reveal the share price and how it was determined. Then, prior to the actual sales of the security, each investor must receive in writing the final price and all required disclosure documents.

Can you imagine sending out all this information to hundreds of investors? What is the true cost to get an investor if he invests $25 or $50? What will be the true cost to maintain an investor over time?

In addition, the start-up may have different rights and limitations. Minority ownership rights, dilution, and potential dilution in the future will need to be addressed. What if a $25 investor claims he did not understand the deal? What if he rallies a bunch of $100 investors to say they were duped? Who foots the cost of potential arbitration?

What happens when a company grows and needs more capital, which is typical of start-ups? Will venture capitalists or angels invest in companies with numerous small shareholders? On what terms? Will the stock of the small investor get substantially diluted? (Source: *United States: Crowdfunding: Boom or Bust for Entrepreneurs and Investors* by Elliot Dater)

There are numerous unknowns, such as whether crowdfunding equity is more suited for local investors in small businesses, where the community members can meet and sort things out. Will a potential growth company, such as a software company, be better suited or worse since it will most likely need additional rounds of financing? Will the crowdfunding investors be ultimately more of a help or hindrance based upon the compliance issues pulling at the company and its costs while the company must focus upon its growth pains and competition?

The funding portal is an intermediary, and it charges an entrepreneur to raise money on its website. However, because of the deal size and the very early stage of most start-ups that will seek crowdfunding equity, I do not believe crowdfunding equity will supplant the better venture capitalist firms and angel investor networks, as I will cover more fully under private placements.

## GOOD DEBT VERSUS BAD DEBT

Despite crowdfunding equity's liabilities, the other ways of finding capital can be far worse. Business owners have to make that sort of calculation all the time. Let's review the basics of financing. From the very beginning of a start-up or some time in the future, companies require money to grow. Whether small or large, companies will turn to the capital markets. For example, large companies may need short-term lines of credit from a bank or other financial lending institutions to bridge the gap between the time goods are sold to the time of collection. Why? During this gap period the company may have to pay suppliers who provided ingredients, parts, or services to create the final goods.

For a small business, the challenge becomes choosing the correct funding source and cost of capital. If a small company raises outside capital from the wrong investors—devils rather than angels—the company may find the terms onerous and the investors may try to take over the business. Or, if the company borrows money, the terms of repayment may impede the company's growth for years or even put it under.

Normally, you seek debt financing from a bank or financial institution. Typically, private individuals do not make loans on cars and houses. But they may guarantee loans for ownership in a business or invest in a business by lending money where they receive warrants to own shares or convertible debt where the investors can convert into equity at a predetermined price or a price to be determined in the future.

Among the pros of borrowing are:

You don't give up any ownership or operational control. Once you repay the loan, the lender's relationship ends.

The interest payment on the loan is tax deductible and you have some degree of certainty as to your obligations.

Among the cons: Debt is tied to a certain date. Payments come due like clockwork whether you possess the means to pay them or not. For a start-up or early stage company with uncertain income, debt financing can be very disruptive and weigh on your team and you. In fact, in our food business, we used asset-based lending against our inventory and our sales had to be deposited in a lock box. The entire process had very onerous terms (covenants) and a lot of costs to account for the flows of money to us and back to the bank.

Let's review quickly the basic elements of getting the money:

In most circumstances, avoid borrowing money, especially when you are starting up a company. Why?

- Debt can be the highest cost if you give additional incentives such as stock options and you still have to pay the debt off.
- Repayment is in after-tax dollars

- Your take on personal liability for repayment of the debt.
- Often the terms are fixed.
- The amount you seek often is not enough to achieve your goals, since you most likely will miss your projections.
- The requirement to repay the debt may make you desperate to bring in equity capital on worse terms than you would have gotten if you sought equity capital in the beginning.
- The terms of the debt may scare away equity capital and/or prevent additional borrowings.

## GOOD DEBT: THE EXCEPTION TO AVOID BORROWING

Good debt is where you have an asset which generates sufficient and consistent income to cover your costs of borrowing. Under this circumstance, good debt allows you to achieve *positive* leverage. Leverage in financial terms means borrowing money. Positive leverage means you make money on every dollar you borrow and you increase your percentage return on your investment more than if you had not borrowed at all.

Here's a simple example of positive leverage:

You buy a house for $100,000 and rent it out to a very creditworthy tenant for $10,000 per year, or a 10% return ($100,000 x 10%). Assume you can borrow from a bank 70% of the house's value at 5% interest only per annum; then you would pay $3,500 in interest: 70% x $100,000 (the house's value) = $70,000 loan at 5% = $3,500 interest payment).

$10,000 Rental Income<br>
- 3,500 Interest<br>
$ 6,500 Net return after interest<br>
$ 6,500/$30,000 net investment ($100,000 - $70,000 loan) = 21.6% rate of return

By borrowing or leveraging, you would increase your return on investment from 10% ($10,000/$100,000) to 21.67%

($6,500/$30,000). How did that happen? Because you are making a spread or a profit on every dollar you are borrowing between the 10% return and the 5% interest cost (10% – 5% = 5% spread or profit). Take the 5% spread times the $70,000 borrowed money and you made $3,500 profit by borrowing. The $3,500 profit/$30,000 net investment equals 11.67% profit. Add your profit to your original 10% return—you got the 10% if you did not borrow at all and invested all the money to buy the house (10% original return + 11.67% profit = 21.67%).

The main point: borrowing when the income is predictable at a favorable rate can create positive leverage. Please note that I left out all the other costs, including taxes, insurance, maintenance, plus there can be different fees up front or during the life of the loan which can make borrowing even more expensive.

**Negative** leverage is just the opposite. Take the same example and imagine you borrowed the same $70,000 at 12% interest only (greater than your 10% overall return by 2%). Now your interest rate is $8,400.

$10,000 Rental Income
- 8,400 Interest
$ 1,600 Net return
$1,600/$30,000 net investment ($100,000 - $70,000 loan) = 5.3% rate of return

In the negative leverage example, you would be losing money on every dollar borrowing because you are getting 10% and borrowing at 12%, or losing 2% on every dollar borrowed. As a result, your rate of return drops to 5.3% from 10%.

## BAD DEBT: BORROWING ON CREDIT CARDS

Many start-ups begin by borrowing on their credit cards. This is extremely dangerous since start-ups typically have no assets and income to borrow against, which will generate consistent stable income to pay down the credit card interest and balances.

Instead of borrowing at 5% or even 12%, now imagine that to start up your business, you borrowed from a credit card company at 20% to 33% interest rate. You would have serious negative leverage. At a 20% rate of interest, in 3.6 years the money you owe will double. If you borrowed $25,000 at 20%, you'd owe $50,000 in 3.6 years.

Let's say you decided to borrow from at online lender such as Prosper, which states it will get a personal loan at a low rate (rates "starting" at 6.59% annual percentage rate for best borrowers). But you are then told in the finer print that these unsecured loans, with easy monthly payments and fixed rates, only start at 6.59% and really may cost you up to 35.36% annual percentage rate. These rates are the same or much higher than your credit card loan.

Next, on Prosper, you are told to check your rate: select the purpose of your loan; enter the amount; and select your credit quality.

I'm told in a note, "A Prosper loan for a small business is a personal loan for business expenses. Individual borrowers will be personally liable for the debt and loans are not related to or guaranteed by the Small Business Association."

Then you must disclose a lot of personal information: to get a Credit Report Authorization. In the fine print, your loan depends upon "credit history, income, loan term, and other factors." All loans are made by a web bank, the Utah-chartered Industrial Bank, Member FDIC.

You can get loans, debt consolidation, home improvement, auto, motorcycle, RV, boat, vacation, household expenses, baby and adoption loans, taxes, and other.

You can get a personal loan for virtually anything if you have the credit score, income, and other criteria they are seeking.

A bunch of investors are crowd loaning or putting up small amounts of money to lend to you. Now institutions are jumping into this lending as well as individuals lending you money because this lending is so lucrative.

You can see quickly how fast you can be in a negative leverage position if you borrow money for your business. How far can $2,500 to $25,000 carry your business? It's a question you must ask yourself. You are personally on the hook for repayment in after-tax dollars, since only the interest rate is tax deductible. This means if you borrow $25,000 and you have a 50% tax rate, then you must generate $50,000 net dollars to pay off the $25,000 loan. If your business had $50,000 in expenses during the year, then you would have to generate $105,000 in gross income to pay off the $25,000 loan.

$105,000
- 50,000 business expenses
55,000 net income
- 5,000 interest on loan (20% interest rate x $25,000 loan)
50,000 net income after interest
- 25,000 taxes at 50%
$25,000 to repay the $25,000 loan

This means you must make $105,000 if you wanted to repay the $25,000 loan in a year at a 20% interest rate. $105,000 is more than four times the loan amount. What if you made little or no money? You'd go out of business and still owe $25,000!

Borrowing to start up a business can truly put you into a difficult financial situation and kill your business before it has a chance to get off the ground.

Be very careful of investors—including family and friends—who want to lend you money in order to start up or expand a business.

As an investor, lending to a start-up with personal guarantees from the business owner is very risky as well. If you do not get paid back, then your options may be limited. Do you take over the business? Can you run it? Will you have to put money in? Will you have to sue—which could drive other investors away? Will the business owner refuse to stay and run the business unless you extend the loss?

Debt can cut both ways. A mentor warned, "Whatever you borrow or guarantee—no matter how remote the risk—almost always comes back to haunt you."

## IS EQUITY CAPITAL BETTER?

Now let's look at the pros of equity capital. You don't have a certain date to pay back the debt. Investors own the company with you and make or lose money with you. This leaves the money in the business rather than being withdrawn to repay the debt. Investors, hopefully, will be patient and give you the time to build the business.

Equity capital also has its cons. The challenge with early-stage investor funding becomes the strings attached to the money, i.e., the terms. Early-stage investors focus upon downside protections such as preferences to get their money out if the business must be sold off or liquidated. It is very easy to sign terms which can wrest control of the company if milestones are not met and the company needs more capital, especially at a lower valuation than the initial investors funded the company.

Suddenly, you have owners and partners in your business with their own ideas, experiences, and levels of greed and honesty telling you what to do. In the beginning, you may have a honeymoon period, but if you don't perform, things can deteriorate into a war and a nasty divorce.

## ADVERTISING

Be aware that advertising by an issuer or company under the JOBS Act Title III is restricted. The Act's limitations make it difficult for a company on a crowdfunding portal to spread the word about its offering. Under the proposed law the issuer (company) may not advertise the terms of the offering, except for notices which direct investors to the funding portal or broker. Also, the issuer (company) may "not compensate or commit to compensate, directly or indirectly, any person to promote its offering through communication channels provided by a broker or funding portal, without taking such steps as the commission shall by rule, require to ensure that such person clearly discloses the receipt, past or prospective, of such compensation, upon each instance of such promotional communication."

These provisions prevent any details of the offering on the crowdfunding portal from being blasted out to the public via emails, faxes, mass direct mailing of a tour sheet, or similar means of communication which promote the investment. Nor can the issuer (company) promote the investment on the web, such as on its website, blog, or any social or mobile sites.

Even though crowdfunding with donations with rewards allows building a crowd of followers, crowdfunding equity limits what you can say or do to mostly what you state on a portal site's page. Only the portal can highlight you, but they cannot advertise your specific deal outside the portal. Thus, your ability to capture attention and a following is much more limited than you might be aware.

## FRAUD FROM UNEXPECTED PLAYERS

Without being too philosophical, the financial press over the past decade has almost daily reported individual and company securities fraud, including insider trading and real estate mortgage-backed securities.

The public's trust in corporations and financial institutions has been at an all-time low. Wall Street and the banks have gained significantly at the expense of Main Street, small businesses, and the entrepreneur.

It is my own observation that the biggest obstacle beyond overregulation and the biggest costs—if not frauds—will come from the service providers who will arise to support the JOBS Act Title III companies and investors.

Many of the companies and people racing into crowdfunding never raised a nickel, or, if they did, not in the $1 million or less early-stage raises. Most of those rushing to the supposed crowdfunding gold mine have no securities licenses and know little about finance or building businesses. Many of the lawyers and accountants that will exact high fees or interest in companies have little experience as well. Many crowdfunding conferences have speakers—promoters—who joined crowdfunding organizations early to give themselves credibility and credentials by association that are as phony as a three-dollar bill, as the saying goes.

Just because a person or company completed large financings as part of a group at an investment banking firm does not qualify them for raising capital, especially on the Internet.

Unsuspecting and inexperienced entrepreneurs will pay a lot for misinformation, including giving the so-called experts an interest in their companies, from many service providers who are charlatans or over-promote limited expertise. I hate to be so harsh but I see this already happening.

On the other hand, investors will be faced with entrepreneurs who lack the skills to start up and build a company.

After 30+ years, in the Reg D private placement area where I have directly raised money mostly in the $500,000 to $3 million range, you see lots of BS.

When you turn back to reviewing the existing funding portals, such as Crowd Cube or Funded By Me, you see the positive of getting your deal exposed potentially to a lot of small investors who could become evangelists and customers. But you also see the negative of the virtual world where you can't promote your company off the portal. For this reason, you are relegated to a bunch of buttons about your company through which the investor has to wade.

Virtually every crowdfunding donations with rewards campaign now uses video. Why? Video naturally engages, and a video is worth a thousand words. In crowdfunding equity, video will become even more important for all the parties involved—the SEC, investor, and entrepreneur. Videos will become interactive. Instead of one-way boring pitches, entrepreneurs will use videos to grab attention, relate emotionally by telling their story, ask questions, and get feedback from investors on their products and deal. These interactions will be recorded and give the SEC and the portals records to reduce fraud and misrepresentations. Portals will be able to ask potential investors if they understand the deal and risks and educate their investors. Mobile video will serve the same purpose but will make visiting a portal page much more convenient.

This means the headline, tag line, and the video(s) will become part of an overall portal page pitch designed to get the investor to take the time to read the deal. If the company can interest the investor, then the investor can engage in an open Q&A (FAQs). The video Q&A can achieve useful feedback, segment investors by how they answer, such as if they want to invest now, and send them responses in real time.

Combining investor video Q&A with FAQs adjusted to the investor feedback will give entrepreneurs a better idea of the attractiveness of their business and the deal terms they are offering.

There is no way to screen bad-intentioned actors—or even competitors—from negative comments that scare off potential or committed investors, or from having competitors scour your information to steal ideas and customers.

The bottom line:

Crowdfunding will pull together many skill sets and strategies from the online and offline world. There will be few short cuts to the hard work it takes to raise capital for early-stage companies. The big advantage I have laid out for you is your deeper understanding of how the different pieces of raising capital fit together. The more you can see the interplay of the rules, players, frameworks, and patterns of starting up, pitching an early-stage company, and the strategies and tactics involved, the greater are your odds of getting the money and building a successful business.

The entrepreneur has to attract enough investors and/or customers and create sufficient momentum for the deal being offered *before* he or she seeks funding on a crowdfunding portal. Ironically, this attraction of investors and customers involves the same tried-and-true, traditional ways to network and meet investors before you go live.

You have to interest people, such as friends, family, and their friends, in your company. With this core group committed to the venture, then you can begin to prepare your crowdfunding equity offering with money "in the bank." These early investors show other investors they are not alone and that people close to you believe in the venture—biased or not. Early investor commitment builds momentum for your deal.

The web, social, and mobile amplify your deal by spreading the word of your products and services to prospects and selling them. How you use the web, social, and mobile also showcases for potential investors who may visit your site, blog, social networks, or mobile offerings your experience in online marketing and sales.

We are going to turn now to a traditional area of investment: private placement. For the start-up company, that still remains the primary way to raise capital. So you should know the ins and outs of what the big investors really want.

## TAKEAWAYS AND INSIGHTS

- The point of the SEC regulations is to define the rules of money raising similar to creating rules for a game. As in any game, if the rules become too onerous, they stop the flow of the action.
- The SEC and other regulatory bodies must balance the cost of over-regulation and protection of the "players" in the money-raising industry.
- Like any endeavor, learn the key rules well. They will surely be tested by the marketplace. Those who understand the rules the best will discover opportunities. For example, as a marketer or an entrepreneur the rules of investment as to income defines different demographics for which you can frame your message, product, and deal.
- The way to succeed at any endeavor, whether as an investor, entrepreneur, creative-type or small business, is to constantly assess the context or landscape within which you are operating. Within this environment, you will need a strong self-belief and the tenacity to push yourself to set goals and stay focused.
- One of the biggest challenges is how to pierce through all the hype; have a vision and purpose; set goals to reach your vision and purpose; and to adjust quickly when things are clearly not working.
- The realization I've discovered is that most people are not capable of performing at their potential because of fear, laziness, and greed. Out of fear, they pass up on opportunities. Out of fear and/or laziness, they avoid taking action. Out of greed, they want more than they deserve and will take advantage of you wherever you are ignorant and vulnerable.

- For these reasons—and many more—the money-raising rules are only guidelines. The waters of business and money-raising are full of sharks. The earlier the stage a company finds itself, the more sharks it attracts who present themselves as dolphins.
- As Napoleon Hill wrote in the *Laws of Success*, the fear of poverty is based upon the predatory nature of most people's desire to part you from your money.
- To this end, be very careful what type of money you take, from whom, and on what terms. Once money controls your actions, it snuffs out your creativity, destroys your vision, and wrests control of your company.
- On the other hand, most people given money will piss it away out of incompetence and/or lack of integrity.
- A former wealthy partner said, when I invest my money in you, I want to know how to protect my downside. If things go wrong, I don't expect to get part of the money back.
- All money comes with terms and conditions—and emotions especially when families and friends are involved. Read the fine print. Avoid bad debt wherever possible. Be very careful of credit cards or other unsecured loans even if they seem cheap.
- As an investor, especially in early-stage companies, buyer beware. Focus on the execution and the time to execute and who will execute.

Click here for additional resources: http://bit.ly/13UnMT2

CHAPTER 15

# PRIVATE PLACEMENTS

Very exciting news. After 80 years, the SEC has ruled that issuers can advertise and generally solicit accredited investor using private placements. This will open up opportunities for companies seeking capital especially for early stage companies.

Increased investment and deal flow will result as companies have the ability to reach, market, advertise present, and pitch to a much larger pool of accredited investors, faster and more efficiently. Likewise, accredited investors will become aware of a larger selection of alternative investments and be able to compare more quickly the merits of one deal against the other. In time, investment unites may become easier to sell because the deals have great visibility and their values may be more easily assessed as information companies become more readily available. Some companies will effectively be quasi-public companies.

In 2012, under the old reg D law, more than $1.3 trillion was funded and more than 37,000 Reg D offerings have funded since 2009 (Reg D Resources).

Keep in mind is that the full SEC registration process is very time consuming laborious, and expensive for early-stage companies.

Now, an early-stage company does not have to go through a full SEC registration like company that wants to offer securities publically. Yet the early-stage company can advertise on the radio, websites, social media, print, mobile, and in other media and formats.

This will allow the market to dictate the level of information it seems necessary for investment decisions to be made.

Simply put, private placements involve selling securities that are not offered through a public offering. To raise capital in the United States, you have to register the securities offering with the SEC or rely on an exemption. Most private placements are offered an exemption from registration under the rules of 506 Regulation D. If the requirements are met, the offering is not deemed to be a public offering.

The types of securities mostly are common or preferred stock, but can be for membership interests (limited liability corporation), warrants, or bonds.

Purchasers can be accredited investors, including wealthy individuals, venture capital funds funded by institutions, and wealthy individuals or institutions directly, such as pension funds, banks, and insurance companies.

In general, Regulation D consists of a series of rules, i.e., Rules 501–506.

The key provision under the JOBS Act comes under Title II (note: Title III defines crowdfunding equity to an unlimited number of non-accredited investors, which we covered under crowdfunding equity).

Under Title II, Regulation D, Rule 506 had prohibited the general solicitation or advertising of private placement securities. Under the JOBS Act, this prohibition has been lifted. You can advertise or generally solicit investors. The ramifications are significant for raising capital.

Let's look at what you could do and not do before the change in the law.

If I wanted to raise money in a private placement, I could under Rule 506 sell the securities—say, common stock—to an unlimited number of accredited investors and 35 non-accredited investors without regard to the size of the transaction. But I could not generally solicit an investor to invest or advertise the transaction to the public.

As I have mentioned before, the SEC gives and takes. Since under the new law, a company (issuer) can advertise its deal publically, the SEC increased the burden on companies to verify that an investor is truly accredited (before companies accepted investor representations), eliminated the solicitation of non-accredited investors, and issued "bad actor" provisions as to who can participate in the offering in an attempt to reduce fraud and ponzi schemes.

In addition, the SEC is requiring temporarily a review of its marketing communications to analyze how the new advertising and general solicitation rules are being applied.

The final rules create a new form of securities offering called 506 (c) but leaves "the existing rules under Section 4 (a) (2) of the Securities Act (which exempts from registration transactions by an issuer" not involving any public offering') and existing Rule 506 (b) (which provides a safe harbor under Section 4 (a) (2) for offerings conducted without general solicitation)

Although new Rule 506 (c) allows for use of advertising in connection with fundraising activities, there are certain limitations.

For private funds relying on Rule 506 (c):

- The inability to rely upon Section 4 (a) (2) as an alternative for inadvertent failure to comply with Rule 506 (c);
- Increased compliance burdens and costs due to the new verification of accredited investor status requirements;
- Proposed filing of an initial form D prior to commencing any general solicitation and heightened disclosure requirements;
    - o Greater risk of funning a foul of the anti-fraud rules while engaging in general solicitation activities; and
    - o Lack of harmonization with the exemptions contained in CFTC Rules 4 7(b) and 4.13 (a) (3) (which include restrictions against "marketing to the public."
    - o The issues to compare between existing Rule 506 (c) are: investor communications, investor qualifications, investor verification requirements, filings and timing, Investment Company Act, Regulation S, Blue Sky and Commodity Exchange Act/ CFTC/NFA. ("Source: Marco V. Masotti, partner law firm Paul, Weiss Rifkind posted by Kobi Kastiel, co-editor, Harvard Law School (Forum)

Under the new Rule 506 (c), (note again: the old rule is now called rule 506 (b), which you can sell follow if you do not advertise or generally solicit accredited investors) general solicitation to accredited investors would be allowed if:

- All purchasers are accredited investors or the issuer reasonably believes they are accredited at the time of the sale.
- The issuer takes reasonable "steps to verify" that purchasers are accredited investors.
- All other requirements of Rules 501 (definitions), 502 (a) (integration) and 502 (d) (resale restrictions) are met.

The key here is the verification that the purchaser is an accredited investor based upon the circumstances of the transaction. For example, did you require the investor to fill out a questionnaire to verify the net worth or income requirements to be an accredited investor? Or, did you ask for tax returns, which is a higher level of due diligence? The amount and type of information counts.

Also, you need to consider the way the investor was solicited and the terms of the offering—such as a minimum investment amount. For example, was the investor pre-screened rather than generally solicited from the public? Can the investor meet the minimum investment amount without the issuer or a third party providing him financing? Can you rely upon the investor's accountant broker-deal or lawyer or lawyer for verification of the investor accredited status? Or, can you verify by public disclosure.

Note that new rule 506 (c) does not apply to non-accredited investors—you cannot generally solicit them. Note also, even though there is no prohibition on general solicitation in Rule 506 (c) offerings, the person who solicits or funds potential purchasers in securities offerings will still need to be registered as broker-dealers under the Securities Exchange Act of 1934 (and applicable blue sky laws) or comply with an appropriate exemption from such registration requirements.

In addition, under the new Rule 506 (d) there are certain individuals under the "bad actor provisions (felons and other bad actors) which may disqualify an issuer from relying upon Rule 506. The test is whether they the bad actors are deemed "Covered Persons" under the new rule 506 (d). For example, is a felon a director, executive officer, general partner, other officer participating in the offering or managing member of the issuer. There are other categories of persons called "Covered Persons" you should review as well as rule 506 (e).

There are disqualifying events under Rule 506 (d) such as criminal convictions related to the purchase and sale of security or various court order, judgments, SEC cease and desist orders. SEC disciplinary orders related to the purchase and sale of securities.

Note that certain provisions time provisions such as criminal convictions within ten years before the sale of securities and five years before the sale of securities where issuers, their predecessors and affiliated issuers are involved.

There are exemptions and waivers under Rule 506 (d) such as reasonable care. Under newly adopted Rule 506 (e) there are guidelines for disclosures of bad actors to accredited and non accredited investors for 506 offerings before the effective dates of this rule you should review carefully.

Let's get beyond the legalities and review where private placements fit in the capital-raising landscape hierarchy and ecosystems:

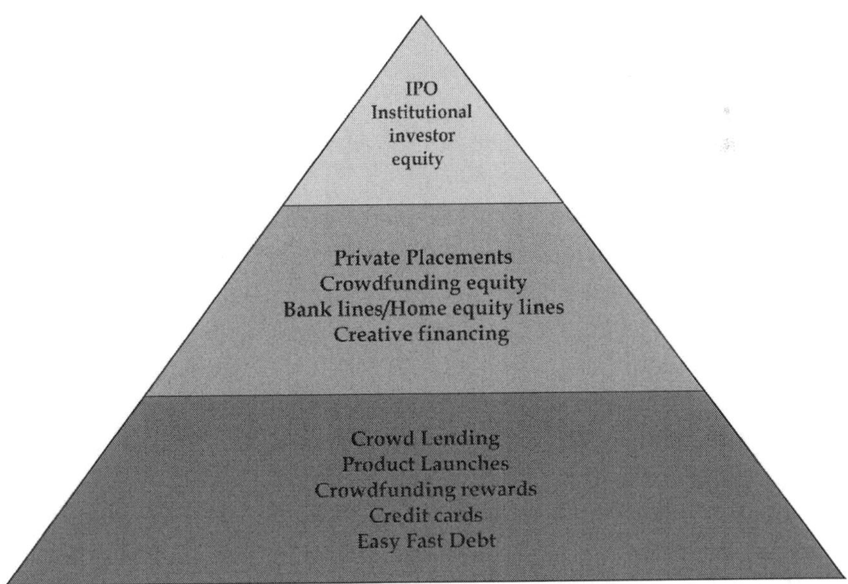

You can view capital-raising as a mountain or pyramid. There are numerous ways to access capital, some easier, simpler and faster at the base and more complex, as you climb the mountain. Many of these approaches depend upon the age of the business; the type of the business; the experience of the management; the amount and quality of hard assets, e.g., well-located real estate (bricks and mortar), fungible inventory, and accounts receivable with financially sound companies; the business models; and the uniqueness and competitive advantage of the business.

For example, at the bottom of the mountain, you might finance your business out of your pocket or by using a credit card or debit card. In effect, you are funding your company with high-priced unsecured debt—rates can exceed 30% per annum. Credit card debt can mount rapidly. At 30% interest per annum, unpaid, your debt balance will double in 2.4 years. Credit card debt affects your credit and credit score. Still, many entrepreneurs use it.

Besides using your own credit or assets, you can turn to family, friends or strangers to get seed or start-up capital in the form of loans or equity investments.

In crowdfunding donations with rewards and product launches, you can pre-sell goods and services. Typically, crowdfunding will take 90 days and product launches from beginning to end can take 30 to 60 days up to six months, depending on the size of the launch and a number of other factors we covered.

As you move up the money-raising mountain, you can get money using creative financing through seller financing (e.g., in real estate the seller takes back a mortgage); leasing rather than buying; exchanging one type of assets for another; second jobs or consulting for stock or a percentage of sales; barter; competitions and awards; factoring receivables; 401(k)s; IRAs grants; borrowing against life insurance; and reverse mergers (backing your company into a "shell" or public company )and selling off shares to investors.

If you have some assets, and/or a wealthy investor or group provides a guarantee, you can get a line of credit from a bank. Or, you might buy a franchise with a similar arrangement and/or get ownership of a franchise or other asset through sweat equity (earning ownership through working hard and taking less than you could earn elsewhere in exchange for ownership of part or even all of the business in the future).

The list of ways to finance your business is not meant to be exhaustive or explain the pros and cons of each funding source. Instead, I want to point out that raising venture capital or angel money through private placements is found near the top of the mountain.

Getting the money from venture capitalists and angel investors via private placements takes a lot of climbing up the mountain. In a way, it's similar to climbing Mount Everest. With the right team and the right planning and preparation and resources, you may get to the top. On the way up the mountain, you face many unknowns which can derail you or even kill you (or your company). Getting to the top—being a "peak" performer (excuse the pun)—is a high-risk, high-return adventure.

Here are some really interesting stats and observations by Shaun So in the *Forbes* article "Raising VC Money—Better Luck Winning the Power Ball?" Instead of doing the pitches and presentations to venture capitalists, working the 100+ hours, cold calling, networking, and pursuing wealthy relatives and angel investors, you can find your business by playing Powerball—odds 1 in 775,223,510, whereas the odds of raising $1 million to start up your company are 1 in 5,152,632.65. If you spend $1 to find your $40,000 minimal viable product following the lean start-up method, then your odds of getting funded increase to 1 out of 648,975.96. The article says that a venture-capitalist-backed company, according to venture capitalist Steve Blank, has a 1 in 500 chance (.2%) of reaching a $100 million valuation.

According to Nathan Kaiser in an npost.com article "Vcodds: what are my chances of raising money from VCs," your chances of getting a meeting with a venture capitalist you don't know are 1 in 100 and 1 in 1,000 of getting funded if you don't know the venture capitalist.

I created for you the following table from the article:

| | **What are the odds of getting a meeting with a venture capitalist** | **Odds of getting a deal done** |
|---|---|---|
| Unsolicited business plan— | 1% | 1% |
| Solicitation by unknown agent— | 2% | 1% |
| Venture fairs and events— | 6.6% | 5% |
| Referral from professionals with fund relationships- | 33% | 20% |
| Referral from current and future investors— | 50% | 33% |
| Referral from executives of a portfolio company or stake-holder in venture capitalist fund—100% (nearly) | 100% | 33% |

These are not hard facts, but from research and interviews with venture capitalists.

What are the industry statistics on the number of companies with whom you are competing?

Depending on which statistics I've researched less than 1% receive VC funding. Kaiser states the following:

- Two to 3% of companies seeking venture capitalist funding are successful.
- 40,000 to 60,000 companies compete for 1,200 to 1,400 first financing deals

Nathan Kaiser on Raising Money from Venture Capitalists adds, "You increase your odds substantially by targeting venture capitalists investing in your market, your region, and your business stage.

Based upon these statistics, your odds increase dramatically by expanding your network of who you know and who makes the introductions.

Plus, venture capitalists claim they will bet on the jockey (team) over the horse (business and its idea), i.e., they prefer an A Team with a B idea over an A idea and a B team. A doctoral study says that beyond a minimal level of trust, companies are funded based more upon the idea's potential than on the founders' credentials.

Yet you still have to ask yourself the question: Does venture capitalist funding increase your chances of success?

In their research of venture capitalists, Kirsch and Goldfarb found that the same 50% of companies survived over a five-year period whether they were funded by venture capitalists or not. Abandoning the chase for venture capitalist money lets the owners focus on bootstrapping or raising smaller amounts of money.

John Tezzi, in *Bloomberg Businessweek*'s article "The Truth About Venture Capital," points out that venture capitalists only fund 10-11% of seed or start-up stage companies seeing financing.

## ANGEL CAPITAL FUNDING

Now let's look at angel capital. Here are some leading stats provided by J. Sohl of the Center for Venture Research:

- 20,000 seed/start ups raise money in U.S. each year.
- 30,000 later-stage raise money in U.S. each year (often who raised seed/startup capital from angels in prior rounds)
- $20 Billion invested annually.
- $300,000 is the average seed/start-up round (ten angels investing $30,000 each, according to Angel Capital Association).

Now let's take a look at the odds of getting funding from angel capital groups. In "Probability of Raising Angel Capital," on billpayne.com, the California Tech Coast Angels found:

- Pre-screening: 1 in 4 proceeds to screening
- Screening: 1 in 3 proceeds to due diligence

- Due diligence: 1 in 3 proceeds to an investment meeting
- Investment meeting: 1 in 2 deals raise money
- Overall: 1 in 72 (1.39%) of companies that apply for funding to angel capital groups are funded

The success rate depends upon the angel group, but the overall rate of funding success is probably about 2%.

Why are the odds so narrow? It's because the top performers—the top income, wealth, performers, and relationships—are found in the top 1/10th of 1%. The top 5% make some money, the top 1% make a lot of money, and the 1/10th of 1% make most of the money.

The same success rate approximates the true numbers of deals funded and even the deals which truly succeed—those that become worth $100 million. That is 12%, which is close to the 0.1% (1/10th of 1%).

## ONE OR THE OTHER?

According to the Center for Research at the New Hampshire University, in an average year 250,000 angel investors will invest $20 billion in 60,000 companies. Compare this to 800 venture capitalists, who according to the National Venture Capital Association will invest the same $20 billion in only 4,000 companies.

What this tells you is that while venture capitalists invest much larger amounts of money per deal, 15 times more companies/entrepreneurs (60,000 angels/4,000 venture capitalists) get funded by angels.

I am a big believer in starting with the end in mind. If you raise capital from angel investors, then you may have to seek larger amounts of money in the future. Venture capitalists normally start to invest money at the $2 million level, and the average deal size is $5-7 million.

Also, most of the same components of a successful deal are sought by venture capitalists and angel investors. Venture capitalists may seek harsher terms or more control and have a less emotional approach to your company than an angel.

Remember, venture capitalists under certain circumstances invest seed money or start-up money, but mostly they come in later. They want to see more proof—your product developed and paying customers—which translates into less risk.

Let's examine how venture capitalists approach private placement investments and then see the similarities and differences in that light.

I went back into the 1990s and examined the venture capitalist model then. Next, I looked at venture capitalists as they operate now. The gist of what follows is covered in an excellent article by Bob Zilder called "How Venture Capital Works" in the *Harvard Business Review* written in 1998.

First off, the venture capitalist approach to investing has not changed that much. That's why some feel that the venture capitalist model is broken and crowdfunding will challenge the venture capitalist control and leverage over entrepreneurs.

Back in the 1990s, venture capitalists invested in inventions and innovations, which still drives the U.S. economy. VC capital has often been viewed as the Wild West, with the entrepreneur being the modern cowboy and the venture capitalist the trusted sidekick. But venture capitalists are more like bankers who invest mainly in a certain part of the growth cycle of a business. VC capital fills a void in funding innovation since the major investors are the government and corporations. Only a small part of venture capitalist money goes into seed or start-up capital, let's say 10%.

Venture capitalist money is not invested long term. The basic goal is to accelerate growth at a certain stage in the company's life and then exit in five to seven years or sooner via a corporate acquisition or public offering. For the venture capitalist, timing is imperative. The VC typically wants to invest where the traditional "S" curve begins to rise—the adolescent stage. The venture capitalist wields a lot of power as the "only bank in town." Banks can't lend under usury laws at the rates they'd need, nor are they comfortable with the overall risk. Plus, start-ups in the information age have few hard assets.

The venture capitalist desires a high ROI (rate of investment) for an acceptable risk. To obtain this ROI, venture capitalists look for high-growth areas. Contrary to popular belief, venture capitalists rarely will invest in low-growth markets even if the management and the idea are very good. Venture capitalists look to avoid the wrong industry or the wrong technology.

Zilder writes: "What is confirmed over and over is that the blockbuster deal—good people, plans, and businesses—succeed one out of ten times. There are many components to a company's success, and a very best company has an 80% chance of succeeding at each component, which means its chances of succeeding will be less than 20%.

| Individual Event | Probability |
|---|---|
| Company has sufficient capital | 80% |
| Management is capable & focused | 80% |
| Product development goes as planned | 80% |
| Production and component sourcing goes as planned | 80% |
| Competitors behave as expected | 80% |
| Customers want product | 80% |
| Pricing is forecast correctly | 80% |
| Patents are issued enforceable | 80% |
| Combined probability of success | 17% |

"If one variable drops to 50%, the combined probability of success drops to 10%!

"But venture capitalists take a portfolio approach and only need 10% to 20% of their companies to be blockbusters to achieve their targeted rate of 25% to 30%.

## HERE'S A TYPICAL PORTFOLIO BREAKOUT:

| | Bad | Alive | Okay | Good | Great | Total |
|---|---|---|---|---|---|---|
| Investment | 200 | 400 | 200 | 100 | 100 | $1,000 |
| Payout years | 0 | 1x | 5x | 10x | 20x | |
| Gross return | 0 | 400 | 1000 | 1000 | 200 | 4,400 |
| Net return | (200) | 0 | 800 | 900 | 1900 | 3,400 |

(Source: "How Venture Capital Works" by Bob Zilder)

Zilder calculated that in 1994, a venture capitalist works 2,000 hours a year and spends 40% of her time acting as a consultant and serving as a director—eight hundred hours per year. He estimates that venture capitalist partners spend 10% of their time soliciting deals, 5% selecting them, 5% analyzing business plans, and 5% negotiating investments. If partners ran more than one fund, then their time became even less.

Now imagine today. The on-the-go, instant-connection world diminishes the time spent on deals even more. The venture capitalist is overwhelmed. He or she has little time to view your pitch and presentation.

Ironically, venture capitalists do what social networkers do. They turn to their peers to evaluate and co-invest in deals. They look for top managers/entrepreneurs to run the companies in which they invest.

That leads to the logical question: Is the venture capitalist model dead?

There has been a lot written about the coming crowdfunding revolution and the death of venture capital as we know it. My own feeling is that the Internet by its nature makes transactions more transparent and lowers costs as alternative sources of capital become available.

Here are some observations:

- The top venture capitalist firms will mostly remain dominant because of their powerful networks and relationships.
- The partners of venture capitalist firms will come under greater scrutiny.
- Fees will be reduced.
- Deal terms may become less onerous or at least more clearly spelled out with a better understanding of their meaning.
- Small, less powerful venture capitalists will find it hard to raise money.
- Venture capitalists, incubators, and crowdfunding equity will become more entwined.
- Crowdfunding equity may become an additional proving ground for product validation and product to marketing fit.

- Crowdfunding equity may become a way for venture capitalists to vet more deals faster, plus learn about competition faster.

## JOBS ACT: TITLE II VERSUS TITLE III

Based upon the proposed law changes, which would allow general solicitation and advertising of Reg. D 506 (c) private placements, the market for private placements may expand globally. Currently, it is over a trillion-dollar market, whereas crowdfunding equity is a $5 billion market. Private placements in 2011 were five times the amount raised by IPOs.

Ironically, the biggest benefit of the JOBS Act would be not to the crowd, but to the traditional investors who have had access to the best early-stage and small business investment opportunities.

Accredited investors—mainly corporations or wealthy individuals—must have a liquid net worth of $1 million or an annual income of greater than $200,000. The SEC presumes that accredited investors can protect themselves, so there is less regulation and less cost compared to crowdfunding equity.

With crowdfunding equity there is a cap of $1 million on the amount of money that can be raised and the amount of money that an individual can invest. With private placements, there is no cap on the amount a start-up can raise or on the amount an accredited investor can invest.

Private placements under Rule 506 will attract more capital since companies can market directly to investors and, in certain instances, may create angel investors—those who qualify as accredited investors but are not aware of their status or the deals available.

If a start-up is able to raise more money from fewer people with less cost and less threat of litigation and less regulatory risk, then more money will flow to private placements than to crowdfunding equity.

On the other hand, some companies may seek crowdfunding equity if they feel they need less money and do not have to give up as much control and ownership.

In addition, certain deals will fit better with crowdfunding equity, such as those that need crowd validating, including local business consumer products, publishing, sports teams, and food.

## THE TERM SHEET

The basis of a deal with a venture capitalist or an angel group comes down to terms. It all starts with the *valuation* of a company, since the amount of money invested divided by the valuation before the investment plus the money invested determines the percentage of ownership.

If you value the company too low, then you will give up a greater ownership percentage and possible control of your company. Value it too high, and the next round of financing could trigger negotiations where you could lose much more control and ownership than if the value was more realistic from the start.

Valuation is more an art than a science. The earlier the stage of the company, the more unknowns, the greater the return investors want, and the more of the company you give up unless the founders are known and the idea and industry match up. You can get a sense of value by comparing similar deals or running discounted cash flow in deals.

The second point to consider is *anti-dilution clauses.* These clauses are triggered when more stock is being issued than anticipated at a lower price per share, which dilutes or reduces the investor's ownership percentage. The normal anti-dilution provision uses a weighted averaged formula, but avoid a full anti-dilution clause, where all shares of prior investors are marked down to the lowest amount of any single subsequent preferred share price regardless of how much is raised. Such a clause is deadly and can reduce your ownership and control substantially.

You need to look at *protective provisions.* These are negative control provisions where you promise not to do things without the consent of the investors, such as future financings or changing the company's bylaws. These provisions can become very restrictive and unwieldy if not examined carefully.

The next area to focus upon is the *option pool.* To avoid dilution and indirectly lower the valuation the investors ask that the option pool be expanded significantly above 20%. Be aware that the options come out of the entrepreneur ownership or shares and/or that of the prior investors. The option pool should be only large enough to create incentives to meet milestones and get to the next round of financing.

Another factor is the *liquidation preference.* You want upon sale for the investors to get their money back and any accrued dividends—sometimes only if declared. But investors may try to get multiples on their investment—avoid this.

You should be wary of *drag-along rights.* This allows investors to force a vote to sell the company if a certain percentage of investors agrees. Avoid this, since the minute things get tough, the investors may try to bail. This can consume time, resources, and the ability to focus. Another drag-along provision may be that if you sell, the investors can sell with you.

I don't like one provision, *financing based on milestones*, since it increases the uncertainty of ever getting the funds and puts you on a leash to the investor. Just when you need money, it's not there, and the investor restricts you from getting additional financing.

The clause *in the ability to shop the deal* can tie you. If the investor drags out his or her due diligence, then he or she can put you in a desperate situation if you need money.

## PRIVATE PLACEMENT DOCUMENTATION

You will have to supply a number of documents and disclosures. The issuer is almost always required to make extensive disclosures about the nature, character, and risk of the offering. The document is at first called an "offering memorandum," or private placement memorandum, which disclosures key information to investors about a company.

In preparation for your private placement memorandum, you will need to address it in a very negative way. That offers an insurance policy to entrepreneurs as long as they do not misrepresent or defraud investors.

Here are some of the items covered in the private placement memorandum:

1. Risk factors
2. State blue sky laws
3. Valuation of company
4. Use of proceeds
5. Stock price, if offering equity and/or debt terms
6. Ownership provisions, if offering equity
7. Capitalization table (who owns what)
8. Financial statement
9. Executive summary and business plan can be referenced or included
10. Number of legal covenants

Here are some things to know about private placements:

- Whether you are a start-up or not, you need a private placement memorandum if you want to protect yourself, even if you have few assets and little revenue.
- Under Reg. D, you can structure your deal any way you want as long as you disclose it. Make sure you review the difference between the old Rule 506 (b) versus the new Role 506 (c) and the new bad actor. Rule 506 (e) as I noted under the legal analysis in the beginning of the chapter.
- Disclosure means you are under the state commercial rule, which is: buyer beware. But you are also under federal law, where the rule is: issuer beware. You must disclose all material issues and facts related to the investment. Again see new Rules 506 (c) (d) and 506 (e)
- You don't have to be a C corp, but it's the best legal structure for private investors.
- What about the number of investors? Under old Rule 506 (b), deals over $1 million require a filing, and there is a limitation on the number of non-accredited (35) investors). Under the new Rule 506 (c), you cannot have non-accredited investors.

- By having a private placement memorandum, you are complying with state and federal rules and regulations for selling securities (debt or equity) when raising capital. With new rule 506 (c) and 506 (d) you have to review carefully state by state whether you have to file any documents and pay additional fees.
- The private placement memorandum ensures you are treating all investors equally.
- You are subject to fines and rescission (giving the investors their money back) as well as investors' or regulatory bodies' lawsuits if you do not comply and sell securities improperly.

As we come full circle, you can see the pitches and presentations from the very beginning cover the key business issues that become the terms in the term sheet and are reflected in the private placement memorandum.

Over and over, the same people, product, potential dance plays out every minute of the day.

But the last piece of the puzzle is the new dimension of raising capital—the crowd and social, content, video, and mobile marketing. The way deals are presented has dramatically changed, and that holds the key to who succeeds and who does not in the digital age of raising capital.

## TAKEAWAYS AND INSIGHTS

- Let's view the changes in the advertising and general solicitation regulations for private placements (Title II of the Jobs Act) under the new rules 506 (c), 506 (d) and 506 (e) as opening up a large spigot or faucet of capital for early stage companies. The private placement market in 2012 was over $1.2 trillion.
- If you view the different capital-raising strategies depicted in the capital-raising mountain, crowdfunding donations with rewards opened up a new source of capital for mainly creative types, small businesses, and non-profits to access project funding or seed capital to get innovative ideas off the ground.
- Product launches can help provide seed capital for companies and test products as well.
- Crowd lending can bring capital to start-ups.
- Crowdfunding donations with rewards and product launches don't give up ownership and you can advertise them across the web, social, and mobile.
- Private placements can sell securities in the form of equity ownership in a company and under Rule 506 (c) can now also advertise and generally solicit only accredited investors.
- Crowdfunding equity under Title III of the Jobs Act for non-accredited (and accredited investors) to invest in early stage companies. But, under Title III, issuers cannot advertise their offerings and crowdfunding portals can only advertise their deals in general across the web, mobile, and social.

- Private placements will stimulate investment activity and bring more investors and money to early-stage companies. View the new investors as new "customers" for entrepreneurs. This will create more start-ups, and the amount of deals funded by VCs and angel investors may grow but percentage-wise still remain relatively low. Or, follow-up rounds may still be difficult.
- As a result, the ability to market, present, and pitch deals will become even more important. More than ever entrepreneurs will have to learn to tell stories both to attract money and demonstrate they understand how to build brands.
- The two-minute video pitch will become more the standard, as well as interactive videos, where time-starved investors can interact and give their feedback. Entrepreneurs can learn from the feedback, hone their pitch, and lead investors by different criteria and level of interest and respond back in real time.

Click here for additional resources: http://bit.ly/16Meq9X

CHAPTER 16

# MARKETING STRATEGIES

The script for raising money or investing in the digital age appears simple on the surface. If you come up with a great idea, build a cool product build a great product, then just show it to investors, and the investors will throw money at you. Yet the reality is the opposite. As *Shark Tank*'s Daymond John remarked, "Cool doesn't sell." "Cool" might get some interest from potential investors and customers, but that's a long way from getting actual investors and customers to invest and buy your product and reorder. You must first get out of your office and discover (Discovery step) your potential customers by listening and learning what product they want. Then build your minimum usable product (MVP). Don't wait for your customers to come to you. Test it by marketing: push your product out (direct market) to potential customers and investors and pull them to you (indirect market) by letting them test-drive your products

Here's the success script you want: An entrepreneur comes up with a great idea; develops it into a working prototype that solves a problem; prices the product to make a profit; and sells enough customers to validate the business model. Even better, he can show investors that more and more customers want the product; will pay a greater average price as the company adds more features and benefits; and sells it more frequently. If a start-up can show it has sales traction like this; the ability to sustain profitability; and the ability to scale the business rapidly with an experienced team of advisers, then investors will line up to provide funding.

In effect, I have summarized again the four business success basics:

1. Can you make money—a profit and positive free cash flow?
2. Can you sustain making money?
3. Can you scale the business?
4. Can you sell shares in your company to investors to get more money (and/or borrow where appropriate against the business/an asset, such as real estate, which generates income to cover with an adequate margin the borrowing costs) to grow your business, or sell part or all of the business to put money in your pocket?

Marketing more and more is becoming the missing ingredient for business success. Marketing strategies and then marketing tactics (discussed later) must be in place to create the awareness, attention, and word of mouth to lead to sales. Keep in mind that marketing is the conversation you initiate by going out to your potential customers, investors, and other stakeholders and asking them what they feel about your product.

Potential is an important concept, but it's up to you to define it for your specific business or project. Don't try to promote a potential outcome which neither is realistic nor one you even want. Whether you are an individual who works from her home, works part-time or full-time, you must define whether you want to grow a large company with lots of other people or stay small. There is no right or wrong. You can make a lot of money in a small profitable company, or maybe you love what you do and making lots of money is not your highest priority. But whatever you decide, you still must go out and market more than ever.

Look at your business-type options this way:

1. Solo business: such as author speaker, consultant, coach, internet marketer, seminar leader business, professional.
2. Instead of solo business, add staff to your author, speaker, consultant, coach, internet marketer, seminar leader business.
3. Grow your business into a lifestyle business that may make you a lot of money but never be the large type of business which VCs and angels are seeking.
4. Build a local small business with a physical locations such as a dress shop, jewelry store, insurance agency.

5. Buy into a franchise or join a direct selling organization, real estate brokerage operation.
6. Build a franchise business or brokerage operation, other, more than one retail location.
7. Look to be an entrepreneur seeking to build a tech or biotech or other fast- growth company which can scale and attract VCs, super angel and angel investors.

Again, no matter what business type become adept at marketing and selling. Without sales, there's no cash flow. Without cash flow, you go out of business sooner than later. You choose to start, you have and carry the business. Investors don't want to be the only source of cash flow. They want to see customers' cash flow take over.

## THE MARKETING ECONOMY

In the Marketing Economy (The Conversation Economy) no matter what business type you choose, you have to let your potential stakeholders know your exist. You can't be shy and feel you are being pushy nor can you be so pushy that you turn people. Like most things in life, marketing is a balance.

Another way to think of marketing is that it's a process of communicating your product's value to customers. According to the American Marketing Association, "Marketing is the activity, set of institutions, and processes for communicating, delivering, and exchanging offerings that have value for customers, clients, partners, and society at large. It includes advertising, selling, and delivering products to people. People who work in marketing departments of companies try to get the attention of targeted audiences by using slogans, packaging design, celebrity endorsement, and general media exposure. The four Ps of marketing are product, place, price, and promotion."

You market *products* to *people* with certain *prices*, in certain *places*, and with certain *promotions*. Weigh the success of these marketing campaigns. They begin to indicate the potential of your business. You discover whether your hypothesis or educated guess as to your business model is being validated in the marketplace by customers and stakeholders. Your objective is to find out whether there is a product to market fit and customers who will readily pay you a price where you can make high margins—not a price at which you give away or highly discount your product.

Remember, a small company has an idea of its product but little idea of its market type until it validates it. Large companies know their markets but must find the product to give their customers which will result in a greater market share.

Now, this may sound a little dry when you define marketing. But you'd be surprised how few people actually understand that marketing is about starting a conversation or dialogue about an idea, then how that idea might solve a problem by reducing a pain or solving a need.

Yet that's not enough. You have to tell a story about what you guess or hypothesize is this solution.

Now you become a storyteller, an entertainer, an artist who can tell a short story really well—so well that potential investors and customers want to know more will test it out and validate it.

No one really knows for sure. There's no hundred percent guarantee.

For some reason, marketing is as much an art as a science. You need both to succeed in today's economy. Why? Let's take a very simple view of our economy. Uncertainty and risk have never been higher. Unemployment has risen as many businesses have failed or can't afford to hire since the Great Recession. Interest rates have been artificially kept low to stimulate the economy. With low interest rates, yields on virtually every investment have dropped sharply.

As a result of these market conditions, consciously or unconsciously, many investors, entrepreneurs, and businesses have become speculators in search of yield and larger returns to offset increased taxes, health care costs, and anticipated increased inflation. Being a patient investor—a buy-and-hold Buffett type— to most investors seems passé. Building a company to last generations rarely is mentioned in investor meetings. Instead, the appeal of investing in an entrepreneurial fast-growth, next-big-thing type of company rests upon how quickly and for how much a company can be built and then sold.

With uncertainty, large businesses invest less and sit on cash. More focus is on short-term earnings reports. High-speed trading has become more attractive. Fractions of a second can mean huge profits with the right trading software in place.

The world has become increasingly more impatient and more demanding. This makes marketing more and more important. You can't sell if potential customers come and leave so fast you don't even have the opportunity to stop them and to tell your story. That is why I have used the word "pitch" so often. You must capture and emotionally graba potential customer in a few seconds. Preparation and practice are everything when you present your company and yourself. As a result, to succeed, you must hone your pitch so that you can strike up a conversation on a moment's notice that incorporates your marketing message, your unique selling proposition, and what's in it for your audience. At times, your presentations must be reduced to sound bites that will immediately grab people's attention. More and more, you recognize why everyone talks about the need to engage and entertain prospects and customers. To win, you must monitor, gauge, and measure who your customers and investors are, what they do, and probe constantly why they do what they do.

Much of the market thrives on the adrenaline rush of the next trade, the next news alert, tweet, text, or email. We are flooded with information, which gives us often a false sense of connection and belonging. For the money crowd and certain entrepreneurs with big dreams, the next big thing is just around the corner. Like speed daters that never stop looking over the current prospect's shoulder, there must be a bigger and better opportunity The challenge for investors becomes: on whom do you bet? Yet the same challenge is faced by all people running any business type. The question becomes, who can you trust and rely upon to achieve your business vision and purpose?

The consequence of low interest rates is that Wall Street inflates assets and stimulates markets such as the stock market. At some point, investors pile in because their hard-earned money yields them little while inflation eats away at its purchasing power like a silent tax. Even worse is the fear of missing the next bull market and seeing others make money while you don't.

In this yield-starved environment, investors turn to crowd lending where they lend unsecured money for a greater yield.

Investors turn to alternative investments such as private placements or other creative financings I've outlined in the financing mountain in Chapter 15.

When it comes to investments, the fear of missing out competes with the fear of loss. Tied to the fear of loss is the worst fear of all of losing everything—the fear of actual poverty or psychological poverty. Psychologically, some investors feel poor with millions of dollars in the bank. We battle the fear of missing out with the fear of poverty.

Napoleon Hill, in *Think and Grow Rich*, stated: "The fear of poverty grew out of the human tendency to prey upon others economically…Nothing brings so much suffering and humility as poverty… So eager are people to possess wealth that they will acquire it in any feasible manner—through legal methods if possible, but through other methods if necessary or expedient."

What does the fear of poverty have to do with marketing, sales, and raising capital from individuals and crowds?

Everything! Much of marketing is fear-based, real or psychologically imagined. You lack this car insurance and can be stuck with tremendous bills suffer actual poverty or lose enough to psychologically feel impoverished if you get into an accident. Or, the burglars will steal from you without the proper alarm system.

Being human, investors have positive and negative emotions. They want to be seen as smart and successful in the eyes of others, and they desire to be financially independent and secure for their lifetime. They want to provide for their family, friends, or others.

To win as an investor or entrepreneur, you must understand the fears, dreams, and greed that underlie the context in which the marketplace transacts. Everyone is pitching to each other in a fiercely competitive market. Most people are smart, but when it comes to money and emotions, they do dumb things. Even the conservative investor may want a shot at the Next Big Thing. There's the allure of the blockbuster deal: just one big hit that covers lots of dumb mistakes and losses. And gives you status, bragging rights, and the ability to do what you want when you want it.

The key of all marketing is to know the conversation going on in the heads of your potential relationships and be able to tune into them at the deepest emotional level.

Most companies don't listen and communicate. They shout and broadcast about themselves. As a result, the marketplace has the feel of a giant bazaar or commodities trading pit where marketing has turned into a frenzy with everyone trying to shout (broadcast and tell) above the other. In the beginning, especially, few early-stage companies have the resources and expertise to market with enough volume to be heard above the crowd.

Like investors chasing after all kinds of deals to get more yield, entrepreneurs, small businesses, and creative types chase after marketing gimmicks that make absurd promises of tons of traffic and sales. The gimmicks emphasize how you can shout better than the next guy, gal or company. Some start-ups and even later stage companies get caught up in this biz-op hype. After being duped and bled of their time and money, some early-stage companies throw up their hands in dismay. The companies begin to take on doubt and the leaders lose confidence in themselves. They start to mistrust others. They become paralyzed by the inability to know what to do, who to trust, and how to make sense of the myriad channels to market their services.

When there you encounter so much market uncertainty, risk, noise, and confusion, I recommend stepping back and being strategic. By strategic I mean working on your business rather than in its look at the big picture. Remove yourself from the noise and static. Realize you can't shout louder than the next guy and win. You have to become customer-focused and start designing a conversation with them based upon what interests them.

Think of why you choose some people as friends or listen to certain music watch certain TV programs or movies.

Just like your potential customers, you want to feel good, look good and reduce some pain or solve some problem. You wouldn't just blurt off in you met someone, "I can solve your problem, take out your wallet and give me your money."

You'd want to build some rapport and trust by telling your story and how it relates to their interests—not yours.

How do you come up with your story and start the conversation? Step back before you do anything. Ask yourself what your overall aim and purpose and what value it brings others. Start with the end in mind. What results are they looking for from you which would make them stop, listen and want to speak with you further.

## MARKETING, CROWDFUNDING, AND MULTIPLE PITCHES

Here's an example of being strategic. You might look at what crowdfunding will demand of you and your company. Ask yourself, how good are you at presenting your story, connecting with people, having an ongoing conversation and being a public figure?

Here's why you should ask: with crowdfunding, you become a public figure what you say you can't take back. It's on the Internet forever—good, bad or ugly. It's your conversation. You are a marketer, a conversationalist, a storyteller, an artist and a data reader/pattern analyzer scientist all in one searching to connect with your audience and bring them value. It's your stage and platform from which you must engage entertain, educate, encourage, and evaluate your prospects and customers.

In addition, you will have to learn the multiple types of pitches and approaches we have covered to target different audiences and different market segments. Not only do you, have to build a product/solution of value and fit the product to a customer base that wants it, but you also have to choose the "right type" of funding strategy and the "right" investor type with the right terms and the right valuation and give up the right ownership percentage. The challenge is, how do you determine what is "right" when there is no exact "right."

There is no right that you can buy in a store or arrive at by some capital-raising recipe or formula. But you can't just wing it or rely totally on your intuition either. In fact, there is a growing science that says you should not rely on intuition alone. There are too many variables. To win at attracting customers and fund raising, you must turn to analytics. As a fund raiser, examine data on venture and angel deals. How many get closed? Learn the valuations at which investors funded deals at the different phases of an early-stage company, from seed to

Series C capital raises. Note: you, as an investor, should study the same data to give you benchmarks as well to negotiate with entrepreneurs or other business opportunities in which you may want to invest.

To market successfully to investors, you must be aware of the data the investors are reviewing. Even if the data they are looking at may be misleading or not representative when applied to your specific deal, you must understand how investors look at the "average" deal of your type to arrive at some benchmark from which to negotiate. It's up to you to persuade them why your deal should not be valued as the average deal. Or, you should recognize that maybe the averages make sense, take the money, and not blow potentially a good deal for your company.

In a meeting with a head of a large angel group, I explained my company to him. He immediately rattled off data on similar companies and the criteria on which his group invested. Then it was up to me whether to accept what he was saying and engage in a conversation. Or, in this instance I realized that his approach to valuing and structuring business didn't appeal to me. I thanked him and declined to pursue any further dialogue with him. This is key to your success as a marketer to investors, customers, and other stakeholders. You have to choose who you want to engage in conversations and enter relationships. Dialogue means a two-way conversation.

Individual investor criteria may include any or all of the following:

- Simple enough to understand your deal (what is it?)Has something proprietary, such as patients
- Fun and excitement of something new and growing
- Proof of concept: customers can attest to value; pay for it
- Being around people they enjoy
- Business model—can make money: good margins; sustainable and business can scale
- Management team: competent; experienced with successful track record; personal investment; enthusiastic and fire in the belly to succeed
- Geographically close—within 200 to 300 miles
- Allows for staged funding against milestones
- Transparent with facts and figures

- Not involved in related companies which are a conflict of interest in terms of time and/or money
- Realistic executive summary, business plan and assumptions
- Clear exit strategy

The bottom line: both you as the company seeking capital and the investor must employ the intuition and creativity of an artist and the discipline and rigorous scrutiny of a scientist examining the data of a well-laid-out experiment. Why?

Because good deals for both sides are made with creativity. They just happen without lots of conversations and creativity and analysis. If one party in the negotiation is desperate or being duped intentionally in a deal, then the outcome will mostly favor the less desperate or dishonest party.

In effect, any person heading up a crowd-funding project or product launch or private placement is a marketer who must understand and learn the art of carrying multiple conversations to satisfy an array of customer, investor, and other stakeholder own internal conversations about the way they see the world and their own priorities. As mentioned, the project leader or CEO might be regarded as running a community or quasi-public entity. This demands that you must look at the new world of crowdfunding as a customer-focused marketer and conversationalist. This requires resources and skill sets which most of us haven't developed but can be learned.

## SOCIAL MARKETING SKILLS

Building an online following on Facebook, Twitter, You Tube, and LinkedIn requires you—and your team members—to be both artists and entertainers as well as more techie scientist types with a deep knowledge of online direct (push) and indirect (pull) marketing. Questions arise, such as: How do you drive traffic to your site? How do you generate and nurture leads to become sales and repeat sales? What content do you write? How should your blog and/or website be structured? How do you design a product launch and a converting sales funnel? How do you create a crowdfunding page that attracts backers? How do you respond to the crowd's criticism? How do you keep them engaged?

With any marketing strategy, you have to begin with the end in mind. What do you want to accomplish and then work backward.

In laying out your strategy, keep in mind there is no free traffic. If you write your own content and post blogs, that costs time and money. Your overhead ticks away. Another point to keep in mind: don't spread yourself thin by trying to marketing on Facebook, YouTube, Twitter, Pinterest, and LinkedIn at the same time.

Pick one social network focus on it and become an expert.

Next, understand that when you pick a marketing strategy, you have to be aware of what your target group expects. Mainly people come onto a site like Facebook to relate, not be hammered by sales pitches.

Your overall goal on social network sites it to build an audience. Your selling is linking them to your own website where you sell yourself.

Many marketers configure where to build an audience by giving them great content and links to resources and where to do your actual selling.

On Facebook, you can buy ads or sponsored stories. From those ads, you drive traffic to your money-making sites. This is what the top marketers do.

Few early-stage companies have the know-how or resources to undertake extensive social media marketing. That's why you must stay focused and be very clear on your marketing objective: aim at the strategy that will get you sales and money. As a result of sales (traction), you can attract the money. But getting sales from social media is not easy because by definition it is is supposed to be about being social.

Strategically as mentioned, you can use social media marketing to sell products and attract investors. But you must understand the difference between marketing on Facebook and marketing on Kickstarter. If you take a step back and look at the big picture, you can use social media as a testing ground to build your audience. On Kickstarter you can develop your customers, your products, and your social networking skills, which you can use on Facebook and other social networking sites.

To get the sales, you must undertake customer development in parallel with your minimal viable product development. Here you want to undertake face-to-face customer development interviews. But you can crowd source ideas and ask a group what they think about your product idea. You can test whether the optimum channels to reach your customers are Facebook, Twitter, YouTube, LinkedIn, direct mail, trade shows, seminars/conferencing, mobile, call centers, online paid media, or traditional media, such as TV, radio, newspapers, magazines. Remember, you are like an explorer going on a journey of discovery. As an explorer, you must use your intuition and be the artist, but you also need a scientific approach to stay on course, which means a lot of data collecting and analyzing. That is why you should recommend a strategy that incorporates the following:

- Start with customer development with face-to-face interview.
- Run video and non-video surveys to supplement your face-to-face interviews.
- Use the feedback to test develop and test your minimal viable product (MVP).
- Once you have your MVP, then you can decide upon your money-raising strategy and product selling strategy as crowdfunding donations with rewards, product launches, private placements, crowd lending or other strategies as I outlined in the money-raising mountain in Chapter 15. Not that you may seek seed money prior to building your MVP but you will most likely only get it from friends and family first unless you have a track record of success in this area.
- Use crowd sourcing and voting to test your ideas, solutions and designs.

This process may seem overwhelming. You may be asking: how can you take on so many roles and possess so many skill sets? If you feel this way, then I've accomplished my purpose: to give you a sense of why being an entrepreneur or investing in an early-stage company is so challenging and risky. But if you know this comes with the turf, you can dramatically increase your odds of succeeding. You have to admit what you don't know. Then you can plan to assemble the best team to supplement your weaknesses.

## THE FOUR START-UP TYPES

As explained in Steve Blank's book *The Four Steps to Epiphany*, an entrepreneur must understand the type of start-up he is creating. *Not all start-ups are the same*. There are four types of start-ups:

1. Entering an existing market
2. Creating an entirely new market
3. Resegmenting an existing market as a low-cost entrant
4. Resegmenting an existing market as a niche player

Each start-up has a different set of requirements to succeed. Your marketing strategy must be attuned to the different market types or you will fail. Marketing types tell you how to evaluate customer needs, what adoption rates are, how the customer understands his needs, how you position the product, how you launch it into the market, and how big the market is. For example, entering an existing market with a new product is easier, since the users and the market are known. The basis of competition rests on the product and the features.

Compare that to entering a new market with a new product, such as when Apple created the tablet computer or Quicken created the home accounting market. "Creating a new market," Steve Blank writes, "requires understanding whether there is a large customer base who couldn't do this before, whether these customers can be convinced they want or need your new product, and whether customer adoption occurs in your lifetime. It also requires rather sophisticated thinking about financing—how you manage and find investors who are patient and have deep pockets."

Low-end cost resegmenting is entering an existing market at the low end, offering a substantially lower price. For example, a company may offer a low-end video hosting solution where price is the main determinant, all other features from competitors being equal. A different market type, niche resegmenting, goes after the profitable core of an existing market rather than the low end of the market. For instance, In-n-out Burger in 2001 offered only a premium burger versus McDonald's, which offered over 55 different items. In-n-Out-burger went after the core profit area of McDonald's business—hamburgers—with a niche offer.

To reiterate, each of these four market types requires different marketing and sales strategies and time horizon. A new venture must know what market type it is going after so it can evaluate its customers, their needs, the product performance it will have to deliver, the competition and their reaction to it, and the risks it is taking to succeed.

Another valuable distinction Steve Blank makes is that big companies develop products for known customers and markets to "maximize market share and profitability. Start-ups begin with known product specs and tailor their Product Development to *unknown* customers and market requirements. In short, in big companies, the product spec is market driven; in start-ups, the marketing is *product-driven*."

If a start-up does not get the first part of its customer development right, then it can't scale and "cross the chasm" into the mainstream. Instead, it will go out of business.

Put another way, start-ups that focus on execution before they discover in customer development what their customer wants will go out of business. "Instead, you need a 'learning and discovery' process so you can get the company to where you know what to execute," Blank states.

You hear the mantra: execute, execute, execute. But the real challenge is to know what to focus upon first to know what to execute upon. There is too much focus upon getting a product launched and marketed before you know whether you have the right approach to the right market type and have developed through a rigorous, iterative process what the customer wants, which can be incorporated into the product and tested as well. This begins to determine your real market and customer base.

## WHY IS ATTENTION AND INTEREST VERY IMPORTANT?

So, how does a start-up get the awareness, attention, interest, and consideration of customers and investors for its products once it has defined its customer needs, the solution, the product, and the market type?

As with so many marketing solutions, you can take the advice of Jay Conrad and Jeannie Levinson in the book *Guerilla Marketing Field Guide*: "Always start with the people and then work backward to the offering. Such a strategy zeros in on the results you want to achieve, the way you plan to obtain those results, and the specific action you want your target audience to take.

"The strategy must be expressed in writing, and it should not contain headlines, theme lines, or copy. The strategy is devoid of specific marketing copy because it must be solid, yet flexible. Specific words and phrases pin you down. A strategy should be developed as your guide, not as your master."

The authors suggest that you ask yourself these questions to create a marketing strategy:

1. What physical act do I want people to take after being exposed to my marketing (click here, call a phone number, complete this coupon, or look for my product next time they're at the store)?
2. What prime benefit do I offer? What competitive advantage do I want to stress?
3. Who is my target audience?
4. What marketing weapons will I use?
5. What will my market niche be?
6. What identity do I want my business to have?
7. My marketing budget will be _______% of our projected gross sales.

Another way of looking at the customer development process is that more traditional marketing kicks in once you really have a sense of what your customer wants—her problem or pain points—and whether she sees you as the solution.

But even more than that, the customer must feel the value is enough that she will make the effort to buy *and* actually use the product.

Placement is another powerful marketing strategy. Direct marketing legend Dan Kennedy told an audience a story of guys that love to buy horses. They tell their wives they are just going to where they sell the horses and promise themselves they won't buy another horse. Soon, they buy a $35,000 horse. To make amends, they turn to a vendor who has the exclusive to sell $3,500 pieces of jewelry. Well, the wife usually forgives the horse-buying husband when she sees the jewelry. Think of airports and those prices you'd never pay for the same thing anywhere else. Now imagine where could you place your product where you'd be in a monopoly position and your customers would be eager to buy your stuff.

## WHAT CHARACTERISTICS OF MARKETING STRATEGIES WORK?

Let's review the common elements of successful marketing strategies. To reiterate, be strategic—define your goals and be clear as to what you want to achieve, such as: sign up 500 monthly customers at $200/per customer. Then be tactical and lay out your tactics to achieve the goals, such as: develop strategic partners who will mail to their customer lists. Give them proven metrics that they can make money with you.

To do business with others and track your progress, you need to define how you will measure results for your partners and your company. You can't be vague. For every $200 sale, I will pay you $30, $40, or $60 for every sale. This means you will net after paying your partners $140, $160 or $170 per sale.

You want to set your goals based upon actions you can take rather than depending on outside market forces, such as a rise in interest rates or ingredient costs. You can deliver your product to affiliates and you can create incentives to motivate strategic partners to mail to their customer base your product offering.

But what if your potential JV or affiliate partners won't mail to their customer list for you without proof that they can make money? How do you get out of this chicken or egg situation?

Strategy one: agree to pay the JV or affiliate partner 50% to 100% of the sale price.

Why would you do this?

- You need to get proof of concept to show other partners you want to mail.
- You can sell those who purchased from you more expensive products.
- For those prospects that signed up but did not buy, you can keep trying to sell them.
- You can negotiate to keep all or most of these proceeds if you gave the majority or 100% of the upfront sales price to your partner who mailed for you.

Strategy two:

- Buy media such as Facebook Ads or Google Ads and test your offer.
- Buying media is a sound strategy since you do not rely upon fickle and often, expensive JV or affiliate partners.
- Whatever strategy and arrangement you choose, you should have a short, specific plan written out of what you want to accomplish, with whom, over what time period at what expense and what defines success. Also, you should have a system in place to send out emails, record opt-ins or sign-ups, measure key metrics and deliver your products and services.

Keep constant checks on what's working and what's not regarding your strategic goals. Learn and adjust incrementally by constantly testing. Be ready to make major changes if your market tests reveal better opportunities.

Try to keep your strategic direction (vision) as consistent as possible and test your assumptions by using various tactics. Think of raising capital and building a business as an ongoing learning and discovery process. Don't confuse getting frustrated—lacking resources—with the impulse to change your strategic vision, e.g., confusion comes from lack of a clear vision and clarity—not a lack of resources. Because of this, changes in strategy should be undertaken only when it's clear that achieving a strategic goal is either impossible or no longer desirable.

## MARKETING HAS EVOLVED

Here's a brief summary of how different media and related technologies have evolved. Years ago in the factory/industrial age, you created a physical company and sought investors in the physical world. Your marketing and advertising was mass market, direct mail/direct response, or telemarketing, where you solicited by phone. Radio advertising ruled, along with billboards and print ads in newspapers and magazines. Then came the three major TV networks—CBS, NBC, and ABC. Soon, cable TV segmented the TV market by interests, and infomercials grew in popularity. Next came the Internet, bringing information/content marketing and paid media, such as targeted online ads and search engine optimization. Direct mail went online, using email rather than snail mail. Social media, such as blogs, exploded along with social networking sites, such as Facebook, LinkedIn, Twitter, and YouTube. Now mobile marketing is emerging with the growth of smart phones.

Marketing now draws upon multiple channels and multimedia multiplying the number of ways to send out marketing, advertising, and sales messages, copy, and content.

There are two types of companies: predominantly physical companies, such as Starbucks or McDonald's, and primarily online companies, such as Google, Microsoft, and Amazon.

For physical world start-ups, which compete with entrenched giants such as Walmart, the challenge is to get foot traffic to stores or dealerships, or attendees to events or meetings to present products and services.

For most online companies other than the giants that dominate the Internet, the challenge is how to get traffic to the website or mobile phone app, and convert the traffic to quality leads and sales.

## GUIDELINES, INSIGHTS, AND STRATEGIES FOR ENTREPRENEURS AND INVESTORS

If you are an entrepreneur, here are some guidelines when working with your team or third parties to implement the marketing and sales strategies that follow what you discovered during your product development processes.

If you are an investor, here are some guidelines you should be aware of—best practices in customer and product development and how they are reflected in the pricing, business model, and go-to-market strategies and assumptions.

The Entrepreneur and Investor Guidelines both of you should know for yourselves and each other:

- No matter what you hear, the time, people, resources, and costs are double or triple anything you estimate to develop repeating customers and a working business model that is sustainable. Start with what you feel are your conservative worst-case estimates and then double the time to get there—even triple it. Cut your sales projections by 50–70%. Then calculate the money you require in years one, two, and three.
- Next, assume what anyone tells you they can do for you will materialize at best 20% of the time.
- Expect few people—investors or customers—to take any real risk on you.
- Most customers will try to reduce you to a commodity and try to diminish your value, especially when they sense you need them.
- Understand that most people have little money, no matter what they say, and they will disappear quickly when they can't make a quick hit off you and your company.

- Whatever you don't understand, those who do understand will usually take advantage of your ignorance, either by overcharging you or hiding their own incompetence because you can't evaluate how little they really know.
- Get three bids for every job and compare apples to apples.
- Normally but not always, you get what you pay for. Just because they are expensive does not mean they are good. If they are cheap, then question why.
- Single practitioners often over-commit and are unreliable. Make an agreement based specifically on the time—exact hours—which they are dedicating to just you and your project.
- Make everyone accountable and her actions measurable.
- Do not sign long-term agreements.
- Have a way to test and evaluate as quickly as possible whatever you agreed upon.
- Be able to terminate an agreement quickly with no penalties.
- Work under non-disclosure agreements and see how people respond to them when you propose they sign on—this typically reveals the way they do business. Even with venture capitalists, if they want to get deeply in your business, then have them sign one.
- One of my favorite rules: whatever someone does up-front, such as miss meetings or deadlines, will only get worse.
- Face-to-face meetings are critical to raising money and building lasting relationships.
- Hire slow; fire fast. Once you see it's not working and you're questioning things, normally it's a big sign saying stop your wishful thinking and cut bait.

## THE PHYSICAL WORLD: DOS AND DON'TS

An entrepreneur can also use the many traditional ways to create awareness and interest, including billboards, TV, radio, and print ads in magazines and newspapers. Most of these traditional approaches should come later, as they are expensive and will only confirm awareness that you have already established. Until you have a working business model and prototype, unless you are famous or have a very successful track record, the publicity may create demand for a product or service that is not ready even for early adoption.

Entrepreneurs who do not develop customers and products as I've described run the risk of running after customers and markets prematurely. Instead, the focus must be on developing early adopter customers who tell you in advance the minimal viable product they need or want. When you have a defined working product and viable pricing and business model, then test your product offering wherever possible. Use selective PR and direct mail to amplify your offer. Again, the strategies and tactics will vary based on the product, market type, physical or online presence, and best media and distribution channels.

Until you are ready with a working product for which customers will pay you money at a profit, you should network, network, and network to learn what it takes to achieve customer acceptance of your product and validation of your value proposition. Network means to get out of your office and test your offer. Potential customers are not waiting for your new product and service. Even if you have the greatest thing since sliced bread, steel yourself for rejections.

Most people err on the side of saying no thanks. With new products, they will say no to you first since they know most products probably won't work as promised. Some will be that polite; many not. You want to find the more patient early adopters. That doesn't mean they will immediately try your product, but they are the most inclined. Keep in mind, early adopters only make up 15% of the population; 85% by definition will reject you because they are not ready for myriad reasons. But you can learn a lot from rejection if you prepare yourself to listen carefully rather than get defensive and tune out.

How many times have you seen people dismiss good feedback? That's not to say the customer is always right. This is where you have to be brutally honest with the feedback you receive. Use your intuition but weigh that with data and evidence which may be counter to your gut.

Your job is to forge ahead even when you receive rejection. But again, try not to forge ahead blindly. Listen. Discuss feedback. Compare notes from as many people as possible.

If you have a physical product, hand out samples and practice explaining what your product does and how it benefits them. Demo your product whenever you get a chance: go to trade shows; attend industry events or conferences; speak about your product and how it can help your industry members grow their revenues or save money and time for their business.

Similarly to an investor, go to investor summits, and join angel networks and mastermind groups where you can expand your network for investors and deals. Whether you are an entrepreneur, small businessperson, creative type, investor, or a combination of these types, listen to others' struggles and solutions.

In addition, you should create a website, a Facebook fan page, a Twitter account, a YouTube channel, and a LinkedIn profile. You must keep writing better and better copy to evoke emotional interest in your product, with attention-grabbing pitches in the form of headlines, tag lines, and clear product or service descriptions. Wherever possible, use video to engage (such as Questionmine.com's interactive video engagement, list building, marketing platform, and analytics). Remember that all these ways to present and pitch your products combine to become your digital business card and enlarge your digital presence and footprint.

In addition, you will need to create a physical handout or flyers for trade shows; business cards (some companies use their business cards to advertise or proclaim their philosophy); a slide presentation of your products and company for investors or customers (can vary some slides to your specific viewer of your presentation); a demo and other materials which also explain your company and its pricing, why it's different, and the overall value proposition. Note: all your communications must be consistent and sell an overriding simple concept so it can be grasped immediately.

## PHYSICAL BUSINESS VERSUS ONLINE BUSINESS

Evaluate your online business or actions by asking the simple question: Would I do this in the physical world? Sometimes you will realize what you are doing online makes no sense when you ask this simple question.

Next, view the means by which you ask your prospects to purchase from you as channels. Think of channels as physical pipes which connect you to where you want to reach and distribute things and vice versa. A multichannel strategy is giving your customers more ways to buy

You can reach people via different channels in the physical world, such as TV (short- and long-form ads, infomercials), radio (short- and long-form ads, sponsorships), newspapers (display ads), billboards, magazines, conferences, seminars, events, parties, meet-ups, direct mail, call centers (teleconferences: free and paid; in and outbound sales).

On the web, use social and content marketing (inbound or indirect marketing) where you use your website, blog, videos (on YouTube, for example), webinars, and social networks such as Facebook, Twitter, YouTube, and LinkedIn to disseminate information in the form of studies, best practices, infographics, white papers, how-tos, and other forms of information tips in order to engage with people. Here, your approach is permission marketing. I get your email and send you stuff I want. If you like it we stay engaged. At some point, I trust you enough (I test drove your products) that I will buy from you.

The online world brings together people searching and visiting all types of sites (the visitors are the traffic) with the different intents or purposes via different media and channels. For example, I can use the *Wall Street Journal* as the media to advertise my raise-money book because it's a financial newspaper. Readers can access my financial raise-money course online; it can be delivered in physical form to their homes, or they can buy it off their mobile phone using Questionmine's interactive mobile video with a call-to-action/buy button in the video.

As a marketer, I must weigh the cost to get my name or brand recognized, say in the *Wall Street Journal*. My question is whether I have developed a proven message to the right audience delivered at the right time. If I did, then can I afford the ad relative to the revenue it generated.

The big challenge for many marketers, advertisers, and e-commerce companies is getting enough eyeballs to their site at a cost that makes economic sense, Even if they do understand traffic generation and getting leads, few are very good at closing sales and up sells.

To make matters worse, search engine optimization (SEO) strategies—getting free traffic based upon keywords—normally takes six to eighteen months to show real results. Because of this lag time between investment and results, many incompetent and untrustworthy practitioners charge high fees based upon exaggerated projections which are rarely going to be met.

What should you do as an investor or entrepreneur? Know that a good sales funnel can take three to four months to build and possibly many more months to achieve sales. The results depend not only on the technology but the copy, offer, and the quality of the list (targeted customers).

For example, you can spend a ton of money putting together a sales funnel. But if you can't write a subject line on an email that gets the recipient to open the email (called open rates), then the entire funnel fails. Or, if you sent an email that said "50% off on world's best cat litter" to dog owners, then virtually no emails will be opened (you sent the email to the wrong list). Or, if you sent a targeted email to dog owners with low incomes that says "$1,000 for world's best dog collar," you might get some opened emails but no sales.

To reiterate, it takes a significant amount of time, money, and resources to develop an online business that converts leads to sales. There are no shortcuts. You must design a compelling offer, write the right copy, and target the right lists to which to mail and to make aware of what you have.

## THE CHICKEN AND EGG PROBLEM

In starting any business, you face the chicken and egg problem. As I mentioned, you want JVs or affiliates to mail and endorse you to their list. But to do this, you have to demonstrate you have a product that makes enough money to be attractive to the owner of the list, who only gets paid if his customers buy your product. The other challenge for potential affiliates or JV partners to mail to their list is they do not want to turn off their customers with bad offers or mail too much to them. Your challenge is to find enough ways to test your offer to see whether enough customers will pay for it. If you can demonstrate to others that there is a demand for your product and they can make money off it, they will mail if they like you: if their calendar is free and if they believe it's a good match with their list. I pointed out some strategies and tactics in the beginning of this chapter to overcome this chicken and egg problem and prove your product can make money for others.

Many people waste tons of time writing blogs which few read. The challenge is that most of your competitors are making the same claims you are and write about what you write in their own style. The majority of information has become more and more a commodity. To rise above the noise, you must really offer a special expertise, positioning, and personality as an expert in your field. The brutal facts remain that others are no instant experts. Even if you are an expert in much better writer and have top information you still have to build a platform or stage and get known. The same if you are selling a physical product, software, or a service.

What to do? If you are better, then you have to use all the means I have described to find ways to distinguish your products as different and find the right audience to validate that.

The secret to the chicken-and-egg problem is creating alliances in which you develop use cases and testimonials. This is a tedious process since you have to get the person or company's attention, time, resources, a test that works, and results that make a difference. Most important, you need the person or company's commitment to try different tests without abandoning you the minute your product does not meet expectations.

Here's a winning strategy that I have mentioned throughout the book but is worth repeating. Whatever you are seeking to accomplish comes down to yourself: the people around you; your product or service; and its potential to bring others value.

From the very state of a business, you are creating an Idea or solution to pain or you are joining someone else who has the Idea in some capacity—partner, employee, investor, supplier, distributor, professional investor or some other stakeholder.

But that's still not enough with so many variables to amass and make sense of.

To get out of the chicken-and-egg problem in building an online business, you need to build systems to handle all your marketing and sales activities an email delivery system, an e-commerce capability, and a means to track affiliate or JV sales so you can pay out commissions. When you first start out, there are a number of e-mail delivery systems, such as AWeber, iContact, Constant Contact, SendGrid, and MailChimp. There are e-commerce/shopping cart systems, such as 1 Shopping Cart, Volusion, Shopify, and Shopping Cart Elite.

The bottom line: marketing and sales are becoming more and more automated more advanced system that does it all for small businesses is InfusionSoft. An example of a this system is more complex but very powerful. What I did is to find the very best companies to map out my sales funnel the sequence of selling low-priced to higher priced products and the emails and other associated marketing sales materials using InfusionSoft. My reasoning: you can lose tons of money if your online business is not set up properly from the very beginning. What I realized after much trial and error was that your overhead expense comes every month while you are making a lot of stabs in the dark trying to figure out for yourself the online business. Instead, make an investment up front to have the best online system built for you that matches your business. You can start with a more basic system or the more advanced. The point is, do not try to do it yourself. Find the best company by reputation for the system you pick.

How? Research the best systems: email, shopping cart, database, affiliate tracking if you want to be an affiliate and/or work with them. Then you will decide if you want only a blog or a website or both. Will you drive traffic to opt-in or squeeze pages? You will need copy for your site or opt-pages. You will need a designer who understands online marketing. Then you will need follow-up emails to those visitors who ask for your free material or free trial.

Note: Infusionsoft is a Customer Relationship Management System, or CRM system. For larger businesses, took at CRM.com (IBM), Eloqua (Oracle), Marketo, Hubspot, Sugar CRM Microsoft Dynamics.

## TO FOLLOW THE CROWD OR NOT

Truly successful companies—small and large—must, contradictorily, both follow the crowd and not follow the crowd.

This outside-inside contradiction is what makes for innovation. The outsider sees value that others do not. To be different, an entrepreneur needs to be the Steve Jobs outsider and then be accepted by the crowds to scale and grow.

In the beginning, most start-ups are regarded as outsiders, interlopers, who are saying things should be different from the status quo. Naturally, people don't like change, especially those in power, i.e., competitors. Remember, most people are creatures of habit. They like the familiar in an uncertain world even if the familiar is an abusive relationship, a boring job, or, overall, a life unexamined.

Why? People like their comfort zones. Getting out of their comfort zones creates uncertainty, risk, frustration, and pain, since people and companies are confronted with things they don't want to see or do, or can't do. Competitors, likewise, don't want to be challenged, since they have a comfort zone with certain customers that they want to maintain.

As I have stressed, a start-up must have a remarkable product that customers want. But that's only the first step. Then you need a message and media to market match. This makes marketing and sales skills vital. If you want to invest (or raise money), you need to know what to look for beneath the hype of the entrepreneur. Similarly, the entrepreneur has to know how to grab and keep an investor's attention and get him to invest, i.e., you must be enthusiastic but do your homework and be able to back up your assertions.

According to the late business guru Peter Drucker, all business comes down to innovation and marketing. How will your customers know you exist? Do they have a way to get your product and have you made that process easy? Let's look at one of the main keys to business success: distribution.

Distribution is getting both your message and your products out. To succeed in business, consumers have to hear about your products before they buy.

You reach them through a channel such as TV. You must get their attention to let them know that your goods exist. As discussed, getting attention is very difficult. You need to have some emotional hook. If you get their attention, then you inform them about the wonders that your items deliver. Prospects tune out online and offline because they've been bombarded with so much advertising, so many sales pitches, offers, and promises, that they've shut their ears.

When you go to YouTube, what are those top-ranking videos getting? Attention and time engagement. So today the company that wins must know how to market and sell, or it will fail even if it has a remarkable product. If you are an entrepreneur, go online and study how cutting-edge companies such as Square are grabbing people's attention emotionally. Look at the way Square's visuals on their site are positioned for maximum emotional effect. Then examine your own site and ask: Does it have a similar attention-grabbing, emotional appeal?

In the book *Contagious*, Jonah Berger seeks to answer the question, "Why do things catch on?" When things catch on, we not only engage with them, but we share them. Sometimes, this word of mouth, as described in Malcolm Gladwell's *Tipping Point*, spreads like a virus or becomes contagious. Berger examines in detail why certain videos or products become popular. For example, "Barclay Prime in Philadelphia offers a hundred-dollar cheese steak, where the standard Philly cheese steak is four to five dollars. The ordinary Philly cheese steak is some chopped steak made on a griddle with some Provolone cheese or Cheez Whiz placed on a hero roll. Howard Wein, the owner of Barclay Prime, substituted Kobe Beef, triple-cream taleggio cheese, caramelized onions, shaved heirloom tomatoes, black truffles, butter-poached Maine Lobster tail, and placed it on a hand-made brioche roll brushed with homemade mustard. To be more outrageous he served it with chilled split of Veuve Clicquot champagne...Wein didn't create just another cheese steak, he created a conversation piece!"

The words "conversation piece" underscore the point I've been making throughout this book. Marketing is a conversation we look to start. Pitching and presenting for free, one dollar, or millions of dollars is still a form of a conversation that you or I or others are trying to start. What drives people do to things is the conversations they play over and over in their minds (conscious and unconscious) and how these images and conversations are influenced by others. To look good and feel good, we socialize and do things or say things. When we think or feel we can gain status or influence, such as sounding smart or looking cool, we pass along or share things with others by word of mouth, text, and emails.

Berger says, "Social influence has a huge impact on whether products, ideas, and behaviors catch on. A word-of-mouth conversation by a new customer leads to almost a $200 increase in restaurant sales. A five-star review on Amazon leads to approximately 20 more books sold than a one-star review...In fact, while traditional advertising is still useful, word of mouth from everyday Joe and James is at least ten times more effective...it's more persuasive...Our friends... tend to tell it to us straight and word of mouth is more targeted." We share things with those we feel will benefit most by the information we are sharing.

This brings us back to the paradox of following the crowd and not following the crowd. Like Steve Jobs, you have to listen to yourself—your internal conversation—and then understand the crowd's conversation.

## SOCIAL NETWORKING AND THE OUTSIDER

Here's an example of how you can reach people through social networking. An associate of mine, Kaisa Kokkonen, 13 years ago came to the U.S. from Finland. She was an outsider. She wanted to meet people in the United States and realized other Europeans like herself did not know of each other or Americans. They too felt isolated like outsiders. So she started a social networking site called EuroCircle for European and American professionals to network at events. She created individual profiles well ahead of Facebook. She was happy just to network with people and create new, interesting, and lasting friendships. Her outsider idea of people seeing and communicating with each other online and offline caught on, by word-of-mouth. Now she has 100,000 people in Europe and in the States that are members of her European-American network. As her network grew, she added business network events, which she also created for free. To kick off her business networking concept in 2008, she invited 300 people to come to the Four Seasons restaurant in New York City—one of the finest restaurants in the world. People had cocktails, and she networked. Her business networks grew around the country and into Europe.

During the 13 years, she added paid events which people gladly attended. She built up trust and a reputation among her professional members. Now she offers paid corporate sponsorships and markets products that her community, through surveys and suggestions to her, has expressed they'd like.

That's what you need to do. Build your customer base by plugging into their needs. Your product then needs to reach the largest number of people you can reach in your target segment. Then you have to find ways to keep that communication going.

## TAKEAWAYS AND INSIGHTS

The emphasis here is on setting forth an integrated marketing or conversation strategy or plan which addresses the many different objectives a company has to meet at the same time. Your objectives include:

- Raising capital.
- Discovering who your customer truly are, asking what they want versus the hypothesis or guess you've made.
- Developing your product based upon your customer interviews, surveys, and test marketing.
- From all these multiple interactions and feedback you create your message—your USP—and other presentation and pitches.
- The challenges for businesses, especially early-stage companies, is how to be heard above the noise, get social proof and validation.
    - To do this in the beginning or to move to the next level of business is a chicken-and-egg problem. How do you get the social proof if you can't get customers to try out your product and validate your claims and your business model?
- Part of your strategy needs to incorporate audience building on social networks, such as Facebook, YouTube, Twitter, or LinkedIn. Learn one very well rather than spreading your resources.
    - Understand that social networks exist to socialize, network, and share information and resources—not sell.

  - Your selling should be from buying ads on these networks or from Google and linking them to landing pages where they sign up and enter your sales funnel to buy your stuff. Kickstarter is a platform for pre-selling stuff.

Click here for additional resources: http://bit.ly/15cXUms

# CHAPTER 17

# KEEPING THE CROWD(ED) CONVERSATION GOING

Social networking and social media marketing are part of an undeniable trend that will keep growing. People want to be introduced and talk among each rather than listen to one-way monologues from corporations and institutions that they do not trust. Peer-to-peer marketing makes more sense, since friends trust the opinions of their friends or friends of their friends more.

People want to get a feel that you're for real and you care about them—not just pushing your own agenda. Kaisa Kokkonen of Eurocircle showed she cared. She put her community's interest above her own. She continued to give free events and free stuff away so her network came to trust and admire her. She listened and learned what her community wanted as they spoke among each other. EuroCircle has expanded across the United States and into Europe.

In 1999, Seth Godin wrote his seminal book *Permission Marketing*. He recommended that businesses create ongoing relationships with potential customers. By creating these relationships, the possible customers would become more comfortable with a business and be more open to buying from it in the future. Godin suggested that businesses lay the groundwork for future sales by engaging potential customers in dialogues and interactive relationships. By building these relationships, businesses could make sure that they didn't get bypassed when the potential customers decided to buy. This is essentially a description of indirect marketing, content marketing, and social marketing.

According to Godin, this interactive process should be continual so that the relationships grow stronger over the years. By maintaining these relationships—keeping your customers engaged—a company can find out and keep abreast of what its customers want and how to provide it.

Many businesses' sole focus is on sales. But the successful and the truly great businesses, like Zappos, Apple, and Amazon, focus on customer retention. The number one reason customers leave a company is they don't feel cared for. Continual customer contact shows customers you care, which maintains their loyalty, which leads to more purchases and referrals. Customer loyalty also helps a business avoid having its offerings commoditized. By staying engaged with customers, the business becomes part of the conversation and finds out what the customers feel and want. They design high-value products based upon their customers' feedback.

The company and customer become engaged in a virtuous feedback loop: customers value the company's input if they feel listened to and if the information or the experiences offered reflect the listening by being relevant and help them reach their goals. Potential customers benefit because the business offers them items that they need and value. As a result of loyal customer, companies can maintain a competitive advantage. Preferred customers—the most loyal—can spend up to 20 times as much as a new customer.

## THE IMPORTANCE OF TWO-WAY COMMUNICATION

Customer loyalty reflects the importance of a business at any stage of development, knowing who its customers are and what they want.

Remember, if you are using any of the five money-raising strategies I've shown you, then you are now aware of the importance of customer development. But the real money is in the repeat sales, since you already paid to acquire the customer. For example, if you pay $100 to acquire a customer (if the cost includes your allocated overhead) and the customer spends $100, then on a marginal basis you have broken even. If the customer comes back and spends another $100, what is your cost of acquisition? Zero.

Also remember that there are three ways to increase revenue:

- Get more customers
- Increase the average amount spent-have the customer spend $150 rather than $100
- More frequency, so the customer keeps buying from you

The process of communication goes both ways. Customers want to express their opinions to brands, but studies show brands only allow 16% of their customers to converse with them. Traditional businesses don't realize that their customers are flattered when they believe that their opinions are considered important. You can build a competitive advantage just by interacting with your customers and investors. Interactivity builds engagement. In turn, engagement builds relationships. Relationships are the new currency—the foundation for getting investors and customers and maintaining their ongoing loyalty.

"A business can now ask a consumer directly if he would like more information," Godin points out. "A business can now reward a consumer for receiving and acknowledging its message, insuring that the consumers' own interest is served by learning about a new product or service."

Any business should ask its customers what they need and what they think they might need in the future. Top marketers and salespeople involve their customers in the planning process. Their customers act like an advisory member of their customers' team.

## FEEDBACK IS KEY

*At every level of business and life, we need feedback.* We operate based upon stimulus/response. Our bodies on an unconscious level monitor and adjust to myriad stimuli to keep us alive. On a conscious level, we can only focus on one thing well at a time. For this reason, we are programmed to screen for the most important items, such as what can harm us or what can give us the most pleasure.

But the problem and pain for most of us is that people and businesses are constantly pitching us. We have little say in what they say to us.

Communication in the real world among people is normally two-way. When I first conceived of Questionmine, my interactive video survey, poll, quiz, and assessment company, I sought to find a way to replicate the way we communicate with our friends and business associates. We communicate back and forth—we interact. To make the interaction more interesting, we try to entertain, educate, and engage. We want to get feedback on what people liked or disliked, often right then—in real time.

Videos are naturally engaging, but I discovered most businesses use videos as one-way pitches. Businesses had no idea who watched their videos and why. There was little or no customer feedback.

The business opportunity: you could turn your videos into money and ongoing relationships by replicating the normal two-way communication which occurs among people. In my customer development process, I found that prospects were very interested in making their videos interactive. They wanted to get active participation and analytics from viewers by asking prospects and customers questions at key moments in the video and having them answer the questions and give their opinions or insights on what they liked or disliked about their products while they watched the video. To motivate active participation by their own customers, prospects liked the ability to give incentives such as loyalty points, coupons, discounts, gift certificates, or free stuff or trials. To make it a fun experience for their prospects and customers, we added to our interactive video surveys and assessments other ways to engage with customers, such as polls, quizzes, and contests.

Recently, Questionmine added video branching or choose-your-own adventure where based upon an answer a question, the video viewer is fed a different video. For example, a prospect may be asked in employee training are you a beginner, intermediate, or expert and be immediately sent a different video related to the answer given. Or, a marketer such as a cosmetic company may want to sell makeup, skin cream, and shampoo. Depending upon the answers, prospects are in real time sent videos as they answer each question until the prospect gets enough information on a product to buy it.

Whether you use Questionmine or any other way to interact and engage prospects and the customers, the goal is to establish an active and caring relationship real-time interactive two-way conversation, which creates trust, loyalty and feedback.

Then you must keep the relationship strong. This is similar to starting and keeping a friendship going. If your customers like and benefit from the relationship (friendship), they will put their trust in you and your business. You will become their favorite, and they will support you by continuing to buy your products and recommending them to others.

## YOU ARE IN THE ENTERTAINMENT RATINGS BUSINESS

Think of Oprah or Ellen DeGeneres. You tune them in because you like what they have to say and the relationship you feel you have with them. This goes back to the *American Idol* model and the Performance Economy. Today virtually all companies are in the entertainment/attention/ratings business. If your business is boring and it has unremarkable products, then it is not going to attract an audience, i.e., customers.

Take Google. Google is really a popularity/relevance ranking service. An online business seeks to be the most popular show in its category or niche. The most popular person, company, or show on a Google results page gets the most free audience or organic traffic. For example, let's say you sell dog training. When customers search the Internet by typing in the keywords "dog training," the top-ranked company or person offering dog training on Google's results page gets a lot of free viewers—40% of the traffic. This means the most popular—those that get the most attention (traffic)—benefit over everyone else.

In addition, Google sells ads to advertisers who want to advertise to people searching for certain keywords or information—in this example, dog training. As discussed, Google auctions and prices its keywords to advertisers depending on a certain mix of quality and relevance of content and demand for certain keywords, such as "dog training." When people searching for keywords such as "dog training" click on a dog training ad tied to the keyword(s), the advertiser pays Google whether the advertiser makes any money off the ad or not.

This is the main source of Google's billions in revenues. Between generating organic or free traffic or paid traffic from ads, when it comes to search, Google is the main arbiter of whose information is most popular, most relevant, and of highest quality, and, thus, who gets the most attention.

## FOCUS ON THE HUMAN CONDITION

What I am reiterating is that the world has little time and attention for us. Most customers and investors are in a rush and overwhelmed by a life where personal and business lines have blurred. Unless you establish quickly—sometimes in a few seconds—what's in it for them, they are gone off to the next best thing or personal challenge in their life.

Crowdfunding reflects this dynamic. Investors have no lack of deals. Customers have no lack of things to buy. Most things are in oversupply, including boredom and change.

The key to grabbing someone's attention in seconds is to focus on what is in short supply. For example, almost everyone needs more time. For many, finding a good, challenging, preferably well-paying job, career, or company to run is a major goal. For others, what is in short supply in their lives is meaning, joy, inspiration, relaxation, time with family and friends, good health, and happiness.

A start-up business seeking investors and customers should keep in mind that crowds are made up of individuals who have the same things in short supply—the same needs, fears, aspirations, and circumstances in varying amounts.

Investors and customers are also emotional creatures. When they feel things are in short supply, investors and customers become frustrated, and often very emotional. When an entrepreneur thinks of attracting customers and investors, he should keep in mind how much human beings are driven by similar positive and negative emotions.

Ask yourself, how do your products and services address and appeal to positive and negative emotions? Does the product or service increase the positive emotions (happiness) or the negative ones (fear)?

## COMBINE ATTENTION MARKETING AND PERMISSION MARKETING

**Customer Questions to Ask:** If you are a start-up or an early-stage company, then you have to think carefully and ask yourself and your team these questions: Who are we seeking to be our customer, for what purpose are we seeking them, and for what amount of commitment of their time and money?

Likewise, you have to ask yourself repeatedly: Why am I doing what I am doing? Have I lost sight of my original purpose? Am I still passionate and committed to what I am doing? Do I feel trapped?

**Fire Your Customers**. Another important point in asking these questions: you can work tirelessly to develop customers to validate you have a working business model. Some customers know you are desperate to get their business and feel they are essential to your survival. As a result, you took on some customers who are over-demanding and never want to pay you for the value you are delivering. At some point, you have to suck it up and ask who your optimum customers are—the ones who will pay you for your true value to their businesses. Fire some of your customers no matter what they say. Tell others you will get rid of them unless they play by your rules.

**Ask for Permission and Be Polite.** Most start-ups have little leverage and awareness when it comes to prospective customers and investors, so start-up entrepreneurs have to be polite and keep asking for help and feedback. For this reason, the start-up that understands customer development as I have described it is forced to engage in permission marketing to listen and learn from others what they need and whether the product offered meets the customer's or investor's needs/emotions. Ask for their advice.

This is how you attract customers and/or investors to your business. You need to be personable to get their permission to enter into a relationship with you.

## THE IMPORTANCE OF GOOD COPY

Once you discover the problem you solve for customers and get a deep understanding of customers who will pay you for your solution, then your marketing positioning and copy take on much greater importance. Now you have to assess how your message, market, and media fit together to spread the word of your product as optimally as possible.

Along with the Internet, mobile, social, and content marketing, writing good copy is another low-cost way to leverage your products and company. Good copywriters can be very expensive. You can write your own copy or alternatively, you can hire on people to write copy or articles. If you write your own copy first, then you get good copywriters to tweak your copy. The better copywriters will do this if they believe you will give them more work as you grow.

Marketing provides often the greatest leverage and returns for the least cost, especially writing good copy. In writing sales copy for your product, simply changing the headline—even a few words—can bring two to ten times the response or sales. Some other ways to increase the response rate and sales are a better guarantee or a longer time to pay for your product. When setting up a crowdfunding portal, the principles for copy on a company website are very similar.

According to SellIt.com, the formula for a successful website is to have: (1) excellent content—including good website copy—and (2) patience to build traffic based upon focused (relevant) content.

The focused content creates a pre-selling of the customer's mind, which enables SellIt.com to turn its offers into money. Why? Because, as I have pointed out, marketing is really made up of various strategies and tactics to predispose an individual or group or company to take an action — in this case buy what Sell It.com is offering.

Clayton Makepeace and Tony Flores, authors of *The Great Copywriting Conspiracy*, believe that content includes and is enhanced by great copywriting, such as emails, that give customers free information and motivate them to go to an online page (landing page) where there is a sales letter. How well the sales letter is written spurs the reader to go to the order page. Now, this is where the tire hits the road. You need good copy on the order page to close the buyer. They believe good copywriting distinguishes them from most entrepreneurs online or offline, who do not present what they are selling in an optimum way.

In *Landing Page Optimization*, Tim Ash and Maura Ginty define a landing page as "any webpage the Internet visitor first arrives on their way to an important action that you want them to take on your site. The landing page can be part of your main website, or a stand-alone page designed specifically to receive traffic from an online marketing campaign.

"Strictly speaking, it is not just the landing page you should be optimizing, but rather the whole path from the landing page to important conversion on actions (such as purchases, form-fills, or downloads) often happening somewhere deeper in your website.

"So why pay so much attention to landing pages and important conversion paths rather than the whole website?

"The Infamous 80-20 rule applies perfectly here—landing page and paths represent your business critical activities. They are the drivers of revenue and business efficiency. They are the 'money' pages."

The irony of many marketers is that they focus so much on marketing gimmicks and techniques to drive traffic to their site or business, they forget that their copy or sales material or presentation and optimized landing pages and conversion paths are what gets people to buy their products and services. More traffic alone does not mean anything unless it is quality traffic—customers that potentially are suited for your product and service. To create top performing web pages, you have to create a platform or stage which spells out clearly and concretely why someone should believe you and delivers a powerful, objection-proof presentation. This presentation should incorporate the following: specific numbers, strong examples, logical arguments, strong testimonials, personal guarantees, track records, case histories, your product or service shown in action, vivid pictures, scientific proof, clinical studies, graphs, strategic media appearances, and celebrity endorsements.

Tony Flores points out, "Copywriting is the language of marketing." All aspects of a company's website—home page, squeeze (opt-in) page, videos, free content, emails, sales letters, auto-responders, new product launches, marketing campaigns, upsells—all involve copywriting. Flores confirms that the best copywriting has basic patterns and models: "The BEST copywriting secrets are those that have been tested over and over again."

## CROWDFUNDING: YOUR CHARACTER VERSUS REPUTATION

Yet all this focus on writing clever copy should not obscure one basic quality in business. To me, character is what you do when no one is looking. It's your integrity. Reputation is your name and how others perceive your actions (or non actions) and talk about you.

With the stakes so high, many of your competitors, given the opening, will look to destroy you and your reputation. Misstatements or stupid posts on Facebook or off-color videos on YouTube can come back to haunt you. Remember the secret recording of Mitt Romney talking at a fund-raiser about the middle class trying to avoid paying taxes. "There are 47% of the people who will vote for the president no matter what…who are dependent upon the government, who believe they are victims." The harm this did, being played over and over on YouTube, was likely fatal to his campaign.

The importance of pitches, positioning, and the places they are given are critical to the marketing and sales, but you have to be very careful what you say, since the Internet is like indelible ink—you can't erase what you did.

## HOW TO CONSTRUCT A SIMPLE DIRECT MARKETING OFFER

Let's examine the direct marketing or response offer.

You used permission marketing to get people on your list. You can choose to keep sending them more and more free content (indirect or inbound marketing) or you can try and push them to take action (respond), such as buying your stuff (direct marketing).

People will purchase from your company if they feel you are offering value. The value fits what they want: it fulfills the images and conversations in their mind at that moment. They feel they bought on their own volition. You didn't sell them. Let's say you have an e-book for sale titled *How the Masters Build Their Wealth*. You would write a simple offer to the new person that just joined your list using the four basic elements of an irresistible offer, such as:

1. **Price**: $99.
2. **What does the product do:** It's a wealth-building system detailed in an e-book.
3. **What's in it for me:** Use the Masters Wealth Building System to grow your net worth faster.
4. **Why you should believe me:** This is a book based upon an extensive study of Master Wealth Builders backed up by their own personal examples. This is how they do it.

Your written copy should have an attention-grabbing headline with an emotional hook. Give benefits, have testimonials, and provide a clear call to action on how to get the lead magnet report and/or CD on the topic sent to you. Then you need a series of emails—the conversation—getting them to know you by giving them additional information related to Master Wealth Builders. By the fourth email you can make an offer via traditional online sales letter or a video sales letter or both. You may need a minimum of seven emails to get a sale. Even if you make the sale, remember to keep up the ongoing conversation and customer retention.

The most successful marketers start a genuine, emotional customer benefit-oriented conversations (presentation or pitch) from the first headline written, and they write in a very conversational language, as if you were speaking to a buddy at a bar and explaining how you discovered a solution to the problem.

So we have:

1. People on your list that have given you permission to get in touch with them.
2. You made a simple offer to them, taking into account the four elements of an irresistible offer, which at its core has a value proposition.
3. You wrote some short copy.
4. You might use a longer form sales letter or video sales letter (20 minutes long, made with Microsoft PowerPoint or Apple Keynote).

You targeted someone and you asked for them to take action:

**Desired Prospect Action #1**
Give me your email in exchange for my free report. With their email, you get permission to stay in touch with them or make an offer in the future.

**Desired Prospect Action #2**
Give me your money—$99—in exchange for my e-book.

By targeting a specific person and asking him or her to take a certain action or response, we have used direct marketing.

## DIRECT MARKETING TO INVESTORS AS CUSTOMERS

You can use a similar direct marketing approach with a potential investor. Ask similar questions in designing your overall conversation and pitch:

1. Is this particular investor (or group of investors) the right person or people to target—the right audience?
2. Is the offer the right offer—is there enough value in the way the company is presented (big enough Potential with the right team and Product)?

In direct marketing to customers, you can often use risk reversal—you get 100% of your money back in 30 days in a risk-free trial. But this is not typical when you pitch investors to invest in your company. You normally don't guarantee an investor his money back unless it's a direct loan to you which you personally guarantee. In addition to the interest on the loan, you might give him a "sweetener" in the form of a percentage ownership in your company.

You are trying to demonstrate to the investor that he has little downside risk, or that you are aware of the investment risk and you are trying to reduce it as much as possible. You often give him a preference in liquidation of the company's assets, including intellectual property or the sale of the company. This preference can be given in the form of preferred stock or a convertible note. In other words, he can convert the note into stock at a predetermined stock price or a price defined by an offering in the future or other events, such as reaching or not reaching a milestone in revenue in a year.

3. With the sale of the e-book, as stated, you'd typically have a sales page with a great headline and sales copy or a video sales letter. You'd tell the person you target and email to click on a link in the email that brings her to a page she lands upon—called a landing page—which has sales copy, testimonials, and all the benefits as to why she should buy your product.

With an investor under the new private placement general solicitation and advertising Rule 506 (c), you can send an accredited investor your deal in an email with a link to a video presentation of your transaction. This would be your equivalent of a sales or money page which you would optimize as well as the entire conversion path. You will be able to apply similar direct marketing (outbound), content marketing (inbound), as well as social and mobile marketing strategies and tactics to money raising.

## DIRECT MARKETING VIA PORTALS TO CROWDFUNDING INVESTORS

Keep in mind that all the strategies I have outlined can be applied to:

- Raising capital under Title 11 (private placements)
- Raising under Title 111 (crowdfunding equity) but with limitations on advertising
- Building your online and off line companies.

Note: under Title 11 you will be able to advertise your deal to accredited investors and under Title III you won't be able to advertise your dealto accredited or non-accredited investors.

In the world of crowdfunding the portal website, is where your company can create a dedicated web page which acts as your direct response sales page to your "targeted investor." Your crowdfunding page explains your company, its products, and its irresistible offer for someone to back/donate, lend to, or invest in the project or company for equity. The portal type and your page setup will be dictated by capital-raising strategy you are using—donations, loans, or equity.

With Title II, private placements, you can elect to post your deal on a portal site or not. You can post your deal terms anywhere you want and advertise them to accredited investors. You can place ads across the web, social, and mobile to drive awareness and traffic to your deal presentation and pitch.

## DIRECT RESPONSE MARKETING AND YOUR WEBSITE

While you are raising capital via crowdfunding, you may also have a separate website that likewise lists your products, your company, who you are, why you exist, and why the prospective customer or investor should engage with you. You can create a sales funnel that sells your company's products and services. Note again: under title III crowd-funding equity, you cannot advertise your organization or project for your business offer to raise money. You can only advertise the products you sell in your business.

Websites are a collection of ideas, concepts, and messages that represent your stage (platform), store front, information center, and calling card to the world. Websites can be very tricky and require some overriding purpose. For example, is your website meant to merely inform, such as "here are directions to my place," educate or teach, entertain, advertise, sell, or direct someone to your blog or to some other site?

A website properly put together must be in alignment with what, where, and why you want a visitor to know and/or do. For example, you could let visitors know you started up a company and you are running a crowd-funding campaign or project on Kickstarter or RocketHub. You provide a link from your website to your campaign page on these sites. Note: you can advertise your crowdfunding donations with rewards site or sites because you are not considered to be selling a security under the SEC, as you are in crowdfunding equity and private placements.

## FEEDER SITES AND THE MONEY SITE

Use this feeder and money site strategy and tactics for crowdfunding donations with rewards, product launches, and private placements under the new rule 506 (c)

Many savvy Internet marketers create a number of feeder sites on the web or social media pages that give you enough information to get your interest. Then you are directed to their money site, where they get your email in exchange for a free e-book or sell you stuff. With your email and implied permission, you are put in a sales funnel or drip campaign that uses Autoresponder systems such as Aweber, iContact, Mail Chimp and Infusionsoft. Autoresponders send prewritten emails automatically on some pre-planned schedule.

## USE TRAFFIC TO FAIL FAST

The idea behind developing customers, investors, and traffic is similar. You have to learn from others their successes and failures and needs and wants. When you test ways to do anything, including get traffic, fail fast, before you spend a ton of money.

Failing to get traffic you want or to make the money if you *pay* for traffic may be a result of your bidding on the wrong keywords, overpaying for them, not having the right ad or the right opt-in page copy consistent with your ad copy, design, and functionality, or the right lead magnet. For getting free or organic traffic, you may fail to figure out the right keywords tied to the right content, the right blog, website, or opt-in page and the overall message and timing of the message.

## CONTENT AND TRAFFIC

When you seek traffic, you are *not* doing this in a vacuum. You have to be aware of the buyers and sellers of products and services in your niche as well as those competing with you for the same keywords in paid traffic and organic traffic. Your competition may be simply too strong and dominate certain keywords on the results page on which you want to rank high. That's because there are a number of criteria which determine your ranking on a results page, such a relevance of your content, the URL of your website or blog, and the number of sites and the influence of those sites that link back to your site.

Every way you seek to get traffic is overrun with competitors, similar to the stock market. Few investors and few traffic seekers make money even if they get traffic. Why? For the same reason people don't buy offline in physical stores: price, presentation, positioning, product, people, terms, competition and trust to name some.

As a result, you have to test each of these variables until you come up with a combination that works. Top online marketers admit most of their companies fail to meet their goals or fail completely.

Instead of one giant rigid plan, if you are seeking online traffic, you need, as for the rest of your business, a series of mini plans that have goals which can be measured. Then the mini traffic-generating plan is tested against your goals—for example, lead generation and list building. You learn and you adjust as you begin to generate traffic. Keep reminding yourself that you are seeking to deliver value to your prospects and existing customers along a path which has a series of steps or actions that you want them to take. If along the path you develop trust and desire, then they will buy. If you are not getting sales and repeat sales, you have to ask: Do my customers feel that I overhyped them and my product is not remarkable? Or, do I have a remarkable product, but I set expectations too high and I have to tone down my marketing copy?

## TOO MANY OPTIONS

What you quickly realize is that there are so many choices for an investor or an entrepreneur that it is very easy to get overwhelmed, even for the most sophisticated, let alone beginners. It is very easy to get caught up in the trees and lose sight of the forest. For this reason, I have advocated a flexible creative but disciplined approach.

The allure and bane of technology is that it is relatively inexpensive to start up companies but increasingly expensive to compete to grow a company against well-staffed and financed competitors.

Crowdfunding will fuel more and more start-ups and increase the number of investment options and competitive products.

Because the marginal cost of communicating (creating a conversation and getting and keeping your audience engaged using emails or links to a blog) has been reduced by technology compared to marginal revenue, there is tremendous noise competing for buyers.

As a result, the question will be less can I get an idea off the ground and more will the idea survive and attract funding.

With so many ideas and so many start-ups using the same low-cost ways to get the word out the ultimate challenge is how to get your message and offer heard. When you multiply the number of companies and individuals doing this at the same time, you come to the realization of how important your presentation pitch, copy, offer, product and overall ability to market and communicate become. To compete on the Internet, you must make your message to your market. Using the three main strategies I showed you are permission/email marketing, search engine optimization, and pay per click. In addition, you can employ strategies using videos on social network sites, such as Facebook and YouTube, to get the message out.

Again, the challenge is that learning these strategies just gets you into the game. But finding the team to come up with a winning sustainable business model against all the competition is what separates you from the pack.

The same low cost of starting up Internet and mobile-based companies is both attractive for innovation and overwhelming for entrepreneurs and investors, since sorting out the best technologies, strategies, tactics, and the winning companies themselves will be very challenging.

What I have been recommending whether you are an investor or entrepreneur is keeping your eye on the basics that underlie all these different offerings and options. For example, there are only so many basic ways to get traffic. There are fundamentals to sales funnels, copy, offers, list building. There are fundamentals to companies. These basics are always present no matter what company or project you build or invest in. There are only so many basic ways or sequences to raise capital. Those who succeed always have strong fundamentals upon which they add their unique style or twist.

The real challenge for startups will be staying power. Will they be able to attract the capital and stakeholders to get to the next stages of growth. The cost of getting follow-up on capital will be higher as much more money will be required to help potential winners compete with more entrenched competitors off- and online. For example, the latest data show that launching a new game app has jumped from almost nothing to $5 million.

In a *Wall Street Journal* article by Jessica Lessin entitled "Expenses Mount for App Launches," game-app maker Zep to Lab's CEO Misha Lyalin says, "It's amazing what it costs to launch a new game. Zep to Lab released its Cut the Rope: Time Travel in April 2013, its first major title in the popular Cut the Rope series since 2011." Overall, Zep to Lab says it will spend $1 million launching Cut the Rope: Time Travel. By contrast, the company spent almost nothing to promote the first Cut the Rope game in 2010.

"As a result, game-app makers, who used to mostly rely upon word of mouth to move their products, have been forced to ratchet up the cost and fanfare of their marketing campaigns to rival those for lower-end video games and books, even borrowing from Hollywood's playbook."

That's why to get above the noise and cut through the clutter of the market place start-ups to more seasoned companies must take on the mind-set of multimedia entertainment companies. No longer can word of mouth be depended upon. You can't wait for your field of dreams to be discovered. You have to make things happen. You have to be and get on your team, find the artist/creator/director and the scientist/data collector/pattern analyst. Online campaigns with video, mobile, and social tied to the web must be created even on the most basic level. Customer data must be gathered through marketing automation and other data collection tools.

## THE MULTIMEDIA MIND-SET

Beyond specifics tactics, you need to adopt what I call the new multimedia mind-set to succeed. The multimedia entertainment approach combines social, mobile, the web, video, images, photos, and multiple channels of distribution to go to where customers are having their conversations and fit into those conversations with the right message delivered at the right time. The objective is to interact, engage, entertain, and educate prospects and customers to get their feedback, opinions, and insights while collecting and analyzing data to know your prospects and customers better.

This multimedia approach will be part of the WOW the prospect and customer want to see. Think of Apple—it wows customers with remarkable products and does it with a multimedia entertainment approach. Products are launched similar to movies with great suspense and anticipation with great design and special effects so they become part of the conversation. The conversation continues about the remarkable products and grows among Apple's followers.

Clearly, most companies, especially early-stage or small businesses, don't have the resources to create the Apple launches. But you would be shocked to see how a little creativity can affect the view of your company and its products.

You can begin to implement this multimedia, multichannel approach right away by simply seeing your entire business through this mindset. The key is to keep this multimedia/multichannel entertaining approach in mind for even the smallest things you do. Each move you make will add to your overall multimedia approach to your business. In a short period of the time the changes will add up and you will suddenly more and more have opportunities as the market comes to realize what you already anticipated. You and your business will have expertise you can share and monetize.

## THE ARTIST AT WORK: THE LEAN CANVAS

To reiterate, in order to accelerate this approach, you must seek the artists—the social conversationalists—who know their craft better than anyone else. You must find the artist/traffic generator, the artist/designer, the artist/data collector, and the artist/predictive analytics master. These artists understand the dynamics of social influence and word of mouth phenomena. They get what arouses people to action. They have the integrity to use their skills to better people's lives and not take from them.

So, the mechanics of starting up an online business, crowdfunding equity and related services, and, more specifically, traffic generation can only go so far. It's the artistry which elevates the mechanics. Mechanics give you the basic fundamentals. When you spend the hours learning the fundamentals through deliberate practice, you elevate your level of mastery. You come to see the nuances—possibly the Next Big Idea—which create the openings or the holes in the market to get the competitive edge and win.

Here's an example of programmers and high-speed traders learning the mechanics and laws related to their business so well that they found an opening to make millions of dollars in seconds. A *Wall Street Journal* front-page headline announced: "Speedy Traders Exploit Loophole." It goes on to report: "High-speed traders are using a hidden facet of the Chicago Mercantile Exchange's Computer system to trade on the direction of the futures market before other investors get the same information...trying to profit from their ability to detect when their own orders for certain commodities are executed a fraction of a second before the rest of the market sees the data traders say, the advantage is just one to ten milliseconds (one thousandth a second)... But that is plenty of time for computer-driven traders....The ability to exploit such small time gaps raises questions about transparency and fairness amid the computer driven, rapid-fire trading that increasingly grips Wall Street and confounds regulators."

The point: someone knew the mechanics of the system so well that he could design a way to master the system and exploit it by one thousandth of a second.

But the story of high-speed trading becomes a metaphor for the entire capital-raising and business-building landscape. Time and speed are challenging every part of business and life. Winning and losing in business can be a matter of fractions of seconds.

The challenge becomes designing a business model that has to engage prospects and customers in seconds, make money be sustainable over time and have the ability to scale.

Whether high-speed trading, traffic generation, raising capital, or observing and testing, there is both a "scientific" lean start-up approach and a creative approach. It's the creative artistry which synthesizes all the variables and sees the wow solution that engages the crowd and converts them to fans and customers, which makes the difference between the winners and losers.

On the Lean Startup investor.com website is an interesting model of this idea. "Step 1, put very simply, is to document your Plan A. Documenting your Plan A is done on what is called a Lean Canvas. The Lean Canvas is a business modeling technique adapted from The Business Model Canvas, specifically for start-ups. The idea of the Lean Canvas is to be able to see, demonstrate, and iterate your entire business model on one clearly understandable sheet of paper.

"This canvas and the business model," the copy goes on to say, "are at the center of the start-up and drive the point home that the you sell to make money is only one product you have to design and build. Your 'business model' itself is also a product you have to design and build too."

In turn, the 7 Steps are another way of answering the questions raised by the Lean Canvas:

1. Idea/Problem/Solution : steps 1-4 in the 7 Step System relate to steps 1-4 in the lean start up canvas
2. Design: You will notice that you design a business and a business model as the "product" (Golden Goose) you are selling as well as the product itself (Golden Eggs).
3. Discovery: Look for the unfair advantage (Unique Value Proposition) and develop your customer segments/target customers and product specifications. You will also begin to look at the competitors' pricing models and start to begin laying out your business model.
4. Development: All the elements of your company from customer to product, and you begin to see the problems, challenges, and solutions and the related time, resources, and costs

to create the Minimal Viable Product and weigh these against the revenues projected.

5. Pre-launch: Line up your channels of distribution and begin testing your Minimal Viable Product and whether people will test it and buy it. You set up initial metrics.
6. Launch: You go to market and see if more early adapters will buy it.
7. Post-launch: You review all your assumptions, including your metrics, and keep making incremental changes, or make more dramatic changes and pivot to Plan B.

## RIGHT MARKETING LEADS TO RIGHT CONVERSATIONS

Throughout the chapters on marketing strategies and marketing tactics, you have seen that marketing is all inclusive—on the web, social and mobile. As an entrepreneur or an investor trying to evaluate a start-up company, you must understand how much marketing can affect the success or failure of a company or its products. When you try to learn and discover who your customers are and their needs and whether you solve them, you are doing market research. If you try to scale your business prematurely and throw money at marketing and PR, you can burn up your cash and then discover you have not matched your product to the right four market types, which Steve Blank defines in his book *The Four Steps To Epiphany*.

None of the capital-raising, marketing, and sales strategies and tactics I have revealed is linear. There is no formula or recipe which says "do this, then that, and so on, and you will have a successful project or business." Instead, creating a business and attracting stakeholders like customers and investors is more a circular or recursive process. You have to keep circling back and forth among each of the 7 Steps and each of the Magical Ps and other models I have presented.

Just as you learn the basics in any discipline or sport, you have to keep reviewing and repeating them, since often a fundamental step is missing or not properly executed. The huge explosion of social media, mobile, and video marketing to get the word out about your products, company, and crowdfunding and other investment opportunities presents too many options unless you have lots of time and resources. Instead, your marketing strategy should be to pick an area of marketing that matches up well with your skill set and liking. For example, if you are passionate about videos, then become a YouTube marketing experts. If you like quick chats and thoughts, then become a Twitter expert. You want to find your marketing niche and to keep the conversation going—and what better place to do that than sites where people are communicating with each other all the time? But make sure you understand how conversations are conducted on these platforms so you can market your platforms like Facebook, YouTube, Twitter, and LinkedIn for products, projects, and the company you are starting and building. By using a selective marketing platform strategy, you can focus your resources and enjoy the process since you are doing what you love—using videos, chatting, or networking more. As a result, you can keep your stakeholders engaged, happy, and supportive.

## TAKEAWAYS AND INSIGHTS

- You need to raise capital and build a business in a global competitive environment that is accelerating in speed, technological innovation, and generating more information and options.
- To counter being overwhelmed, individuals and business (the crowd) must collaborate and share ideas, information solutions, insights, reviews, and opinions.
- Google, Facebook and others want to find ways for us to give information about ourselves. Such as "who we are, where we are, what we like, whom we like, what we buy, what we want, what we know, what we want to know—so they can serve us more relevant and valuable content, services and advertising" Jarvis states.
- To compete and win you must understand how important Conversation Intelligence is—the ability to interact face-to-face and duplicate that humanness in any of your non face-to-face interactions.
- Within this context, your objective is to engage people, find out what they want, and share information with them that gives them value. When you meet their needs emotionally and you build trust through your communications, then they will buy.
- In effect, you want to create a true dialogue and exchange that from the moment you engage a person, you are allowing them to get to know you.
- Everything surrounding your engagement and interaction must support your ongoing conversations, such as your profile on LinkedIn, Facebook, and Twitter.

- All your keywords, copy, offers, write ups, material, positioning must be integrated so show clearly what you and your business are.
- All your traffic driving and conversions strategies—inbound or outbound marketing—must have a clear focus on message to defend audience and niche.
- To get above the noise and static, you need the perspective of a multimedia company that looks not only to engage but entertain, educate and encourage your audience to interact and share with you and your community.
- With the understanding of the sharing economy, you can evaluate the product you sell for money and your business model itself as a product and how it interacts and share with others.
- To build your business, you need to be or find the artists and the scientists to help to build, monitor, and measure your conversations.

Click here for additional resources: http://bit.ly/18gwIhx

Printed in Great Britain
by Amazon.co.uk, Ltd.,
Marston Gate.